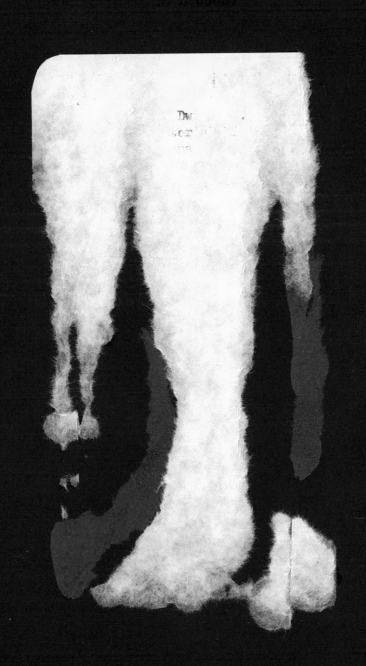

A Pictorial History of
INDIANA

A

Pictorial History

OF

INDIANA

Dwight W. Hoover

WITH THE ASSISTANCE OF

Jane Rodman

Indiana University Press   Bloomington

Indiana University Press gratefully acknowledges the financial assistance of the Lilly Endowment, Inc., Indianapolis, Indiana, which has helped make the publication of this work possible.

Copyright © 1980 by Dwight W. Hoover

All rights reserved

Manufactured in the United States of America

Hoover, Dwight W   1926–
    A pictorial history of Indiana.

SUMMARY: Text accompanied by photographs, drawings, cartoons, maps, and paintings traces the history of the Hoosier state from the time of the first inhabitants to the present.
    1. Indiana—History.   2. Indiana—Description and travel. [1. Indiana—History]   I. Rodman, Jane, 1921–   joint author. II. Title.
F526,H66   977.2   80–7806
ISBNO–253–14693–3   1 2 3 4 5 84 83 82 81 80

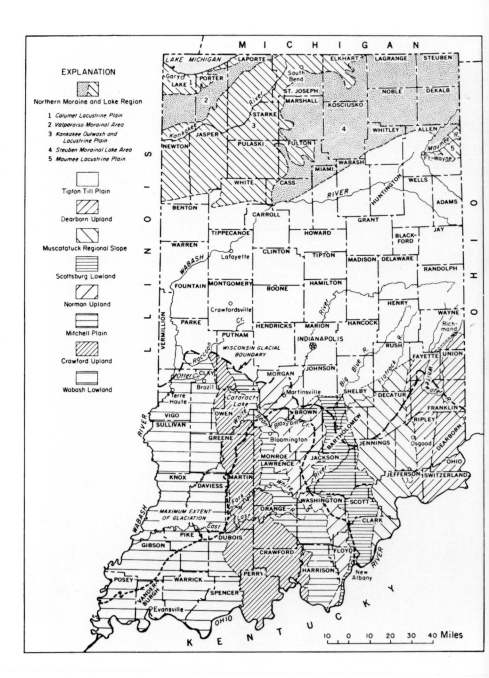

Crosby asked me what my name was. . . . I
told him, and his wife Hazel recognized my name
as an Indiana name. She was from Indiana, too.

"My God," she said, "are you a *Hoosier?*"

I admitted I was.

"I'm a Hoosier, too," she crowed. "Nobody
has to be ashamed of being a Hoosier."

"I'm not," I said. "I never knew anybody who
was."

—Kurt Vonnegut, Jr.,
Cat's Cradle

Contents

The Land

Indiana's history has been shaped by its physical features and natural resources, which make it both a beautiful and rich state. The process of creating this beauty and riches took thousands of years.

The land which was to become Indiana was originally submerged under an inland sea. It then became elevated and was shaped by wind and water. Streams, the major one of which was the Teays, which ran from the western part of Ohio to the Mahomet River in Illinois, eroded the landscape into a form still visible in the south-central portion of Indiana. Here are sandstone uplands cut into knobs and ridges, limestone plains, and shale lowlands.

The landscape of Indiana underwent a considerable transformation beginning about 400,000 years ago when the first of three waves of glaciers began to cover the state. These glaciers approached from the north and leveled the knobs and hills, filled in the river valleys, and created a flat plain. They, in turn, carved out lakes and new rivers. The existing vegetation became peat and marl. Most importantly, the glaciers resulted in better soils, either directly under the glaciated area or in those unglaciated areas covered by loess, wind-blown dust.

Indiana is a much more fertile state because of the glaciers, and those areas of the state not covered by glaciers have the least fertile soils. The soils, which are the major agricultural resource, range from sandy ones in southern Indiana to clayey ones along the Ohio River; they also include silt loams and muck. All are suitable for some kind of cultivation, provided the proper preparation has been made.

Beneath the layers of soil lie substantive mineral resources which include fossil fuels and industrial minerals, but few deposits of metallic ore. Small quantities of copper, gold, silver, lead, and iron are present in the state. The Indians worked

lead and silver, either from mines now lost or from nuggets they found washed from the sand of riverbeds. The early settlers of the state smelted iron. As late as 1900, iron ore from local mines supplied small furnaces but the competition from richer sources and larger smelters forced the closing of both the mines and the furnaces.

Far more plentiful than metallic ores are such minerals as limestone, sandstone, and dolomite, all of which have commercial potential. Of these the most significant is limestone. The Salem Limestone Belt, which underlies portions of Monroe and Lawrence counties, provides handsome stone which was avidly sought by builders until the advent of the steel and glass skyscraper diminished demand. Other limestone quarries can be found in Harrison, Crawford, Perry, and Putnam counties. The stone from these quarries, however, is used, in crushed form, to make concrete, to surface roads, and, when spread on the soil, to neutralize excess acidity.

Other mineral resources include sand, gravel, shale, clay, gypsum, lime, and quartz. These, too, are of considerable use. Sand and gravel pits dot the state and furnish the base for making cement. Clay mines in Adams, Blackford, and Huntington counties enable Hoosiers to make tile and sewer pipe, bricks, insulators, and ceramic pots. Gypsum mines in Martin County provide a basis for making plaster and plasterboard; quartz mines in the same region produce a material used in making refractory products.

The greatest mineral wealth of Indiana is in fossil fuels, the most plentiful of which is coal. Indiana's coal reserves are the fourteenth largest in the United States and its production is seventh largest. While approximately one-fifth of the state has coal under it, mining occurs primarily in the southwestern part of the state, from Warrick and Spencer counties on a line as far north as Fountain County. The coal is soft, or bituminous coal, seventy percent of which goes to generate electricity.

While Indiana has less in the way of petroleum resources, the state does produce oil and natural gas. The major source of both was the Trenton

Field in east-central Indiana which underlay Jay, Blackford, Grant, Madison, and Delaware counties. Another, less rich source is in southwestern Indiana. Primary production of oil has largely ceased in the state as drilled wells cannot be pumped. Oil can still be recovered through the use of such secondary production methods as flooding the oil-bearing rocks with water to force out the oil.

Indiana has another vital physical resource in its ample supply of water contained in lakes and streams. Its northwestern border touches the southern tip of Lake Michigan, and the Ohio River forms its southern border. Because the highest point of the state is at the east-central border and the lowest points are at the far northern and southwestern edges, the principal rivers within the state run from east to west, before turning south. These are the Wabash River, with its major tributary, the Tippecanoe, and the White River, with its two forks. Other rivers are the Kankakee, which originates in northwestern Indiana and ends in the Illinois River, the Whitewater, which terminates in the Ohio River, and three rivers in the northeastern part of the state—the Maumee, St. Joseph, and Elkhart—which flow north into Ohio and Michigan.

The early history of Indiana is tied to the systems of rivers. The early French explorers came down the St. Joseph or Maumee and then portaged to a river, the Kankakee or the Wabash, which flowed south. The English or American settlers, coming from the east on the Ohio River or the south to the Ohio River, followed the river valleys—the Whitewater, the Maumee, and the Wabash—into the territory. Finally, the major cities of the state, with the exception of those in the Gary-Hammond region which are on Lake Michigan, are to be found on rivers.

In addition to its rivers, Indiana has numerous lakes, both natural and artificial, which add to its beauty and enhance the lives of natives and tourists as well. The natural lakes—Wawasee, Webster, Barbee, Tippecanoe, James, and Sylvan—are in northeastern Indiana. The artificial impoundments,

13

which include developments such as Monroe, Patoka, Whitewater, Mississinewa, and Salamonie reservoirs, were created in the twentieth century.

The conjunction of water and limestone in the state has resulted in the creation of numerous caves, another significant feature of the Indiana landscape. Water dissolved the limestone, creating what geologists call karst topography characterized by sinkholes, caverns, and ridges. While it is possible that caves may exist in many parts of the state, only two areas have known caves. Both are in the south-central part of the state which was unglaciated, leading to the supposition that glaciers covered the mouths of others. Indiana's more than 700 caves are located on a line beginning in Harrison County and ending in Putnam County.

Three of the most famous are Wyandotte and Marengo caves in Crawford County and Blue Springs Cave in Lawrence County. Knowledge of Wyandotte Cave predates European settlement, and at one time it was thought to be the largest in the nation, which it is not. It is unique because it lacks the water or mud usually associated with caves. Additionally, it has the largest passages, including the spectacular Rothrock's Cathedral, of any cave in the state. Blue Springs Cave, a more recent discovery, is also a significant cave. It lays claim to being the fifth longest cave in the United States and the eighth longest cave in the world.

The limestone bedrock which made cave formation possible also led to the founding of distilleries, an important industry of the state. Distillers claim that limestone-based water makes the best bourbon whiskey. Whether this claim is true or not, the fact remains that Indiana shares with Kentucky a disproportionate number of whiskey distilleries in the United States.

Equally important for Hoosier agriculture and industry is the climate, which is basically a humid continental one. Each month of the year can bring high humidity because of rainfall or snowfall; the summers are hot and the winters cold. Within the state, average temperatures vary considerably. The frost-free periods, important for the maturation of

crops, range from a 150-day minimum in the extreme northern portion to a 200-day maximum in the extreme southern portion.

The growing season is adequate for most crops and, combined with the plentiful rainfall, allows the raising of almost all cereal crops plus other products such as tobacco. The continental climate system, which brings this bounty, also brings disturbances in the form of violent storms. As low-pressure centers move across Indiana, they bring thunderstorms, accompanied by much thunder and lightning and sometimes hail, or tornadoes in the summer and blizzards in the winter. Frightening to the uninitiated and veteran alike, these storms can be extremely destructive.

All of the natural features—soil, water, and climate—combined to produce a distinctive flora and fauna in the state. The first settlers found a land heavily forested with three combinations of trees being predominant. Over fifty percent of the forest consisted of a mix of beech and maple trees interspersed with elm, redbud, dogwood, or blue beech which covered the area from Clark and Jefferson counties as far north as DeKalb County. The second distinct forest, found in the northern and southwestern regions, combined oak and hickory trees while the third, the mixed forest, included such trees as beech, maple, yellow buckeye, white basswood, black gum, ash, tulip poplar, hickory, and oak.

Little of the original forest remains. One survivor is a segment of mixed forest in Donaldson's Woods in Spring Mill State Park consisting mainly of beech and maple. Another is a segment in Pine Hills along Sugar Creek near Turkey Run State Park containing black walnut, ash, sycamore, and hackberry trees. In these two areas one can gain some idea of Indiana's appearance when forests extended mile after mile.

Not all the land was forested. Wetlands and dry prairies were found in the northwestern part of the state. The wetlands included bogs, swamps, marshes, and wet prairies, all formed by glacial action and all characterized by high water content.

While the wetlands may have had underlying fertile soils, they were unsuitable for cultivation in their original state, requiring drainage in preparation for use. Lacking capital or labor for such projects, early settlers passed the wetlands by, calling them "the lost land." A few sections of the wetlands remain as they were prior to the drainage which took place in the late nineteenth and early twentieth centuries. Jasper-Pulaski and Willow Slough State Fish and Wildlife areas near the Kankakee River are good examples of original marshes, while Little Cypress Swamp near the Wabash River and Leesburg Swamp in Kosciusco County are characteristic of the many swamps which previously existed in the area.

In contrast to the wetlands was the dry prairie which covered 13 percent of the state, primarily in the northwest, prior to settlement. Consisting of a variety of grasses, including big bluestem, little bluestem, prairie dropseed, and slough grass, the prairie was an impressive sight. Travelers in LaPorte, Benton, Jasper, and Newton counties reported that the grasses contained wild flowers of great variety and reached over the heads of horseback riders. In common with the wetlands the prairie was bypassed by early settlers, who called the lands "the barrens," reflecting the relative absence of trees. The scarcity of trees meant the settler had to find other building materials and fuel than wood. Nor was this the only disadvantage. The accumulated thatch and root systems in the grass proved impervious to the crude plows of the early pioneer. The coming of the steel plow and more adequate methods of pulling it spelled the end of the original prairie which remains only in isolated patches in such areas as cemeteries, railroad rights of way, highway shoulders, and ditches.

The natural landscape of Indiana has changed significantly from its original form, yet the underlying structure can be found beneath the surface or in untouched places which the plow and ax have missed. From these few examples the natural past can be reconstructed.

16

The First Inhabitants

Adena burials in Burkam Stone Mound, Dearborn County.

THE ORIGINAL OCCUPANTS OF INDIANA WERE THE NATIVE AMERICANS OR INDIANS, AS THE EUROPEANS NAMED THEM. The first Indians for whom we have evidence of a stay in the area were the Indians of the late Lithic Stage (15,000–5000 B.C.). These people left fluted points from the weapons they used to hunt large Late Pleistocene mammals in the lower tiers of counties along the Wabash and Ohio rivers as well as in some locations in central Indiana and Lake County.

The Indians of that period appear to have been supplanted by another cultural group beginning about 8000 B.C. as the large mammals disappeared. This cultural group, called the Plano, left a different kind of point, called unfluted lanceolate, used to hunt deer and elk in the northern part of the state. The Plano Indians were, in turn, succeeded by the Archaic culture which became dominant in the years from 5000 to 1000 B.C. and which left a much greater number of relics than the cultures it replaced.

The Archaic Indians hunted small animals, fished, and gathered food from the edible plants in the area. This diversity of foodstuffs resulted in a proliferation of stone artifacts dedicated to the preparation of food. These included choppers and scrapers, pestles and grinders to mill wild seeds and grains, axes and wedges to work wood, as well as needles, awls, and hooks of bone or antler to fashion clothes, drill holes, and catch fish. In addition, they crafted atlatl weights (bannerstones) of slate or igneous stone to use on their spear throwers, as well as stone pipes.

All of these artifacts have been found in Indiana, but these are not the only evidence of Indian occupation. Because of the way Indians lived, in caves or open sites, the food they ate, and the way in which they buried their dead, Indian remains of this period are varied and available. Near their living sites are deposits of fish and animal bones, of

Turkey tails, narrow bi-pointed blades, from
Randolph County.

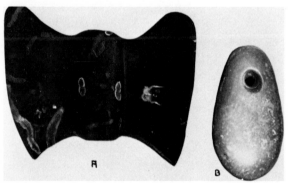

Bannerstone, a weight often added to a spear
thrower, and stone pendant from Randolph
County.

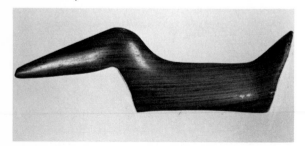

Birdstone of banded slate from Decatur
County.

Copper and antler headdress from Posey County.

Platform pipe from Weise Mound, Porter County.

Hopewell vessel from LaPorte County.

Three Hopewell vessels from LaPorte County.

Large incised jar from Yankeetown site, Warrick County.

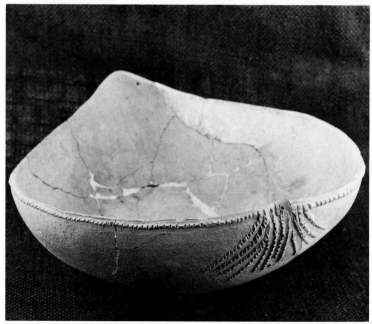

Large incised bowl from Yankeetown site, Warrick County.

19

Owl effigy bottle from Angel Mounds, Vanderburgh County.

ashes from fires, and tools lost, broken, or discarded. Shell mounds mark where the people lived on the rivers and discarded their shells. Burial sites located near living sites or shell mounds reveal the skeletal remains of the dead lying either fully flexed or in circular pits, occasionally accompanied by dogs.

Sometime between the years 1500 and 800 B.C. a new stage of Indian culture called the late Archaic or Intermediate Stage appeared. Characteristics of this stage are the first evidence of pottery—crude though it was—along with more elaborate burial sites, and greater cultural variations from one group to another. Four traditions of this stage have been identified. They are Glacial Kame (northern Indiana), Fayette, also called early Adena (southeastern Indiana), Baumer (southwestern Indiana), and Red Ocher (western Indiana). Of these forms, two are most distinctive; they are Glacial Kame and Red Ocher. The Glacial Kame people earned their name from the use of sand and gravel ridges formed by glacial outwash (kames) for their burials; and the Red Ocher from the custom of decorating their graves with that substance. The Glacial Kame people also made a distinctive form of artifact, the birdstone, of polished banded slate carved to resemble birds, while the Red Ocher Indians chipped points into a peculiar shape called a "turkey tail."

The next cultural stage in Indiana was the Woodland which dates from 800 B.C. down to A.D. 900. The Woodland Indians lived in more permanent locations in the villages, a characteristic made possible by the cultivation of plants for food. They built large ceremonial structures for the dead which earned them the alternate name of Burial Mound culture, and made elaborately decorated pottery. The Woodland Stage has been subdivided into early, middle, and late. The most significant Early Woodland is called the Adena (a late development of the latter is called Robbins). The most significant Middle Woodland is called the Hopewell.

Effigy figurine from Posey County.

Human effigy bowl from Posey County.

Fluorspar figurine from Angel Mounds, Vanderburgh County. It shows the outstanding artistic skill of the Middle Mississippi people.

20

Pinnacle Mound, Angel Mounds site, Vanderburgh County.

Beehive Mound, Vanderburgh County.

Anderson Mound, Mounds State Park, Madison County.

The mounds associated with the Adena Indians are most significant and impressive. Made of earth in a variety of shapes and sizes, ranging in height from a few feet to over seventy feet, and in shape from circles to other geometric forms, these mounds contain those dead considered to be of enough significance to deserve special attention. Buried within log-lined pits covered with logs and layers of earth are skeletons, sometimes showing signs of cremation, along with stone pipes or other ornaments, mica, or carved animal bones. Shards or whole pottery, decorated by cordmaking, incising, or stamping, also have been found. In the village sites, seeds of gourds, squash, sunflowers, and probably maize attest to the supposition that these Indians were farmers.

Several such mounds have been discovered and excavated in Indiana. One is the White site near the Upper Big Blue River on the grounds of the New Castle State Hospital in Henry County; another is the Nowlin Mound near the Whitewater River in Dearborn County; and a third is the C. L. Lewis Stone Mound near the Flat Rock River in Shelby County.

The Hopewell culture or Middle Woodland seems to have coexisted with the Adena. Indeed, the two often are difficult to distinguish as they share many of the same cultural traits. The Hopewell Indian mounds sometimes were larger, and their pottery was more ornate, as were their platform pipes.

Unlike the Adena sites, which so far have been found only in the southeastern segment of Indiana, Hopewell sites have been found in three parts of the state. The Havana Hopewell left evidence of occupation in the Kankakee River valley. The Crab Orchard Hopewell and Wabash Hopewell occupied the southwestern area of the state. It is here in Posey County that the largest known Hopewell site consisting of over two hundred acres has been found. The last area containing Hopewell mounds is the

Excavating the village floor at Angel Mounds site, Vanderburgh County.

southeastern part of the state, almost exactly duplicating the Adena occupation. The best-known site of the Scioto Hopewell is in Mounds State Park near Anderson, which contains the remains of several earthworks, the largest of which is 360 feet in diameter.

The last stage of Woodland culture, Late Woodland, left little evidence for the archaeologists to find. Small mounds, probably representative of this culture, have been found near the Whitewater, Ohio, lower Wabash, and White rivers. In this stage, Indians ceased their extensive ceremonial burials and no longer provided large mounds for later excavation. While scholars assume that cultural practices of earlier stages continued, they have even less grounds than before for their assumptions.

The Mississippian culture superseded the Woodland about A.D. 900 and lasted to about A.D. 1600. The origin of the culture is obscure, but because the physical remains resemble those of Mexico and Central America, archaeologists assume it came from the south. Regardless of their origin, the people of the Mississippian culture left the most spectacular remains of any of the prehistoric Indians. They were farmers who settled in more or less permanent sites along the river bottoms to cultivate maize, beans, and squash. They hunted and fished to supplement their cereal diet. Since earlier Indians had done the same, the tools of the Mississippian people are like those of the Woodland Indians. The major and distinctive feature is the temple mound, which is used as a descriptive term for these Indians.

The Mississippians lived in compounds surrounded by an earthen wall topped with palisades. Contained within the compound were flat-topped mounds arranged in a square around a central plaza. The temple mounds, unlike the earlier burial mounds, supported structures on top which were presumably used for religious purposes. These structures, which were constructed of wattle with

Aerial view of Mann site, Posey County.

Archaeologists sifting soil with a screen at Fort Ouiatenon site, Tippecanoe County.

mud daubed in the cracks, of course, have not survived. Also within the compound are found burial mounds similar in shape and contents to those of earlier cultures.

As with the earlier occupations, the latecomers merged with the Indians already there and exchanged traits, resulting in a mixture too difficult to classify. Such is the case with Yankeetown, a site in southwestern Indiana in Warrick County. The excavated village has a plaza in its center but the pottery show characteristics of both the Woodland and Mississippian. The points, however, are Mississippian. As a result, Yankeetown has been classified as either Late Woodland or Early Mississippian.

The only extensive Mississippian settlement (about A.D. 1200) in Indiana and perhaps the most famous prehistoric site in the state is Angel Mounds near Evansville. Angel Mounds covers an area of approximately 100 acres close to a narrow island in the Ohio River which served as a barrier for one side of the settlement while the remaining sides were defended with palisades. Archaeologists estimate that the settlement contained approximately 1,000 inhabitants who centered their lives around the temple pyramids, the largest of which was three terraces high and measured 650 by 300 by 44 feet. The site has been extensively excavated and is the source of a variety of beautiful artifacts.

In the rest of Indiana, the Woodland and Mississippian seem to have fused, creating mixed cultural manifestations. By the time the first Europeans came to the New World, the temple builders had disappeared from the Indiana scene. No explorer ever reported finding Indians living in the villages containing temple mounds in the Indiana area, although DeSoto did describe such villages in southeastern United States.

What happened to these prehistoric Indians? They were not, as many eighteenth-century thinkers believed, a separate race which disappeared before the Europeans came. What happened was that Indians living in the area abandoned parts of their culture and accepted parts of others. Moreover, there was considerable mobility from one location to another. The Indians the Europeans found in Indiana, for example, had come from Wisconsin and Illinois in the late seventeenth century; the Potawatomi moved south from Michigan about the same time. The Shawnees and Delawares came even later, arriving from Ohio and Western Pennsylvania in the middle of the eighteenth century.

The later Indian migration came as a result of French and English rivalry. The Iroquois, who were allies of Great Britain, forced the Miami out of Wisconsin in 1649. The French, anxious to frustrate the English, urged the Miami and the Potawatomi to move into Indiana. By 1725, they complied.

It is the Miami, Wea, Piankashaw, Potawatomi, Shawnee, and Delaware Indians who claimed Indiana and whose life was observed by the European explorers. Much of that life was misunderstood and some of it was condemned. Although Indians were farmers, they held land as a common possession, a notion unacceptable to the French or the English. The practice of polygamy was offensive to the Christian belief in monogamy. Even the political and social ties that bound these Indians together were misunderstood.

Despite the cultural differences, Europeans and Indians conjoined in a symbiotic relationship which altered both groups. The furs provided by the Indians became the basis of a well-developed trade, while the guns, steel knives, and cloth sold by the Europeans became Indian necessities. This mutual dependence led to intermarriage and commingling, the influence of which still remains.

Explorers, Fur Traders, and Empire Builders

George Croghan, deputy superintendent of the northern department of Indian affairs, and Pontiac, the Ottawa chief, meet in council at Fort Ouiatenon in 1765.

THE FIRST WHITE MAN WHO IS RECORDED AS HAVING REACHED WHAT IS NOW INDIANA WAS RENÉ-ROBERT CAVELIER, SIEUR DE La Salle. In 1679 La Salle led twenty-nine companions down the St. Joseph River of the Lake. He then portaged to the Kankakee River, which took him to his destination in the Illinois country.

La Salle's expedition coincided with the reorganization of New France, of which Indiana was a part, in order to increase the contribution of the colony to the French. What the French wished to accomplish was an increase in the quantity of raw materials from New France and a corresponding increase of sales of manufactured goods to the natives. In addition, they hoped to encourage more French immigration to New France and the conversion of the Indians to Catholicism. Finally, they wished to block English attempts to penetrate the Mississippi Valley.

Colbert, the principal adviser to Louis XIV, had granted La Salle the right to establish trading posts in the Mississippi Valley to further the French imperial design. La Salle, who with the Comte de Frontenac, governor of New France, had earlier built Fort Frontenac on Lake Ontario as well as a trading post at Niagara, hoped to dominate the fur trade from the Great Lakes down the Illinois River to the mouth of the Mississippi. To do that they had to have friendly Indians in the area and had to pacify the Iroquois, who were traditionally allied with the English. La Salle and Frontenac began this project and achieved limited success.

Not until 1713 were the French able to devote men and money to the development of New France. It was then the French government began to subsidize the fur trade by selling manufactured goods at just above costs through posts at Fort Frontenac, Fort Niagara, and Fort Detroit. As part of the increased interest in the Indiana region, the French established three new posts in the area. They were Post Ouiatenon (near Lafayette) in 1717, Fort

25

René-Robert Cavelier, sieur de La Salle, explorer of the Great Lakes and the Mississippi Valley.

Voyageur's pirogue made of tulip poplar. It was found buried in the silt of the West Fork of White River near Conner Prairie.

Saint Philippe des Miamis at Kekionga (now Fort Wayne) in 1722, and Post Vincennes in 1732.

The purposes of Post Ouiatenon were to insure harmonious relations with the Illinois Indians, and to entice the Wea Indians away from British influence. But the fur trade was not forgotten. In 1718, a year after Ensign François-Marie Picoté, sieur de Belestre, was sent to build the post, four trading licenses were issued to five traders from Quebec and Montreal, authorizing them to go to Post Ouiatenon and deal with the Indians.

Fort St. Philippe des Miamis was built for similar reasons. The French had sent Jean-Baptiste Bissot, sieur de Vincennes, to Kekionga, one of the principal villages of the Miami, as their agent with instructions to move the Miami north to the St. Joseph of the Lake, where the Indians would be under more certain French control. Vincennes died in the winter of 1718–19 and was succeeded by his son, François-Marie Bissot, who had no more luck than his father in persuading the Miami to move. So the French sent Captain Charles-Renaud du Buisson to Kekionga in 1721 to build a fort. He was also put in command of Post Ouiatenon. When Fort St. Philippe des Miamis, or Fort Miamis, was completed in 1722, Du Buisson took command and sent the junior Vincennes to be in charge of Post Ouiatenon.

Sieur de Vincennes' record at Post Ouiatenon was outstanding, so he earned the right to build the third fort, Vincennes. A southern fort was needed farther down the Wabash to counter English fur traders. The construction of Post Vincennes was delayed because of a jurisdictional dispute between New Orleans and Quebec, but was finally finished in 1732. The following year Vincennes went to Canada, probably to get married, but returned in 1734. Two years later Vincennes was dead, burned at the stake by the Chickasaws after being captured following a military defeat by this southern tribe allied with the English.

La Salle explored near the site of South Bend in December 1679.

Jacques Marquette in a sail-assisted canoe. Some think the Jesuit explorer may have visited Indiana in 1675.

Father Pierre Gibault came to Vincennes in October 1769.

The Brouillette house in Vincennes.

The first St. Francis Xavier Church in Vincennes, built about 1749.

None of the French settlements grew very rapidly; most of the population was Indian. In 1746 Ouiatenon consisted of 20 Frenchmen and 600 Indians; Vincennes had 40 Frenchmen, 5 blacks, and 750 Indians. Each settlement, however, followed approximately the same pattern of life.

The French practiced social segregation; there was a post for the French and a village for the Indians. Within the post each person chose what land he wanted for his house. There was no regular system of land ownership so the situation was always confused, but legal rights in general derived from first possession. The houses were crudely constructed of stakes, with no windows and only a dirt floor. Outside the post was a common plot of land to grow foodstuffs to supplement those not obtained by hunting, trade, or purchase. The land was little utilized as there was no incentive to raise more than could be eaten or preserved. Instead, economic life centered upon the twice-yearly visits of traders from New Orleans or Quebec who brought trade goods in their piroques or canoes to exchange for furs.

Because of the seasonal nature of trapping, the French habitants earned the reputation of being lazy, as individuals who lay around, drank, fought, or sponsored fights (cock or human), and raced horses. They also cohabited with the Indians, a practice which greatly concerned the Catholic clergy who insisted upon legal marriages to maintain the faith and to regularize property transfer. As soon as it was feasible, the church sent missionaries to supervise the religious lives of the settlers in the wilderness. In 1734, for example, Father Xavier de Givinne, a Jesuit, went to Vincennes. In 1749 a parish church, St. Francis Xavier, was built. Even in places where there was no parish church, as at Ouiatenon, pressure was applied for parishioners to go to Sainte Anne de Detroit for baptism and marriage ceremonies.

A common belief is that the descendants of the

Death of François-Marie Bissot, sieur de Vincennes, in 1736.

`Two crosses and two brooches from the "Little Turtle Grave" site, Fort Wayne.

Lead cross and brass crucifix, Fort Ouiatenon site, Tippecanoe County.

Bone-handled sheath knife and four-tined iron fork, Ouiatenon.

Indians who lived in Indiana in the eighteenth century all moved to the trans-Mississippi West. That belief fails to take into account the numerous liaisons between French and Indians which produced offspring whose names are still to be found in the state. A good example is that of the Richardville family. In 1748 Claude-Joseph la Gravière Drouet, sieur de Richardville, came to Post Ouiatenon to oversee the fur trade. One of his descendants was Jean-Baptiste Richardville, known by the Miami, of whom he was chief, as "Pe-che-wa." Born about 1761, he was the son of Joseph Drouet de Richardville and the sister of Little Turtle; he died in 1841. Richardville's name, somewhat garbled, gave Russiaville its name. Other families of similar ancestry are Godfroy, LaFontaine, Cicott, Burnett, Langlois, and Hackley. When the federal government removed the Indians in the nineteenth century, many of these families were exempt from removal and retained land upon which to live.

Had the French continued to control the area, Indiana might have had a mixed society similar to that of Mexico. Such, however, was not to be the case. In 1756 England declared war on France and, in what was known as the French and Indian War in North America, defeated the combined allies to win control of the Old Northwest and Canada.

Part of the British strategy in the war was to detach the Indian allies from the French. This was the brainchild of George Croghan, an ex-fur trader in Pennsylvania and deputy superintendent of the northern department for Indian affairs of the British government. Croghan convinced the Ohio tribes to sue for peace in 1758. This abandonment, plus military success in capturing French forts such as Duquesne (renamed Fort Pitt) and Niagara, Montreal and Quebec, led to the French defeat in 1760 and a subsequent peace treaty in 1763.

A detachment of Rogers' Rangers took Fort Miamis in 1760 and the following year British troops occupied Post Ouiatenon. The French in-

Iron hoe, worn along one edge of the blade, Ouiatenon.

Iron lockplate fragment from flintlock musket, Ouiatenon. In the center is the mark of the British maker, "Galton" of Birmingham, England.

Jesuit trade ring, Ouiatenon.

Jetton, a counting piece, with a profile of "Lvdovicvs Magnvs Rex," dated 1687, Ouiatenon.

Tail fragment of iron lockplate from flintlock musket marked with the name of the gunsmith of Birmingham, England, and the date, "Farmer 1747," Ouiatenon.

Iron door handle assembly with key from semi-subterranean storehouse, Ouiatenon.

habitants were given the choice of leaving or staying. If they chose to stay, they could remain Catholic and could retain their property but they were required to pledge their loyalty to the English crown. Some left, but many stayed.

No sooner had the French and Indian War ended than a new one erupted. This was Pontiac's uprising of 1763, which was brought on by Indian dissatisfaction with English attempts to take over the French fur trade. The English were not equipped to assume the full burden immediately; they lacked the subsidy used by the French to keep prices low; and they had a policy of not selling arms and ammunition to the Indians, a policy which was contrary to French practice. Attempts to change the policy failed because of English suspicion of Indian motives based on the failure of the Indians to return all the prisoners taken in the French and Indian War.

In 1763 Indian discontent boiled over into war. An Ottawa named Pontiac fashioned a confederation of tribes which included the Ottawa, the Potawatomi, the Chippewa, and the Wyandots with the avowed purpose of attacking the English forts in the trans-Appalachian West. These forts were poorly garrisoned; in most only a token force of an ensign and fifteen men composed the garrison. The Indians were quite successful, capturing all of the forts, including Miamis and Ouiatenon, with the exception of Detroit and Pitt. Frustrated by their failure to take Detroit, the Indians stopped fighting and asked for peace. George Croghan came to Indiana in the spring of 1765 and met with Pontiac at Ouiatenon. At the council Pontiac promised no further resistance to the British.

The English were uncertain as to what to do with their conquest. They did close the territory to settlement with the Proclamation of 1763, hoping that this action would help pacify the Indians. They debated the fate of three former French forts in Indiana. Fort Ouiatenon still was occupied by Indians; Fort Miamis was a candidate for abandonment; Fort

St. Vincent, as Vincennes was renamed, seemed quiet. The English dallied with the decision until 1768, when they abandoned their plan of rigid control of the fur trade and did not strengthen the forts.

As a result, the English made little impact on the area; few settled in the territory and the settlements remained French. The case of Vincennes is typical. Drouet de Richardville served as a mayor from 1764 to 1765 and was succeeded by another Frenchman, Nicholas Chapport, who governed until 1770 in the traditional French way. Religious services were provided by Father Pierre Gibault, who arrived in Vincennes in 1769 and who was under the jurisdiction of Bishop Briand of Quebec. The social and economic life of Vincennes, such as it was, was dominated still by families named La Salle, Dubois, Campagniott, LaPlante, and Bosseron.

The first one hundred years of European penetration of the Indiana country had resulted in a permanent settlement totaling three small villages plus a few nearby farms. While many Europeans had crossed the land to fight, trade, and die, few had stayed. The next one hundred years were to be different, much to the disadvantage of the Indians who still thought in 1775 that the land was theirs.

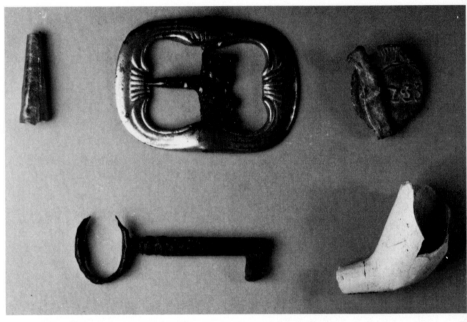

Miscellany, Ouiatenon: tinkling cone; pewter buckle; lead seal, dated 1733; key; and clay pipebowl.

The Americans

Clark statue in George Rogers Clark Memorial, Vincennes.

WITHIN THE TOWN OF VINCENNES STANDS A STATUE OF GEORGE ROGERS CLARK COMMEMORATING HIS CAPTURE OF THE town, thus helping wrest the Northwest Territory from the English. It was this success that made Indiana American.

The Revolution began in 1775 but the trans-Appalachian West did not become an active theater of war until 1777. The British encouraged the Indians to attack the exposed areas of the settlements on the frontier and sparked American concern for the safety of supply lines from New Orleans up the Mississippi and Ohio. As a result, the colonists determined to end English control and the Indian threat by attacking Detroit and other frontier posts.

The English, in turn, tried to strengthen their control in the West. Lieutenant Governor Edward Abbott of the Province of Quebec left Detroit for Vincennes in April 1777. He had no regular troops but recruited some Canadian and Indian irregular forces and hoped to recruit more from his stops at Fort Miamis and Ouiatenon, as well as in Vincennes. When he arrived in Vincennes in May, he was the first English official to appear in the formerly French town. Utilizing such resources as he could muster, Abbott commissioned three companies of militia consisting of fifty men each and built a stockade which he named Fort Sackville in honor of Lord George Sackville, British Secretary for the Colonies. Abbott had two purposes in mind for the stockade: one was to defend against the colonists, and the other was to defend against the Indians who were still unhappy over the English failure to give them gifts. For his pains, Abbott encountered criticism from Governor Guy Carleton of the Province and, as a result, returned to Quebec in 1778 to resign.

Meanwhile, the man who was to take Vincennes had already begun to plan his attack. George Rogers Clark, a native Virginian, had gone west in 1773 to settle in what is now West Virginia and then

George Rogers Clark, Revolutionary War General in the Old Northwest.

Francis Vigo, a trader who had settled in Vincennes and a friend of George Rogers Clark.

Father Gibault blessing Clark's army.

in Kentucky. In 1776 Clark became involved in a dispute over land claims and was chosen by his fellow-settlers as a delegate to the Virginia House of Burgesses to request that Kentucky be made a separate county and have more protection against Indian raids. Clark not only obtained the desired governmental change but was made a major in the Kentucky County militia and was given 500 pounds of powder for use in defending the settlers.

Clark's initial forays against the Indians convinced him that the only way to finally end the raids would be to capture the English forts in Indiana, Illinois, and Michigan. He returned to Virginia in the fall of 1777 to persuade the state to finance his proposed expedition. Once again he was successful in obtaining money and orders to raise seven companies of troops and to attack the English post at Kaskaskia. Clark recruited troops in Western Pennsylvania and Virginia, took them down the Ohio to the falls (present-day Louisville), and camped on Corn Island. When Clark revealed his plans to invade the Illinois country, many men deserted but, with the remaining 175, Clark continued downriver on June 26, 1778, before marching north across Illinois to Kaskaskia.

He captured Kaskaskia on July 4, 1778, without a struggle as the commandant, Philippe François de Rastel, chevalier de Rocheblave, and the garrison were asleep. He informed the French residents that the change in control would not change their status and that France had become the ally of the Americans. He even persuaded Father Gibault, who was present at Kaskaskia, to return to Vincennes to encourage it to surrender as well. The garrison at Vincennes, lacking a commander, also surrendered without a shot. When Clark successfully arranged a council at Cahokia with the Chippewa, Ottawa, Potawatomi, Sioux, Fox, and Miami, in which the Indians agreed to stop supporting the English, it looked as if the war in the West was over.

Plan of Fort Sackville, December 22, 1778, drawn by Lieutenant Henry Duvernet of the King's Regiment, who came with Lieutenant Governor Henry Hamilton to Vincennes in the fall of 1778.

Fort Sackville, Vincennes, 1778.

Clark's winter march through the flooded lands from Kaskaskia to Vincennes, February 5–23, 1779. During the last three days he and his men waded, without food, through water that was never below their knees. The panel is part of the mural in the George Rogers Clark Memorial, Vincennes.

Such was not to be the case. The English Lieutenant Governor at Detroit, Colonel Henry Hamilton, organized an expedition to retake the lost posts. In October he left Detroit with 171 English soldiers and 70 Indians. Gathering other Indians as he crossed Indiana, Hamilton arrived at Vincennes on December 17 with 350 men and forced a surrender, again without the firing of a shot. Fortunately, Clark was not there; he had sent Captain Leonard Helm to command the post.

Hamilton decided to wait until spring to attack Kaskaskia because of the flooding of the Vincennes area and because his available forces had melted away in the winter. When spring came, he hoped to muster his troops once again and defeat Clark.

Clark, however, thought otherwise. Learning of Hamilton's plans in January and that the size of his forces was only eighty men from Francis Vigo (originally named Giuseppe Maria Francesco Vigo), a Sardinian-born merchant from Vincennes, Clark determined to strike quickly. Mustering 170 men, many of whom were French, Clark left Kaskaskia on February 5 and arrived at Vincennes on the twenty-second. He quickly occupied the town and began to attack Fort Sackville. On February 25, Hamilton, convinced of Clark's resolution, surrendered the fort which Clark renamed Fort Patrick Henry.

After the capture of Vincennes, Clark wished to take Detroit but never received the necessary troops. Instead he garrisoned the towns he had taken—Vincennes, Kaskaskia, and Cahokia—and returned to Louisville. The British mounted four campaigns to retake the frontier forts; none was successful. Nor was Clark successful in trying to take Detroit in 1781. As a result, neither side really controlled the Northwest when the Treaty of Paris concluded the Revolutionary War. Still, the United States was able to gain legal control of the area, even though the English refused to relinquish military control of the forts they still held.

33

Little Turtle, chief of the Miami at Kekionga, fought against three armies of the United States.

General Josiah Harmar led troops against the Miami towns in October 1790. They burned the villages but could not defeat the Indians. The Indians defeated a second army led by Governor Arthur St. Clair a year later.

Having gained control of the trans-Appalachian West, the United States faced pressing problems which had to be solved prior to the peaceful settlement of the region. The first was how to govern the area.

During the war, the Continental Congress resolved that the "territory northwest of the River Ohio" would be organized into separate states, thus negating the claims of Virginia, Connecticut, New York, and Massachusetts. In 1785 the Congress passed a land ordinance which regularized the sale of land by dividing it into townships and sections. Of the thirty-six sections in a township, four were retained by the federal government and one was granted to the local government to be used to support education. In July 1787 Congress passed the Northwest Ordinance. This provided that the territory should be divided into no less than three and no more than five states. Until statehood, the territory would be governed by a governor, secretary, and three judges, all appointed by Congress (after the Constitution was ratified, the President assumed the power of appointment with the consent of the Senate). When the territory contained 5,000 free male adults, it could elect a bicameral legislature. When the territory had 60,000 free inhabitants, it could apply for statehood. Finally, the ordinance prohibited slavery in the territory.

The first government of the Northwest Territory began in Marietta, Ohio, on July 15, 1788, with the arrival there of the new governor, Arthur St. Clair, a Scotsman and Revolutionary War general. It was not until 1798 that a territorial legislature was elected.

Part of the reason for the delay was that St. Clair dragged his feet and part was the fact that the Indians both owned and occupied the land. Many white Americans had concluded by 1783 that the Indians had forfeited the right to their land because of their support of the English in the Revolutionary War. As a result, Congress appointed commission-

Colonel Henry Hamilton surrendered Fort Sackville to Colonel George Rogers Clark on the morning of February 25, 1779. Clark then renamed the fort for Patrick Henry, governor of Virginia.

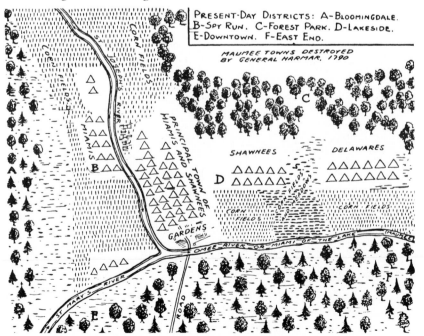

Map of Kekionga (now Fort Wayne) in October 1790, drawn by Major Ebenezer Denny of General Harmar's army.

General Anthony Wayne was appointed commander in chief of the American armies by President George Washington in 1792 and given the task of bringing peace to the Northwest Territory by building an effective fighting force. The Indians soon called him the chief who never sleeps. He decisively defeated the Indians at Fallen Timbers on August 20, 1794. He then marched to the Maumee River and built a fort which was named in his honor on October 22.

Fort Knox near Vincennes, Indiana.

Fort Knox, near Vincennes, named for Henry Knox, Secretary of War under President Washington, was built by troops under the command of Major John Francis Hamtramck in 1787–88.

Wayne held a council with the Indians at Greenville in the summer of 1795. The treaty with the Wyandots, Delawares, Shawnee, Miami, Ottawa, Chippewa, Potawatomi, Kickapoo, Wea, Eel River Miami, Piankashaw, and Kaskaskia was signed on August 3, 1795.

ers to negotiate with the Indians to persuade them to alienate their lands. By 1786 much of what is now Ohio had been opened to white settlement. Although no land was yet for sale in Indiana, a tract had been surveyed that same year to reward George Rogers Clark's little army. Clark's Grant consisted of 150,000 acres, located primarily in Clark, Floyd, and Scott counties. Within the grant was Clarksville, platted in 1784, the first town to be founded in Indiana since Vincennes.

The Indians resisted white encroachments and sporadic fighting between the white settlers and Indians occurred from 1786 on. Clark went back to Vincennes in 1786 to respond to attacks by the Wabash Indians; he arranged to garrison the town and called for a council with the Indians. The next year Colonel Josiah Harmar came to Vincennes with Major John Francis Hamtramck, who stayed there to build Fort Knox. In the fall of 1790, General Harmar led a punitive force from Fort Washington (Cincinnati) to attack the Miami towns near the present Fort Wayne. Harmar found no Indians there, but the Indians found him—and chased his troops back to Cincinnati. In September of the following year, Governor St. Clair was appointed a major general and led another force north from Fort Washington. His force was surprised by an early morning Indian attack on November 4; panicked by the attack, the troops fled, losing one-third of their number. St. Clair's defeat was the worst suffered by Americans in a battle with the Indians up to that time.

In 1794 the Indian confederacy was broken up by "Mad Anthony" Wayne, who had carefully trained his Legion of the United States for two years. Responding to the building of a new Fort Miamis in July, which had been ordered by the English Governor of Canada, General Wayne marched north from his post at Fort Greenville to Fort Recovery (erected at the site of St. Clair's defeat) and on to the Maumee where he built Fort

William Henry Harrison, a young army officer who had served under General Wayne, resigned in 1798 to become secretary of the Northwest Territory and then its delegate to Congress in 1799–1800. He was appointed governor of Indiana Territory on May 13, 1800.

John Gibson, a Pennsylvanian, was secretary of Indiana Territory, 1800–16.

Defiance. He defeated the Indians at the Battle of Fallen Timbers, near the British fort, on August 20, 1794. He threatened Fort Miamis but did not attack it, marching instead to the headwaters of the Maumee to build a fort which was to bear his name.

As a result of their defeat at Fallen Timbers, the Indians gathered at Greenville for a council with Wayne and accepted a boundary between their lands and the area to be opened for settlement in the treaty that was signed on August 3, 1795. Included in the area was land east of a line drawn from Fort Recovery to the Ohio River across from the mouth of the Kentucky River, which is now a triangular strip in southeastern Indiana.

On May 7, 1800, an act of Congress divided the Northwest Territory and created the Indiana Territory. It included Indiana, Illinois, Wisconsin, and the western half of Michigan. The governor of the new territory was William Henry Harrison, who came to Vincennes, the territorial capital, in January 1801, and carved out a 300-acre estate he called Grouseland. The same year the federal land office at Cincinnati opened the sale of land in Indiana subject to its being surveyed. By 1804 land offices would be established at Vincennes and Kaskaskia.

William Henry Harrison, the new governor, was to leave his mark on the state of Indiana and the nation. Born February 9, 1773, in Virginia, Harrison had become an ensign in the army and had been sent to Fort Washington. He served as aide-de-camp to General Wayne in his campaign that led to the Battle of Fallen Timbers and during the council meeting at Greenville. He resigned with the rank of captain from the army in 1797 to become secretary of the Northwest Territory. He was elected the first delegate to Congress from the Northwest Territory in October 1799, and eventually he was to be elected President of the United States. His major tasks in Indiana Territory were,

Grouseland, the home of William Henry Harrison in Vincennes, was built in 1803–4.

A bedroom at Grouseland, Vincennes.

Thomas Posey, a Virginian, was governor of Indiana Territory, 1813–16.

The *Indiana Gazette,* August 7, 1804, Indiana Territory, printed by Elihu Stout. The office was destroyed by fire in 1806, but Stout began publishing *The Western Sun* the next year. This copy was found beneath a window sill of an old house that was being razed.

Indiana territorial capitol and *The Western Sun* newspaper office in Vincennes. Grouseland is in the background between the two buildings.

The printing press in *The Western Sun* office in Vincennes. Abraham Lincoln is said to have visited the office when he and his family were on their way to Illinois.

first, to establish a working government and, second, to persuade the Indians to alienate their land.

As a result of his negotiations with the Indians, Harrison signed two separate treaties with the Delawares and Piankashaws in August 1804, in which they ceded lands between the Ohio and the Wabash rivers south of Vincennes and the road leading to Clarksville. The next year the Wea and Miami ratified the pact, opening about one-fourth of present-day Indiana to settlement.

The first period of the territory ended on September 11, 1804, when Harrison called for an election to determine if the territory wished a territorial assembly. The vote was favorable, and the first territorial assembly met on July 29, 1805. On June 30, Indiana Territory had been diminished by the removal of the Michigan Territory and was somewhat more manageable in size.

In the early territorial assemblies the most controversial question was slavery. Early settlers divided on the question, with Quaker settlers in such areas as Dearborn County opposed and settlers in the western reaches supporting. The Indenture Law of 1805 allowed slavery under the guise of indenture (a servant could sign a lifelong agreement of servitude). The debate over slavery diminished considerably after February 3, 1809, when Congress created Illinois Territory, which separated the most rabid proslavery advocates from Indiana Territory.

While the slavery question cooled, the Indian question heated up. On September 30, 1809, Harrison persuaded Little Turtle, Chief of the Miami, and representatives of the Delawares and Potawatomi to sign a treaty at Fort Wayne which ceded three million acres on the White and Wabash rivers to the United States. The Wea and Kickapoo signed later. The Indian reaction, however, was not entirely favorable, and there was a renewal of hostilities.

The two brothers who led the delayed reaction against white encroachment were Tecumseh and

Tecumseh, a Shawnee chief, dreamed of a federation of the Indians west of the Alleghenies and east of the Mississippi.

The Prophet, brother of Tecumseh, who led the Shawnee in the Battle of Tippecanoe in 1811.

the Prophet, Ohio-born Shawnees who had been forced to move westward by the Treaty of Greenville. Tecumseh fervently hated the American settlers and declared that since the Indians owned the land collectively, no single Indian could alienate it, a challenge to the legitimacy of all the Indian treaties. He was an outstanding speaker; this quality, along with his ideas, won him a wide following among Indians. His ability to attract followers, however, was at first eclipsed by that of his brother, who had begun life as a misfit and who had earned the name of Loud Mouth. Addicted to whiskey, Loud Mouth underwent a religious transformation and became the Prophet who inveighed against white ways and urged Indians to return to traditional tribal living. In 1808 the Prophet had moved with his followers to the junction of the Wabash and Tippecanoe rivers above Ouiatenon to found a settlement called Prophet's Town.

In the summer of 1810 Harrison tried to lower tensions by inviting Tecumseh to a council at Vincennes. Tecumseh came but refused to compromise. After the conference's failure, Harrison came to believe that the influence of the Prophet was pernicious and that Prophet's Town had to be destroyed. The following summer Tecumseh again came to Vincennes to discuss issues with Harrison. No agreement had been reached when Tecumseh left to try to unite the tribes in the South.

Harrison moved his militia and the U.S. Army's Fourth Regiment, which had arrived in Vincennes on September 19, north to Terre Haute and, while building Fort Harrison, the troops came under sniper fire from Indians. Harrison regarded this as an act of war and marched his forces up the Wabash close to Prophet's Town. The Prophet, ignoring the explicit instructions of Tecumseh, decided to attack before Harrison did. The attack failed and Harrison's counterattack succeeded. Thus did Harrison win his military reputation at the Battle of Tippecanoe on November 7, 1811.

Tecumseh and William Henry Harrison failed to agree at a council in Vincennes in August 1810.

Fort Harrison, near Terre Haute, was built in October 1811 to keep watch over Indian movements. The Seventh U.S. Regiment under Captain Zachary Taylor arrived to garrison the fort in July 1812.

General William Henry Harrison and his army fought the Indians led by the Prophet at the Battle of Tippecanoe, November 7, 1811. The Indian attack was beaten back and Prophet's Town was razed.

General William Henry Harrison and the army won the Battle of the Thames, in which Tecumseh was killed, October 5, 1813. By defeating the British and their Indian allies in western Canada, Harrison brought peace to the northwestern frontier.

In June of 1812 the United States declared war on Great Britain. Harrison, who had accepted a commission as major general in the Kentucky militia, was appointed by the federal government in September to command the Northwestern army, with orders to retake Detroit, which had been surrendered to the British in August, and to invade Canada. Late in December 1812 he resigned as governor of Indiana Territory. Harrison and his army marched north during the winter but failed to take Detroit after a detachment of his forces was defeated at the River Raisin in January 1813. Regrouping his forces, Harrison built Fort Meigs at the rapids of the Maumee to await the attack he knew would come. It came and failed. After Oliver Hazard Perry had defeated the British on Lake Erie in September, Harrison was able to retake Detroit and invade Canada. At the Thames on October 5, he defeated a combined force of British and Indians, and in the battle Tecumseh was killed. The Battle of the Thames ended the Indian threat in the Old Northwest.

Meanwhile, the progress toward statehood had continued. The 1811 Territorial Assembly had tried to achieve it but failed. In March 1813 a new governor, Thomas Posey, a Virginian who had lived in Kentucky and Louisiana, began his term which was to last until 1816. On May 1, 1813, the assembly succeeded in moving the territorial capital from Vincennes to Corydon; two years earlier, when the assembly had tried to move the capital to Madison, the attempt had been blocked by Harrison. The 1815 Territorial Assembly was able to persuade Congress to initiate the process of statehood, and delegates met in Corydon on June 10, 1816, to draft a constitution, which was approved on June 27.

Patterned after the constitutions of Ohio and Kentucky, Indiana's constitution gave more power to the legislature and less to the governor and the courts. It provided for free white manhood suffrage and required militia duty of all such citizens be-

William Wells, an Indian captive, was adopted into the family of Little Turtle. He fought with the Indians against Harmar and St. Clair, but then it was agreed that he should join his own people. He served the United States as interpreter, Indian agent at Fort Wayne, and in 1812 lost his life at the hands of the Indians.

tween the ages of eighteen and forty-five but blacks, mulattoes, and Indians were exempted. It promised a system of public schools ranging from township schools to a state university but did not set a time limit for the creation of the system, indicating instead that the system would be created "as soon as circumstances will permit." The constitution did allow counties to use fines to support education. It affirmed that there should be neither slavery nor involuntary servitude in the state, and that indentures of Negroes and mulattoes outside the state would be illegal within the state. Some thought the section did not define the status of slaves already in the soon-to-be state. The constitution also continued Corydon as the capital until 1825 and provided that every twelve years an election should be held to decide whether to amend the old constitution or substitute a new one.

On August 5, 1816, five weeks after the end of the convention, the first state officials were elected. The first two candidates for governor of the state were Thomas Posey and Jonathan Jennings. The winner, Jennings, was a young lawyer who had opposed both Harrison and the introduction of slavery by any pretext into the state. William Hendricks, a newspaperman from Madison, was elected the representative to the U.S. Congress. James Noble from Franklin County was selected by the General Assembly to become a U.S. senator, as was Waller Taylor from Jeffersonville. Although both senators were Virginia-born, they held diametrically opposed positions. Noble was a Jennings partisan while Taylor supported Harrison.

One of the first tests of the constitution came in 1820 when a slave named Polly sued her master, Hyacinth Lasselle, on the grounds that she had been freed according to the terms of the state constitution. The Knox Circuit Court ruled Polly was still a slave because she had been enslaved prior to 1816. The Indiana Supreme Court overruled the circuit court on appeal, and this decision settled the ques-

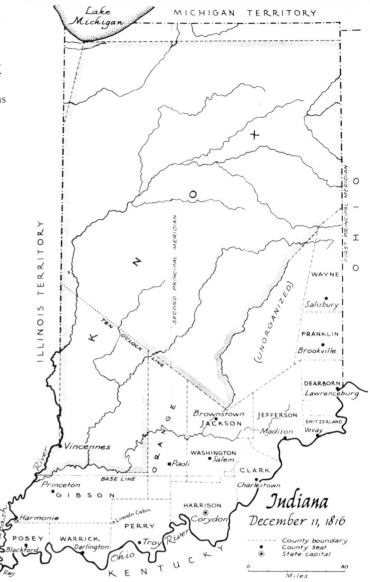

Indiana when it became a state, December 11, 1816. Map by Clark Ray.

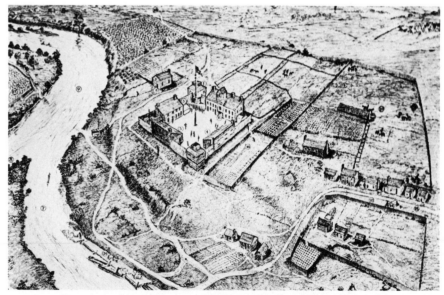

Drawing of Fort Wayne made from the plans of the fort and its surroundings recorded by Major John Whistler in 1815.

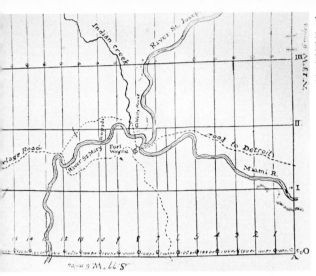

The first government survey map of the region that is now Fort Wayne. William Wells' house is located across the St. Mary's River from Fort Wayne.

Jonathan Jennings, the leader of the anti-Harrison faction, was elected the first governor of Indiana in 1816.

The home of Governor Jennings in Corydon.

The first state capitol, Corydon.

tion of legal right, though it did not end the debate within the state.

The process of creating local governments continued under the new state constitution by the act of designating new counties and towns. As a result, the names of Indiana's first political leaders were enshrined in county designations. At the time of statehood Indiana had 15 counties but by mid-century the present number of counties, 92, had been created.

The method of creating new counties was uniform. Taking an area from a large county or from virgin territory, a state representative would introduce an act which specified the boundaries and name of the county. Once the act passed, the county could elect the necessary officials, including a coroner and sheriff, and begin operations. The existence of the new county, like the old, however, depended entirely upon the state which could expand, contract, or abolish it.

The same may be said for towns which were creatures first of the territorial and then the state government. Often the product of a local promoter, towns were created or legalized by acts of the legislature. The acts specified names and forms of government and, unlike the acts creating counties, continued after the Civil War. Even more than the counties, the towns were subject to state interference and control.

The establishment of state government and the ways of local governance did promote white settlement, but the presence of large numbers of Indians discouraged it. As a result, the first thirty years of statehood saw the gradual removal of the Indians to lands west of the Mississippi. Those who stayed had intermarried with whites and were able to retain some of the tribal lands.

The Treaty of St. Mary's, signed in 1818, gave the United States the central third of Indiana, land held by such groups as the Miami, the Wea, the Wyandots, Seneca, Shawnee, Delawares, and

Notes.

Washington Street is 120 feet wide.
Circle .... 80 ....
North & South Carolina Streets are 60.
Alleys are 30 & 15 feet wide.
Regular lots abut on 30 feet alleys in
general, and have 67½ feet front by
105 feet depth, content ¼ acre.
Irregular lots generally contain acres.

Notes.

The shaded square No.º 12,
are reserved for religious pur
Every lot numbered 1, 5, 9,
ed for some future sale.
Squares 45, 46, 55, 56, are c
gether, "Governers Square."
White River is ½ a mile west
line of the town.

PLAT OF THE TOWN OF INDIANAPOLIS.

Plat of the Town of Indianapolis, December 1821.

Potawatomi. The Delawares were forced to move west by 1821. Others were not removed but saw their land holdings restricted. The Miami, for example, retained six reservations located on the Maumee, St. Mary's, Wabash, and Mississinewa rivers as well as private holdings. In return, these tribes were given an annual subsidy by the federal government.

Among those who retained individual holdings were two leaders of the Miami, Jean-Baptiste Richardville (also known as Pe-che-wa or the Wildcat), who was the principal chief after 1814, and Francis Godfroy, who was elected war chief in 1830. Both were as much French as they were Indian. They had fought on the Indian and English side in the War of 1812, they could speak French and English, and they were comfortable with the customs of European society. Richardville, for example, frequently wore European clothing until the Treaty of St. Mary's, after which he wore Indian dress exclusively.

By 1818 the relationship between the Indians and the United States government had become a symbiotic one which was made possible by a system of Indian agents acting under the authority of the Secretary of War. The Indian agents paid the subsidies and regulated the trade with the Indians which was financed in part by federal money. The appointed day for subsidy payment became a dreaded one for respectable Indians and whites alike. Gathered at agencies such as Fort Wayne and Logansport were white traders eager to sell guns, traps, blankets, and cloth, commodities which the federal government permitted to be sold to the Indians. Others sold whiskey which was not. The whiskey loosened restraints, and violence often ensued with resultant mayhem and death. Because of these drunken spectacles, white pressure increased to move the Indians entirely.

Treaty negotiations continued. In 1820 the Wea ceded all their lands on the Wabash River. The fol-

Indianapolis in 1820.

Marker commemorating the justice meted out to whites in 1825 for killing Indians in the Fall Creek Massacre.

William Henry Harrison was elected President in 1840, after the "log cabin and cider" campaign.

Announcement of the Harrison and Tyler Rally at the Tippecanoe Battle Ground, May 29, 1840.

The second state capitol, Indianapolis.

lowing year, the Ottawa, Potawatomi, and Chippewa signed a treaty at Chicago abrogating their claims to land located between that city and Detroit. It had two results: one was to open the northern edge of Indiana for settlement; the second was to render the claims of other Indians, and the Miami in particular, more tenuous. In 1828 a major treaty, the Treaty of the Mississinewa, was signed with the Miami and Potawatomi. This alienated more land and increased the subsidy.

Although most Indians assumed that the Treaty of the Mississinewa was to end the matter, a change in national policy in 1830 was to correct that assumption. Believing that the conversion of the Indian into a yeoman farmer would not work because of the evils associated with coexisting with whites, the administration of Andrew Jackson had the Federal Removal Act of 1830 passed; it provided reservations west of the Mississippi River for the settlement of those Indians who could be persuaded to move.

The act was designated to relieve two criticisms of the Indians by whites. The first was produced by envy. Tribal leaders regarded themselves as a kind of nobility, which they probably were. They dressed in clothes of the latest style, imported from New Orleans, and adorned themselves with massive and impressive silver jewelry. They owned land which was farmed by tenants and trading posts which competed with white ones. The second criticism was that the Indians were lazy and drunken; this came from observation of the ordinary Indian who did not work, had no land to cultivate, save perhaps a garden plot, but who lounged around the agency or trading post waiting for his annual subsidy in order to buy whiskey. If the Indians were taken away, it was said, both the Indian and the white would benefit.

Despite federal pressure, the Indians had grown more sophisticated and were less trusting of white negotiators. In 1833 the Potawatomi in In-

Jean Baptiste Richardville
(Pe-che-wa), chief of the Miami.

Francis La Fontaine, son-in-law of
Richardville and a Miami chief.

Leopold Pokagon, chief of the
Potawatomi.

diana finally agreed to partial removal to the West, but in 1834 the Miami, led by Richardville, refused to move west but did cede more land, some even from the Big Miami Reserve. The Miami treaty displeased President Jackson because of the failure to remove the Indians, and it remained unsigned until Martin Van Buren took office.

By 1840 Miami resistance had lowered and, against Richardville's advice, about one-half of the Miami were slated to move to a reservation west of Missouri. Interestingly enough, the four signatory chiefs—Richardville, Godfroy, LaFontaine (the son-in-law of Richardville who became principal chief of the Miami when Richardville died in 1841), and Meskingomesia, in whose name a reserve was created—all remained in Indiana. Not until 1846 did the last of the agreed number of Miami leave on the Wabash and Erie Canal.

Many Miami remained in Indiana to be absorbed into life and society. These persons had separate grants of land or were connected with those who did. When state laws permitted Indians to sell land, the Miami remnant had become, except for its heritage, an indistinguishable part of Indiana life. All that remained were the names on the land and the stories which lingered on.

Two of the most famous stories concern the Fall Creek Massacre and the captivity of Frances Slocum. The massacre occurred in 1824 and involved the killing of ten Indians—two men, three women, and five children—by five whites at Fall Creek near Pendleton. The Indians were peaceable Miami and Shawnee; the motive for the crime was robbery. Four of the five men were captured, tried, and sentenced to be hanged. Three were hanged while the fourth, a teen-age boy, had his sentence commuted by Governor James Brown Ray. The story has been told several times; the first by Oliver Hampton Smith in *Indiana Trials and Sketches* (1857) and the last to date by Jessamyn West in *The Massacre at Fall Creek* (1974). Both emphasize the justice meted out to whites for killing Indians.

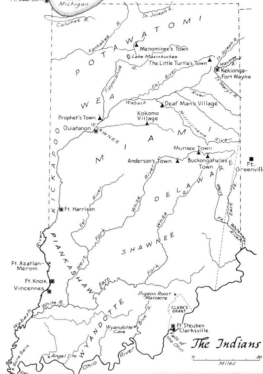

The Indians in Indiana.
Map by Clark Ray.

Francis Godfroy, war chief of the Miami.

44

Frances Slocum (Maconaquah or Little Bear) was the most famous of the Indian captives. The fact that Indian captives sometimes preferred to remain Indian raised both fear and curiosity among those who believed in the superiority of European ways. Slocum was one such.

Born of Quaker parents in the Wyoming Valley of Pennsylvania, Frances Slocum was five years old when three Delawares abducted her in 1778. She came west with the Delawares as they were pushed in that direction. She was first seen by a white man in 1791 in Cornplanter's Town on the Allegheny. She was rediscovered in 1838 by George W. Ewing, an Indian trader, in "Deaf Man's Village," a Miami town on the Mississinewa. At that time, she identified herself as Slocum. Ewing's letter of inquiry east attracted the attention of the Slocum family and two brothers and a sister came west to meet her.

After persuading her that their relationship was genuine, the Slocums learned of her new experiences. Her marriage to a Delaware had not lasted, and she later married a Miami named Shepocanah, or the Deaf Man. She had four children, two of whom survived and with whom she lived. She refused to go east to live or even to visit despite pleas from her white family, then and later. She remained in Indiana after the treaty of 1840 as one of the petitioners who successfully obtained an exemption to removal. She died in 1847 in her Indian home.

The story of Frances Slocum typifies the dilemma of white-Indian relations in pioneer Indiana. Both cultures attracted and repelled the other and, in the process, each group often misunderstood the other's values. Neither culture seemed able to exist in close proximity to the other without innumerable problems. In the end, the Indian disappeared and Indiana became the domain of the white settler. The way was now clear for the white American to populate the state.

Watercolor paintings by George Winter:
—Deaf Man's Village on the Mississinewa River.
—Bishop Bruté speaking to the Potawatomi, 1838.
—Frances Slocum (Maconaquah) lived in Deaf Man's Village with her two daughters.
—An Indian family at their campsite.

45

The Pioneers

This idealized picture of pioneer life was once described as "Domestic architecture in the backwoods."

THE LEGAL SETTLEMENT OF INDIANA TERRITORY TOOK PLACE, WITH SOME EXCEPTIONS, IN THE NINETEENTH CENTURY. BEFORE THE LAND was available at the federal land offices, it had to be obtained from the Indians, surveyed, and granted or sold. This meant that unless the settler wished to be a trader or to squat on land he had to wait until after 1800 to obtain title to the land. Nonetheless, when the newly created Indiana Territory was opened to settlement, it had a population of approximately 2,500 white residents.

Among these white residents were two brothers who had spent most of their lives among the Moravian-taught Delawares in Ohio and Michigan. They followed the Delawares to the West Fork of the White River in Indiana. William Conner married Chief Anderson's daughter and built a double log cabin for a trading post on land near the present site of Noblesville. Meanwhile, his brother John, who also married a Delaware, moved to the Whitewater River to open a trading post there. Both brothers served as scouts and interpreters for William Henry Harrison for many years.

After John's wife died, he married a white wife and became a town founder—Connersville—an entrepreneur, and a merchant with sawmills, gristmills, and later a general store in Indianapolis. He was a state senator in the first General Assembly that met at Corydon and also served as a state representative in the first General Assembly that met at Indianapolis. He died at the age of 50 in 1826.

When the commissioners who were to choose the site for the new state capital, and one of them was John Conner, came to central Indiana in May 1820, they met at William Conner's trading post. In the latter part of that year William's Indian wife and their children followed tribal law and her father and migrated with the Delawares to western Missouri. Later, William married a white wife and began building a two-story brick house which was completed in 1823. He also served as a representative in

47

the General Assembly, but his chief interests were his farms, sawmill, gristmill, and a general store in Noblesville. He died in 1855 when he was about 82 years old.

Many of the earliest travelers and settlers traveled down the Ohio River. The numbers increased gradually after 1750 until the American Revolution. By 1800 the numbers had rapidly increased. Most of the travelers lived off the land, stopping at sites along the river to hunt bison, bear, deer, and turkey. Excavations in 1978 by Resource Analysts, Inc., at a tract near Rockport uncovered one of the sites used by travelers to camp, kill, and butcher game animals as they journeyed down the Ohio River.

The early American pioneers were entrepreneurs determined to seek their advantage and to become rich in the new land. Typically, the first settlers who came down the Ohio River or from the South settled along that river or along the Whitewater River in southeastern Indiana or along the Wabash River in the southwestern part of the state. While some settlers were primarily traders and speculators, others were determined to work their own farms. Sometimes their motives went beyond economic ones. Among the latter group were the Quakers who settled near Richmond. They came from North Carolina because slavery was odious to their religious beliefs as well as because the land in Indiana attracted them. One such move by a Quaker family is detailed in the *Memoir of David Hoover* (1857), an account of its journey to Indiana in 1806.

Regardless of other motives, the desire for land was fundamental and universal. The earliest settlers had in mind an ideal location. It would be land which was close to water and which had an ample supply of trees and stones for buildings. More fertile land lacking these resources would be scorned for less fertile containing them.

Once the land was selected, the owner had to

The house of William Conner at Conner Prairie on the White River.

William Conner, an Indiana pioneer.

Elizabeth Chapman Conner, second wife of William Conner.

An Indiana pioneer and his cabin on the banks of the Ohio River, May 5, 1828, drawn by Basil Hall.

Henry Harden's log cabin in Brown County.

begin to clear the trees. The first trees went to construct the original dwelling which, according to Logan Esarey in *The Indiana Home,* was a "half-faced" camp. This was a lean-to consisting of three walls made of logs or poles which were, in turn, covered with brush. It lacked a fireplace and all other amenities and was freezing cold in winter, though a log fire was kept burning on the open side. The Lincoln family lived in such a camp when it moved to Indiana in November 1816, and the young Abraham was a boy of seven.

The half-faced camp was succeeded by the log cabin. Constructed of logs and chinked with crude mortar, the log cabin was commonly no more than 20 feet long and 10 to 15 feet wide, providing a maximum floor space of 300 square feet. Part of this limited space was taken by a fireplace and a built-in bed. Variations on this basic design might be a sleeping loft or another cabin connected by an open runway, but usually the one room was the house.

That fact complicated pioneer life for, although the population was quite young (in the 1814 census less than 20 percent of the men were over 21 and the largest number of persons in any category were in that of under 10), it clustered in families. Families were large with many children. Added to the natural offspring were those homeless children who were apprenticed out for their training and support in lieu of any institutional provision for their care. Families did not usually include three generations, although sometimes grandparents did live with their children. Few lived to an advanced age; in 1814 only 5 percent of the persons in the territory were men over 45 and women of that age were even rarer.

Given large families and a small house, two comments are in order. The first is that there could be no sense of personal privacy, as all essential human activities, including procreation, occurred in the same room where parents slept in a bed sur-

Woven coverlet, "made by T. H. Miller, Lafayette, 1857."

rounded by children on pallets. The second is that powerful coping mechanisms to handle interpersonal tensions must have been developed. Aggression against fellow family members was controlled and perhaps displaced against outsiders—Indians, strangers, for instance.

Still, it must have been hard to have been an adolescent boy who did a man's work without having the status, or an adolescent girl who had to entertain her suitor in front of her entire family. The enforced intimacy no doubt hurried the departure of children from the family cabin. For a boy it was easier. He could take up land nearby or apprentice out to learn a trade. For a girl it was harder. She could apprentice out, but to learn housewifery. Her main hope was to marry, to set up her own family.

Even marriage was not an ideal solution. Pioneer life was especially hard on women. If they survived the repeated childbirths, they were worn down by the constant hard work, so that the diseases endemic to the frontier found them easy prey. The life was also hard on children and infant mortality was high.

Pioneers were often victims of disease, although their isolation may have made them healthier than their urban counterparts who faced the health problems caused by polluted water systems and inadequate sanitary facilities. The pioneers suffered from the ague, an illness characterized by chills and fever, from the "milk sick," a disease associated with cows that had eaten snakeroot, from typhoid fever, pneumonia, mumps, scarlet fever, and tuberculosis.

There were few doctors and no adequate medical facilities. The doctors were ill-trained itinerant travelers who often contributed to rather than relieved the patient's distress. Covering a territory on horseback, the doctor carried his help in a black bag, a lancet to bleed the sick or to cut boils, medicinal syrups, perhaps a stethoscope, or a forceps to

The Lincoln cabin at Lincoln Boyhood National Memorial, Spencer County (a restoration).

Muzzle-loading rifles at the Muzzle-Loading Rifles Association meeting, Freedom.

50

An early woven coverlet.

Coverlet, "wove by Charles Adolph at Williamsburgh, Wayne Co., 1852."

Coverlet, woven by "Henry Adolf, Wayne County, 1849."

pull teeth, or even to assist in childbirth, if the ministrations of the neighborhood midwife were inadequate.

Along with building a cabin, the pioneer needed a continuing supply of food. Fortunately, the pioneer diet was simple, consisting essentially of corn and meat. The corn was eaten as mush or "pone" (cornbread) for three meals a day, or it was drunk as whiskey. The meat was found in the forests around him.

The frontiersman was as much hunter as farmer. He hunted the deer and bear which were native in Indiana, either one of which would supply enough meat to last a month. The deer hides served as a source of clothes; the bearskins could be used as rugs or bedcovers. The fat could be used for cooking or for making soap or candles or for lubricating wheels and guns. The early settlers also hunted birds and small game. The most common wild birds were turkeys and ducks, but pigeons, prairie hens, geese, and quail were also plentiful. Included among the small game were rabbits, squirrels, and coons. Small game and birds were often trapped or snared in order to save the precious powder and shot for larger game. Finally, Indiana lakes and streams contained catfish, black bass, pike, and sturgeon, which were fished for by the sons in the family.

The main source of meat as the game diminished under the pressure of hunting was the hog which thrived on frontier conditions by eating the natural provender found in the woods—roots, herbs, and nuts. The hog was permitted to run wild and was induced to return to the cabin area by regular feeding of grain. When fattened, the hog could be butchered or sold to the packing houses which soon sprang up on the frontier. Early hog drives to Lawrenceburg, Madison, and Cincinnati became common and salt pork, either processed there or at home, became the second most important dietary staple after corn.

Hand tools of the pioneer: broad axe, frame saw, and drawknife, laid across a sawbuck.

The early settler rarely owned other domestic animals except an occasional yoke of oxen and a horse or two which were confined within a rail fence. The oxen were used to break ground and the horse to ride. At the start, few settlers had sheep or chickens because they were less self-sufficient, were more often prey to predators, and required tighter enclosures.

In addition to the wild game in Indiana, pioneers relied heavily upon wild fruits and vegetables which were gathered by the children. Indeed, a certain progression of fruit ripening marked the annual season. The Juneberry was followed by the mulberry which was followed by the wild strawberry which was followed by the wild blackberry which was followed by the dewberry. Then, when the berry season was over, the pawpaws, crab apples, grapes, plums, and persimmons became ripe enough to eat.

Despite the gathering of wild game, fruits, and vegetables and despite the presence of the domestic hog, the settler had to clear the land so that he could grow more food. Clearing the land began at once; the trees which were cut to be made into logs for the cabin left only a small open space in the woods. It had to be expanded.

The first year, the space cleared would probably be no more than two or three acres, and these few acres would still contain large trees around which the farmer worked. These trees would be girdled by cutting a ring in the bark around them, thus eventually killing them. The next year, the trees would be cut, the logs rolled into piles and burned. Log rollings often became community efforts with neighbors joining in the work with their oxen and families. The process of felling the trees continued through successive years as the pioneer family expanded its arable land.

Once the trees were cleared, the farmer would plow the land with a team of oxen which were used because of their great strength, an advantage when

Harvesting wheat with cradle and scythe.

Doctor's medicines and medical bags, Madison.

Tools used to split wood: wedge, splitting maul, and axe.

Plowing with oxen.

Making clapboards.

tilling land filled with roots and snags. Once the ground had been plowed and the roots dug up with a grubbing hoe, it was harrowed with a wooden harrow and planted.

Every pioneer family had a garden plot devoted to vegetables of various kinds. Oliver Johnson, writing of his pioneer family that lived where the Indiana State Fairgrounds are now located, said his mother favored potatoes and pumpkins. Other staple items were beans, cabbages and cucumbers—both usable in preserved form as sauerkraut and pickles—onions, peas, turnips, and peppers.

The remainder of the land was devoted to three crops: corn, flax, and tobacco. Corn was the major crop, grown to feed both humans and animals; tobacco was enjoyed by both sexes, either to smoke or dip as snuff; and flax served as the main textile source until sheep arrived to provide wool. All the crops were labor intensive, requiring hard work by the entire family. The flax, in particular, required considerable processing before being transformed into linen suitable for dresses, shirts, or trousers.

Each cabin possessed the necessary tools for self-sufficiency. The traps, guns, hoes, cradles, and other farming tools shared space with the spinning wheel or loom, if the family were affluent enough. The fireplace contained a cooking pot, a spider (a three-legged, long-handled frying pan), and often an iron Dutch oven for baking. The table would be set with pewter plates and cups and iron utensils.

Pioneer life on the farm was hard. Everyone had to work and every season had its tasks which had to be completed. If they were not, everyone in the family suffered. Despite the work, the close confinement, and other difficulties, the pioneers survived.

As solitary farms dotted the landscape, small hamlets began to grow. These settlements provided the minimal services which the pioneer family could

Great Inland Sea Serpent, in the Wabash River, 1838. Watercolor by George Winter.

not provide itself. Quite often the first service would be a water-powered gristmill to grind the farmer's corn into meal. Next door would be a store to sell such essential provisions as salt, powder, iron and steel knives, axes, and other tools, and such manufactured goods as factory-made cloth. Another fixture was the tavern which provided food, drink, and overnight accommodations for everyone from the hog drover to the stagecoach passenger. As the hamlet grew, new specialties would appear: a distillery to make whiskey, a blacksmith shop to make and repair tools and shoe horses and oxen, a furniture store and an undertaking establishment. Professionals such as lawyers and doctors might become convinced of the need for their services and would open offices, usually in the county seat. Two other stimuli to growth were the location of county seats and of Indian trading posts.

After the General Assembly created a new county, a seat had to be established. If a hamlet succeeded in being chosen, it could expect to grow because the courthouse, the jail, and the estray pen (for lost animals) would be located in it, and because their location required legal and other services. As a result, there was intense competition for the county seat with the competitors recognizing that failure sometimes meant the death of a hamlet.

A good example of the rivalry is in the early history of Wayne County. When the county was organized in 1810, Salisbury, a town existing only on paper, was designated the county seat despite the fact that Cox's Settlement (Richmond) was the largest town in the area. Cox's Settlement lost because of its location at the eastern edge of the county; the argument that the county seat ought to be nearly equidistant from the outer boundaries was persuasive in an era of primitive transportation. In 1814 citizens of Centerville began to lobby to remove the seat to their town. They convinced the legislature in 1816 and were given the preference, provided they built public facilities equal to those in

Beck's Mill, near Salem.

Early Indianapolis mills, drawn by Christian Schrader: Morris' gristmill on east side of Meridian, north of Pogue's Run; Smock and Nagley's sawmill to the east in the hollow.

Johnny Appleseed, who signed himself "John Chapman (by occupation a gatherer and planter of apple seeds)," died in Fort Wayne in March 1845.

The lower Wabash, 1832. Karl Bodmer, a Swiss artist, visited New Harmony, 1832–33.

Prairie scene. From a painting by George Winter.

Salisbury by August of the following year. The citizens of Salisbury, indignant over the transfer, then refused to allow Centerville's building committee to inspect their buildings, but to no avail. Centerville became the county seat in 1817, and Salisbury gradually decayed.

In the northeastern part of the state urban growth came not from services, either political or economic, provided the surrounding farmers but from services connected with the Indians and the U.S. government. An example is Fort Wayne. Although the French and English had occupied a fort in this area of Indian towns, it had been destroyed. In 1794 General Anthony Wayne built a stockade fort which was named for him and which continued as a protector of the fur-trading post nearby. In 1815 Fort Wayne became the center for annuity payments to the Indians in the area, and the possibility of making money by selling goods to the Indians for their payments and of investing the profits in town promotion became evident.

One person who recognized the opportunity was Alexander Ewing, a second-generation American of Scotch-Irish descent. Ewing moved to Fort Wayne in 1822 to open a trading house, run by his two sons, William Griffith and George Washington, and a tavern, Washington Hall, which he supervised himself. In their trading house the Ewings extended credit to the Indians on the basis of expected annuity payments. When the Indian agency moved to Logansport in 1828, the Ewings established a branch store there.

In both Fort Wayne and Logansport, the Ewings participated in the formation of government and in town promotion. In 1823 Alexander Ewing bought 80 acres adjacent to the original townsite of Fort Wayne, which he platted into town lots and which the Ewings began to sell in 1829. In 1823 they helped organize Allen County and donated the use of Washington Hall for the circuit court when it met. In Logansport they bought land to be sold as

The Scribner house, New Albany, was built in 1814. The Scribner Brothers, who founded the town, named it for the capital of New York State.

town lots. They were aided in this endeavor by the fact that the land reserved for individual Indians in treaties could only be sold with consent of the President of the United States, who then delegated the consent right to the Indian agent in the area. The Ewings were friends of John Tipton, who was the agent of Logansport.

Nor did the Ewings stop with Fort Wayne and Logansport. They bought land in anticipation of urban growth resulting from the construction of the Michigan Road in what is now LaPorte, which they then platted. They opened another branch post in Goshen and speculated in land there. Finally, they planned a town to be called Tippecanoe in Marshall County in 1833, but the town did not grow as they anticipated.

The usual assumption that town growth came only after rural settlement is negated by Indiana's history. Towns grew up before farms were even settled and, as much as the farms, were the spearheads of the frontier.

Nor were all towns the products of unplanned growth and land promotion. Two towns planned in Indiana had a vision of a future society no longer rustic but one in which Indiana might have cities rivaling those of the East. These two towns were Jeffersonville and Indianapolis.

Jeffersonville's plan originated in 1802 according to an idea expressed by Thomas Jefferson, then President of the United States. Jefferson believed, in consonance with the best medical opinion of the time, that the periodic waves of diseases which swept cities could be alleviated by building cities with alternate squares of buildings and natural vegetation. The underdeveloped squares would act as the town's lungs and breathe out the miasmas which had collected. Jeffersonville never quite met Jefferson's standards, and by 1817 pressure to sell lots resulted in the almost complete abandonment of them.

Indianapolis also had an advanced plan for its

Governor's house in Indianapolis. Drawing by Christian Schrader.

Stump speaking in early Bloomington. Painting by Theophilus Adam Wylie.

Jeremiah Sullivan, a Madison attorney and Indiana Supreme Court judge, 1837–46.

The Sullivan house, Madison, was built in 1818.

A family in early Bloomington. Painting by Theophilus Adam Wylie.

day. In 1821 three commissioners laid out the site for the new capital to be called Indianapolis, after the legislature had rejected names such as Tecumseh and Suwarro. The man who designed the city was Alexander Ralston, who helped survey Washington, D.C., under the direction of L'Enfant. Indianapolis, as Ralston planned it, shared the characteristics of the nation's capital city as it had four diagonal streets which converged in a circle which was to be dominated in the center by monumental buildings. Originally, the governor's house, built in 1827, stood in the circle, and was replaced by the Soldiers' and Sailors' Monument after the Civil War. In addition, Ralston named some of the streets after the states as L'Enfant had in Washington. The plan was an interesting and good one which did center attention on the middle of the city with ample room for the development of governmental activities.

While most Hoosier towns were planned with the hope that settlers would come, fill the area, and develop a community, one town on the Indiana frontier came as an already developed community. This was Harmonie, later known as New Harmony.

The first settlers of Harmonie were members of the Harmony Society, a pietistic group which had migrated from Württemberg under the leadership of Father George Rapp. Known as Rappites after their leader, the members of the Harmony Society shared a belief in the imminent second coming of Christ and had separated from the world to form a community where God's love would prevail and the human ego, bloated by individual property ownership, would be diminished.

Originally settling in Beaver County, Pennsylvania, the Rappites moved to Harmonie in Posey County, Indiana, in 1814. There they built a town and prospered greatly. Indeed, their prosperity seemed more of a threat to their community than failure would have been, since success might lead to worldliness. As a result, in 1824 the Rappites sold

57

George Rapp, founder of
the Harmony Society.

Robert Owen founded the Community
of Equality in New Harmony.

Robert Dale Owen.

Harmonie to Robert Owen and moved to Economy, Pennsylvania.

Robert Owen was a native of Wales who migrated at a young age to London and from London to Manchester before going to New Lanark, Scotland, where he became a prosperous mill owner. Owen, depressed by the human misery he had found in rapidly industrializing Great Britain, began to search for some way to improve society by eliminating drunkenness, crime, poverty, and ignorance.

The solution, Owen decided, would be to create villages, ranging in size from 500 to 2,500 persons, which would be group efforts in manufacturing, commerce, or agriculture. They would be voluntary and independent; the inhabitants would use communal facilities for cooking, laundry, and other domestic necessities. They would live in specially designed facilities constructed in the shape of a parallelogram which would contain living quarters and which would enclose a space for a school, dining hall, and other public buildings.

When Richard Flower, who had been visiting the English Settlement in southern Illinois not far from Harmonie, returned to England in 1824, he agreed to act as an agent of the Rapps in selling the community's land and found an interested prospect in Owen. Owen had hoped to create an ideal community in Scotland, but the ideal had not come to fruition, and he was now convinced he ought to come to America. Come he did and bought Harmonie, which consisted of 20,000 acres of land and 180 buildings, reportedly for a sum of $125,000.

Owen had acquired a community but had no settlers nor a very clear idea of how his community would work. He proceeded to remedy both deficiencies by writing a constitution and by propagandizing his way across the United States to England and back. He succeeded in attracting settlers, among them 40 persons who embarked on a keelboat, the *Philanthropist,* at Pittsburgh to travel down

George Rapp's home in Harmonie.

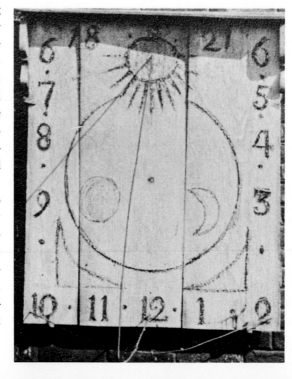

The sundial of the Harmony Society.

David Dale Owen.

Richard Owen.

William Owen.

David Dale Owen's house, New Harmony.

the Ohio and up the Wabash to New Harmony. Called the "Boatload of Knowledge" because it contained so many highly educated and respected individuals, such as William Maclure, a wealthy geologist and mineralogist, Thomas Say, an entomologist and conchologist, Charles Alexandre Lesueur, a French naturalist and inveterate sketcher, Dr. Philip Price, a Quaker doctor, and Madame Fretageot, an educator, the *Philanthropist* arrived in New Harmony in time to begin the year of 1826.

The first year was not a successful one, and by its end Owen had almost given up on New Harmony. The community suffered from disputes, schisms, and falling away, partly inspired by Owen's religious liberality and his indecision as to how to transform his capitalistic investment into a socialistic society, and partly by the contentiousness of the individual members. There were successes: education advanced as New Harmony had the first free public school, the first kindergarten, and the first trade school in the United States. The community had two newspapers, a Female Social Society begun in 1825 by Frances Wright, and a Thespian Society founded by William Owen, Robert Owen's son.

New Harmony began to decay in 1827 as financial problems multiplied. Owen left in June 1827 and, except for an occasional visit, never returned. The land he sold to William Maclure, his erstwhile partner, to settle Owen's debts, or sold to other residents, or deeded to his children who remained in Indiana.

These children, it can be argued, contributed as much to Indiana's history as did the community itself. They were Robert Dale, William, David Dale, Richard, and Jane. Robert Dale was a writer who promoted education and prison reform and women's rights. He served as a congressman in Washington for two terms and was a delegate to the convention of 1850 that drafted the Indiana Constitution of 1851. David Dale made the first geolog-

F. RAPP,

Will always have on hand, *and for sale,*

THE FIRST QUALITY OF

STRONG BEER,

by the Barrel, at

HARMONIE, INDIANA.

April 30, 1819. 18—4t

ADMINISTRATOR'S SALE.

A. Whitlock & T. Dubois, ADMINISTRATORS of all and singular the Goods, Chattels, Rights and Credits of WILLIAM JONES, late of the town of Vincennes deceased, will on

FRIDAY, THE 14TH MAY, 1819,

at the store door of the deceased, opposite the tavern of JOHN MYER's, ON WATER STREET, sell (*without reserve*) all the Goods and Chattels of the deceased, to wit:

A small assortment of

MERCHANDIZE,

CONSISTING OF

Fancy Goods, Calico, Cambric Muslins, Cloths, Hard-Ware, &c. &c. All the Kitchen and House-

Harmonie beer was advertised in *The Western Sun*, Vincennes, April 30, 1819.

William Maclure.

ical study of Indiana in 1837 and became the United States Geologist in 1839. New Harmony thus became the home of the U.S. Geological Survey until 1856. Richard was a scientist, soldier, and educator. He was professor of natural science at Indiana University beginning in 1864 and was the first president of Purdue University for a very short time, although he never lived in Lafayette. William's early death in 1842 probably prevented his acquiring renown comparable to that of his brothers. Jane, who married Robert Henry Fauntleroy in 1835, remained in New Harmony after her husband's death in 1850.

Few religious communities were as successful as the Rappites'. A Shaker settlement was established on Busseron Creek near Vincennes, but it lasted only from 1815 to 1822. And few pioneer communities could boast the amenities of New Harmony. Indeed, the early settlers had to struggle hard to achieve those forms of community life which New Harmonists took for granted. From the beginning of pioneer settlement, however, the drive for more community activities was evident.

The institutions which tied a community together were political, religious, and educational. The settlers met more or less regularly to decide political questions. When the courts were in session, they would meet in the county seat to discuss politics, watch the cases, and learn the news. Twice a year the militia met as required by state law. Muster days came in the fall and the spring. Each white settler between 18 and 45 was obliged to participate unless he was a conscientious objector, in which case he paid a fine. Of the two, the fall muster was more important as it lasted several days and was a prime field for political campaigning. Would-be candidates circulated near the marching troops, making speeches and buying drinks to further their own interests. Surrounded by their families, militiamen had a real sense of their own importance and value as well as a sense of participating in a

Women and children aboard the *Philanthropist,* January 1826. Drawing by Charles-Alexandre Lesueur.

The *Philanthropist,* or the "Boatload of Knowledge," halted by ice in the Ohio River. Drawing by Charles-Alexandre Lesueur.

Thomas Say.

Charles-Alexandre Lesueur,
drawn by Karl Bodmer.

Frances Wright in the costume of
the Community of Equality, 1826.

New Harmony in 1832. Watercolor by Karl Bodmer.

collective political process and defense effort. Then came election day, when interested voters gathered to cast their votes for the party of their choice.

Another institution which, at the start, was as infrequent as muster day but which also strengthened the sense of community life was the religious revival as expressed in the camp meeting. The camp meeting brought settlers to an appointed place, usually for a weekend or longer. At these places, up to a dozen preachers thundered at sinners around the clock. Music filled the ears of those starved for it and urged them to be saved. Converted sinners sometimes jerked convulsively, talked in tongues, or rolled on the ground. All attending were profoundly affected, one way or another. The churches which were the most successful in exploiting the revival technique were the Methodists, Baptists, and Campbellites (Disciples of Christ).

As a result, although Catholicism was the first to come to the Indiana area and Quakerism dominated the early southeast, the three revival churches became more significant. In particular, Methodism became the Indiana religion which gradually transformed an unchurched population into a churched one. It did this through the agency of the circuit rider.

The circuit rider was an itinerant minister who rode his horse through a specific district on a certain schedule. The first such circuit was the Whitewater Circuit, begun in 1806 by a minister named Oglesby. This circuit started in Hamilton, Ohio, came into Indiana near Richmond, turned south to Lawrenceburg, and then back to Hamilton. The stops were sometimes in log meeting houses in the country such as the Cain Meeting House near Richmond; sometimes they were in taverns in towns. The circuit riders were strong men, both physically and spiritually, who fulfilled their mission in all kinds of weather, leading to the saying that the weather was so cold that there was "nothing out today but crows and Methodist preachers."

61

Isaac McCoy, a pioneer Baptist preacher, established the Fort Wayne Indian mission in 1820.

Soon, however, it became apparent to the Methodists, as to other denominations, that permanent ministers would be more effective. Accordingly, certain towns such as Salem and Madison were made into stations, defined as locations with assigned ministers, in 1825. The next step was to build a church to replace the temporary meeting place of the tavern, trading post, or private home. Now towns boasted churches to add to the already existing facilities. These churches not only began to press for reforms such as temperance or abolition of gambling but helped to educate the children of the area.

Such was the case in Indianapolis. In 1823 the Presbyterians started a Sabbath School which was open to members of other denominations and non-church members. This school taught reading and spelling, as well as religious principles. At the same time the Presbyterians started a more secular school devoted to "Reading, Writing, Arithmetic, English Grammar, and Geography." Attendance fees totaled $2 per quarter; two scholarships, one for ringing the bell and the other for making the fire, were offered.

Two other kinds of schools might be available. One was the district or township school, the other was the county seminary. The first taught the rudiments of learning; the second prepared students for college or the professions.

Oliver Johnson describes the founding of a district school near his father's farm in Marion County in 1828. Interested neighbors met and elected trustees to build and staff a school. Johnson's father donated the land, and the patrons built the log schoolhouse. When the school opened, the students were charged $50 to $70 per term, which usually ran for the three winter months—December, January, and February. Since there was no age limit for entry or leaving, full-grown adults attended alongside small children, often in the same class.

Camp meeting in Indiana, 1829. An illustration in Mrs. Frances Trollope's *Domestic Manners of the Americans, 1832.*

A circuit rider on the Indiana frontier.

Martin Hauser led the
Moravians to Indiana in
1829.

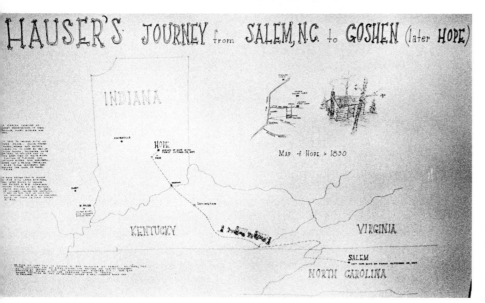

Map of Moravians' journey from Salem, North Carolina, to
Goshen (now Hope) in 1829.

The first Methodist Episcopal Church in Indiana, built in
Charlestown in 1807.

The Indiana Constitution of 1816 permitted each county to build a seminary with the funds collected from fines for crimes and exemption from militia service. The seminaries were not free; their continuation, like that of the township school, depended upon the fees collected from the male students (women were not accepted in the early seminaries). A seminary located in the county seat would add to its growth as sons of farmers and families with eligible children moved into the town for the educational opportunities there.

Equally promotive of town growth were colleges. If a college located in a town, it would mean increased population and revenues. So town promoters strove mightily for the locations of the state college by the General Assembly and the seven colleges founded by religious organizations prior to the Civil War.

As the religious groups moved into the state, they felt the need to have a source of trained ministers for the perpetuation of their faith. Foremost among these groups were the Presbyterians who had the most highly trained ministers and who controlled the first three colleges founded in the state—Indiana (1820), Hanover (1827), and Wabash (1832). Even though Indiana College was chartered as a state institution, its administration was dominated by the Presbyterians. In the 1830s when Methodist legislators remonstrated against this domination, a Presbyterian member claimed, "There is not one Methodist in America with sufficient learning to fill a professor's chair if it were tendered to him."

Somewhat reluctantly, Methodists founded their own institution, Asbury University, at Greencastle, in 1837, despite the opposition of many circuit riders and their followers. One such opponent was Peter Cartwright, one of the most noted circuit riders, who said in his *Autobiography:* "I awfully fear for our beloved Methodism. Multiply colleges, universities, seminaries, and academies;

Henry Ward Beecher, a Presbyterian pastor in Indiana, 1837–47.

Bishop Jackson Kemper, missionary bishop of Indiana and Missouri of the Episcopal Church.

multiply our agencies and editorships, and fill them with our best and most efficient preachers, and you localize the ministry and secularize them too; then farewell to itineracy and when this fails we plunge right into Congregationalism, and stop precisely where all other denominations started. . . ."

The Baptists also took action, founding Franklin College in 1834. The first Catholic college was Notre Dame, which was begun at South Bend by eight French priests of the Congregation of the Holy Cross in 1842. The Quakers gave in to progress and started Earlham College at Richmond in 1847, while the Disciples of Christ founded North Western Christian University at Indianapolis in 1855.

These colleges began modestly, often with no buildings, faculty, or students. As they acquired a president and perhaps a professor or two, they began their own seminaries or academies to equip students for entry into collegiate-level work. Their importance to the towns where they were located was well expressed by W.W. Sweet in commenting about Asbury University: "It was exceedingly fortunate for Greencastle that it secured the location of the college, for had it failed, the county seat would probably have been moved to Putnamville, and the influence given to the town by the University made it a point on the Indianapolis and Terre Haute Railroad and later gained for it also the New Albany and Michigan City Railroad."

Although the word "Hoosier," meaning a rough countryman, was in use as early as 1830, its application to all Indiana residents was less than fair. To be sure, there were isolated settlers living a crude and primitive existence, but there were also people of education and culture living in places such as New Harmony, Vincennes, and Madison, and even those who lived in the woods dreamed of a future when cities such as Indianapolis would be the equal of any in the nation.

The first Episcopal Church in Indiana, built in Crawfordsville in 1837.

Indiana Yearly Meeting of Friends, Richmond, 1844.

The first college building at Vincennes University.

The Second Presbyterian Church, Indianapolis.

The first Wabash College building, 1832. It is still in use on the campus.

The first Indiana University building.

Reunion of former students at a one-room schoolhouse in Allen County.

Unity and Division

Stagecoach crossing Pogue's Run, Indianapolis. Drawing by Christian Schrader.

THE HISTORY OF INDIANA FROM 1830 TO 1870 IS A HISTORY OF GROWTH, BOTH IN TECHNOLOGY AND POPULATION, RESULTING IN greater unity and sense of common purpose. It is also a history of disunity, with the Civil War setting one Hoosier against another and casting doubts upon the ability of the state, and of the nation, to withstand divisive pressures. As the people of the state grew closer together because of an improved system of transportation, they remained apart in their values.

From the beginning of the state the settlers realized that the success of frontier enterprise depended upon the development of adequate transit links. There were several stages of growth, each emphasizing a different form of transportation but each having the same goal—to connect the state to other states and to connect the communities of the state with each other.

At the beginning of settlement there were only a few crude trails cut through the woods which provided room for persons walking or riding on horseback. These connected to more established roads or to navigable rivers. Gradually, a network of roads came into being. Originally constructed of dirt, the roads next were made of corduroy, the name given to the bumpiness of the roads made of logs. By 1830 macadamization came into use; this involved the covering of the roadway with layers of crushed rock. Even these roads, however, would contain stumps and trees too big to cut down.

The first search was for money for better roads. Recognizing the limits of local financing, settlers pushed for federal aid in the form of the National Road. Beginning in Cumberland, Maryland, the National Road, which connected the state capitals on its way to St. Louis, had come as far west as Ohio by 1827, and surveyors had already plotted the best route across Indiana. The National Road (now U.S. 40) went through Richmond, Centerville, and Indianapolis to Terre Haute and was completed in the state by 1834.

A keelboat and a flatboat.
Drawings by Charles-Alexandre Lesueur.

The state also aided road construction. Using funds from the sale of land, the General Assembly authorized construction to begin on the Michigan Road in 1832. The road which connected Madison to Lake Michigan went through such towns as Logansport and South Bend.

The major amount of state aid, however, went to build canals, making the 1830s the canal era. In part, this was because of the recognition that canalboats could haul goods and passengers much more effectively and cheaply than wagons. Fired by the success of the Erie Canal, which was finished in 1825, Hoosiers began to seek funds to create a canal system in the state.

In 1827 the U.S. Congress granted over half a million acres of land to the state to help finance the Wabash and Erie Canal with a proviso that construction had to begin within five years. In 1832 the General Assembly created a canal board and authorized the sale of land to raise the necessary money to begin. By 1835 the first nine miles of canal had been completed and the first canalboat had splashed into the water at Fort Wayne.

The following year the General Assembly permitted a $10,000,000 bond issue for the state's internal improvements. The plans included an extension of the Wabash and Erie Canal from the mouth of the Tippecanoe River to Terre Haute and from there to join the Central Canal; the Central Canal to be built from a point on the Wabash River between Fort Wayne and Logansport to Evansville passing through Indianapolis; the Whitewater Canal to run from Canbridge City to Lawrenceburg; a railroad from Madison to Indianapolis; and a macadamized turnpike from New Albany to Vincennes.

By 1836 the Wabash and Erie Canal had reached Wabash and surveyors had plotted the route to Lafayette. Construction of the Brookville to Lawrenceburg section of the Whitewater Canal had also begun. These projects, however, received a se-

Notice to Travellers & Movers.

The subscriber having purchased the FERRY, crossing the Wabash from Market street, Vincennes, and the farm opposite, on the state road leading to St. Louis, formerly owned by Mr. Gibson—where

Corn, Hay & Oats

will be kept, and sold low for cash; a lot will be prepared for the accommodation of Drovers, Movers, &c.—new and substantial BOATS will be soon completed, one for the conveyance of heavy teams, one for carriages & light waggons, and the best skiffs. The ferry will be attended by experienced and trusty hands, and all damages that may result from the neglect or bad management of the hands will be paid for upon demand, by the proprietor, living at the Ferry landing, corner of Market & Water streets, Vincennes, where he has, connected with Mr. B. Olney, a general assortment of Groceries, Liquors, Druggs, Patent Medicines, Salt, Tar, &c.

WILLIAM MIEURE.

Vincennes, August 13, 1825.

Wabash River Ferry broadside, circulated by a ferry owner on the Louisville–St. Louis stageroad.

Fording the Wabash River. From a painting by George Winter.

Passengers sitting on top of a canalboat.

The *New Orleans,* the first steamboat in the West, 1811.

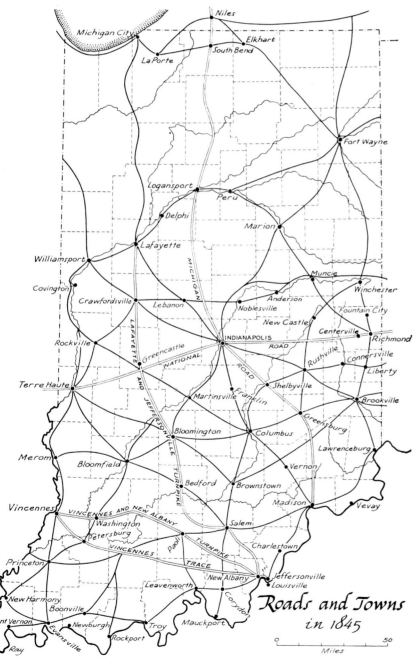

Roads and Towns in 1845. Map by Clark Ray.

vere setback in 1837 when, because of the nationwide panic of that year, the state became both unwilling and unable to pay the interest on the bonds voted in 1836, let alone to finance further efforts. Indeed, the state would long remember the financial defeats and compromises of the next ten years. The second constitution drawn up and ratified in 1850–51 denied the General Assembly the power to incur "any debt, except to meet casual deficits in the revenue, to pay the interest on the present state debt, or to repel invasion, or suppress insurrection."

By 1839 the whole tottering financial structure collapsed, due in part to bad investments by the clerk of the canal commissioners, Isaac Coe. Work ceased on all lines except on the Wabash and Erie Canal, which was permitted to complete the section from the Ohio line to Lafayette, and the Whitewater Canal, which was permitted to complete the Brookville to Lawrenceburg connection. Construction on the Central Canal, which had almost forty-five miles completed between Noblesville and Martinsville, stopped even though nine miles of canal between Indianapolis and Broad Ripple had water in it.

While canal construction continued in the 1840s, the impetus had lessened. But canal traffic on the Wabash and Erie continued. By 1840 regular packet runs were scheduled from Lafayette to Fort Wayne; in 1843 the *Albert S. White* traveled all the way from Lafayette to Toledo, Ohio. Extensions of the Wabash and Erie Canal continued even after the state deeded it to bondholders in return for one-half the debt owed them. By 1853 the *Pennsylvania* went all the way from Toledo to Evansville on the longest canal in the United States.

The canals died before they were fully finished, but, even when newly constructed, canals posed problems of maintenance, as the dirt canal banks and the wooden locks required constant repair. Because of these and other problems, the volume of canal traffic dropped below that which was neces-

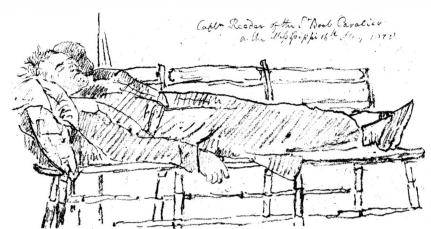

sary for survival. While a few boats operated until the 1870s, canal traffic had been drastically reduced by the time of the Civil War.

The demise of the canal system occurred in part because of the growth of railroads in Indiana. By the time the Wabash and Erie had been completed, Indiana had one thousand miles of railroad built and over twice that either in the planning or construction phase. The railroad was to become the significant mode of transportation for the last half of the nineteenth century, binding the state in bonds of steel, promoting the interests of some towns and decreasing the interests of others, and making all of Indiana part of a regional and national market.

The first railroad built in the state was the Madison and Indianapolis, which was completed in 1847. Originally owned by the state, it was sold to private investors in 1853 pursuant to the provision of the Indiana Constitution of 1851 which forbade state competition with private enterprise.

The decade of the 1850s saw as much frantic building of railroads as the decade of the 1830s had seen of canals. Raising capital by pledging cash or land, the promoters approached county and town governments for their support. Since railway connections often meant life or death for their communities, money was usually forthcoming.

The number of railroads grew rapidly. By 1852 there was a line from Indianapolis to Lafayette and one from Indianapolis to Bellefontaine, Ohio, which passed through Muncie and Winchester. By 1854 rails stretched from New Albany on the Ohio River to Lake Michigan on what was to be the Louisville, New Albany, and Chicago (Monon) Railroad. By 1858 service from Richmond to Chicago could be had on the Pittsburgh, Logansport, and Chicago Railroad and passengers could ride from the Wabash to St. Louis on the Lake Erie and Mississippi (later the Lake Erie, Wabash, and St. Louis Railroad, and then the Wabash line). Rapid expansion created concomitant prob-

Steamboats on the Ohio River, 1859. Watercolor and ink by Lefevre Cranstone.

The steam packet *Governor Morton,* passing under the Old National Road bridge over the White River, Indianapolis, 1865.

Building the Wabash and Erie Canal, near Lafayette. Painting by Wils Burry.

A wedding party on a canalboat.

lems. Railroads were oversold and overbuilt; consequently, most were unprofitable because of rate slashing. As a result, the process of consolidating small lines into larger ones—such as the Pennsylvania, the Wabash, and the Monon—began soon after the Civil War.

Both the canals and the railroads transformed the Hoosier landscape and population. The canals stimulated the growth of livery stables, dock facilities, taverns, and chandler shops near their stops. The railroads also created demands for services. As in Europe, a hotel near the railroad station to accommodate overnight guests, the salesmen and businessmen intent on furthering their interests, became commonplace. Warehouses, taverns, and other facilities also multiplied, making the station a place of excitement, variety, and fun, the focus of the town's attention.

In order to build the canals and railroads, contractors imported labor from outside the state. Because of the scarcity of labor, the competing demands of construction, and the attraction of other places, a number of Irishmen came to be employed in construction jobs. By 1850 the Irish represented 23 percent of the foreign born in Indiana. They joined the Germans who were the major non-native group, constituting 53 percent of the foreign born. Evansville was the entry point into Indiana for European immigrants coming by way of New Orleans, and by 1856 it had become a U.S. port city.

The paths these immigrants took can be traced in towns along the Ohio River or the Wabash and Erie Canal or the Madison and Indianapolis Railroad. Within these towns there will often be two Catholic churches, one serving the Germans and the other the Irish. Although the Germans were more numerous, the Irish became more successful in using the church as an instrument of mobility. As a result, even though Notre Dame was founded by the French and the Germans were predominant in the state, the university is not known as the home

of "the fighting French" or "the fighting Germans."

The influx of people into the area made Indiana the sixth largest state in the United States by 1860. It was the highest national rank in population Indiana was to achieve. While the Irish and Germans made a significant contribution to the state's growth, Indiana had the lowest percentage of foreign-born inhabitants of any state in the Midwest. The major migration into the state was from other states to the east and the south. Moreover, the natural increase was such that approximately half of the population had been born in the state. A few enclaves of English, French, Scandinavians, Swiss, or Dutch could be found in Indiana, but there was an identifiable native-born group which already was the majority.

The state's economy at this time was still basically agricultural. Although most of the land had been surveyed, only about one-third of it was under cultivation. The rest was still in native forest or uncleared and undrained. By far the largest number of farms was in the southern part of the state, despite the fact that this land was less fertile. The delay in settling the Indian claims and the Indian removal from the state had consequently delayed settlement in central and northern Indiana. The land farther north was either prairie or more swampy and marshy, needing drainage and the capital that process entailed to become tillable. Moreover, the river towns of southern Indiana were larger and provided markets for farmers because of their location which more northern towns could not match.

By midcentury Indiana had approximately 100,000 farms. They did not differ much from those of the early settlers, except that houses constructed of sawed lumber were replacing log cabins and new outbuildings, such as barns and springhouses, could be seen. Although the average-sized farm was 136 acres, much of the land remained uncultivated because of the lack of labor

RATES OF TOLL

On the Wabash and Erie Canal, in Indiana, as established by the General Superintendent of said Canal.

Ordered, That from and after the 15th day of March, A. D. 1845, on each article of property transported on the Wabash and Erie Canal, in Indiana, there shall be charged and collected the rates of toll hereinafter affixed to such articles, in lieu of the rates heretofore charged.

Property charged with Toll according to Weight.

ARTICLES.	FOR EACH MILE NOT EXCEEDING 100.	FOR EACH MILE EXCEEDING 100.	ARTICLES.	FOR EACH MILE NOT EXCEEDING 100.	FOR EACH MILE EXCEEDING 100.
	Mills.	*Mills.*		*Mills.*	*Mills.*
On each 1,000 pounds, and in the same proportion for a lesser or greater weight of			On each 1,000 pounds, and in the same proportion for a lesser or greater weight, of		
Ale, - - - -	11	8	*Bacon, - - -	11	8
Ashes, - - -	5	3	Broom handles, -	11	8
Animals, (domestic) -	11	8	Bristles, - -	11	8
Apples, - - -	8	5	Buhr-blocks, U. S., and mill stones made	11	8
Agricultural implements, -	11	8	therefrom, -	11	8
Bread, - - -	11	8	*Barley, - -	8	5
Beans, - - -	11	8	*Buckwheat, - -	8	5
Beer, - - -	11	8	Barrels, (empty) -	8	5
Butter, - - -	11	8	Boxes, (empty) - -	8	5
Baggage, - - -	30	22	Blooms, - - -	19	12
Beeswax, - - -	11	8	Bark, (tanner's) -	8	5
Brooms, - - -	11	8	Bran, - - -	8	5

Rates of Toll on the Wabash and Erie Canal, March 15, 1845.

Horses pulling a canalboat under the
Washington Street bridge on the
Central Canal, Indianapolis.
Drawing by Christian Schrader.

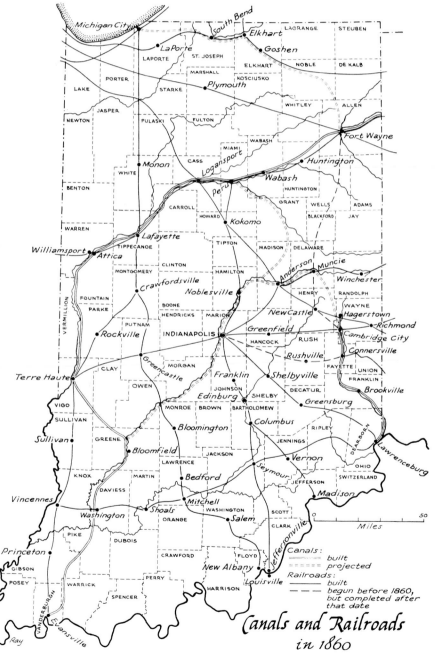

Canals and Railroads
in 1860

or effective equipment. Gradually, farmers were
enclosing their fields with rail fences to contain the
cattle and sheep which had joined the hogs, still the
principal meat animal, down on the farm. Wheat
and corn still constituted the major cereal crops in
the state, but farmers now were growing hay to
feed the livestock in winter.

Because of the need for labor and because of
the dearth of charitable organizations to provide for
orphans and poor children, farm households tended
to be large. Children had to help to make the farms
successful. Natural offspring were joined by ap-
prentices who served as hired girls or boys until
mature enough to venture out into the world on
their own. The farms of Indiana provided the population of the cities as well as the fodder for the can-
nons of the Civil War.

By 1850 Indiana had over two hundred villages, towns, or cities, the largest of which was
New Albany, followed closely by Madison, each of
which had over eight thousand inhabitants. By
1860, however, Indianapolis was the largest city in
the state, with a population of 18,611, making it
equivalent in size to Dayton and Columbus, Ohio,
and forty-eighth in size in the entire country.

Indianapolis' urban growth is typical of the
Old Northwest. Early towns succeeded where
others failed because they obtained transportation
links providing services to the region which were
superior to those of their competitors. These services might be in the form of financial or political
institutions. Indianapolis became the hub of the railroads in the state. The building of the Madison and
Indianapolis Railroad provided a link to the Ohio
River. Two years after that connection, seven others
had been added, to the east, west, and north. No
other city in Indiana could match that record.

Railroad development was not a product of
natural growth; it was the result of skillful promotion. No more colorful promoter, or more representative one, lived in Indiana than Oliver H.

73

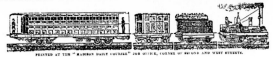

Waybill of the Madison and Indianapolis Railroad, May 22, 1857.

Smith, a Pennsylvanian, who came to Connersville originally, where he was a successful lawyer and politician, serving in the United States Congress first as a Democrat and then as a Whig. Moving to Indianapolis, he began boosting railroads and helped complete the Indianapolis and Bellefontaine Railroad. He then began to promote the Evansville, Indianapolis, and Cleveland Straight Line Railroad. He died before this road was finished.

The political connection also boosted the size and services of Indianapolis. Home of the General Assembly and the federal land office, Indianapolis became the site of the welfare institutions created in the reform fervor of the 1840s, the State School for the Deaf in 1844, the State School for the Blind in 1847, and the Indianapolis Hospital for the Insane opened in 1848 (technically, the latter was two miles out of the city). These institutions improved the lot of their residents, and they also swelled the population of the capital city.

So also did the burgeoning banking business. Both the Second State Bank of Indiana and its successor, the Bank of the State of Indiana, were in Indianapolis. When free banking became possible under the Constitution of 1851, several banks took advantage of the law to open in the city where banks were expected to be; and when the National Banking Act of 1863 permitted the charter of national banks, Calvin Fletcher and Thomas Sharpe established the Indianapolis National Bank, which soon became a significant financial institution in the state. Fletcher had a long career in both political and financial enterprises. A lawyer, Methodist, anti-slavery advocate, Fletcher eventually joined the Republican party and became a staunch supporter of Governor Oliver P. Morton during the Civil War.

Despite its growth, Indianapolis had still not surpassed the importance of the towns on the southern border. Utilizing the Ohio River, towns such as Madison, New Albany, Jeffersonville, and Evansville capitalized upon the trade with the

Broadside of the Louisville, New Albany & Chicago Railroad, with a drawing of the "Traveler," an express passenger engine.

Old Union Station, Indianapolis, in the 1850s. Drawing by Christian Schrader.

The first train robbery was at Seymour, Indiana, by the four Reno brothers, October 6, 1866.

"M.G. Bright" engine and crew of the Jeffersonville, Madison & Indianapolis Railroad.

Monon depot and hotel, Monon, Indiana, 1880.

South. They built steamboats to ply the Ohio and the Mississippi. They sold farm produce from the inland farms and packed salt pork for sale to the southern plantations, using the hogs driven to their slaughterhouses. There was even an attempt at Cannelton to duplicate the success of manufacturing centers in New England. The Indiana Cotton Mills, the largest factory in Indiana in 1850, took cotton from the South to process into cloth. It had between 300 and 400 employees and 372 looms. The coming of the Civil War interrupted the lucrative trade, and other Indiana towns began to grow more than those on the river.

Northern Indiana towns had already begun to develop industrially. Good examples are South Bend and Mishawaka. Both towns began with basic industries oriented to the regional markets. These produced such items as iron, textiles, flour, and lumber. In 1836, for example, the St. Joseph Iron Company dammed the St. Joseph River to provide power for its mills. By 1850 the company was producing 1,100 tons of pig iron per year. In South Bend, the St. Joseph was dammed by the South Bend Manufacturing Company, a corporation still in existence and owned by Indiana and Michigan Electric. The power provided went to several firms, the largest of which was the South Bend Woolen Manufacturing Company. In 1850 this company produced 15,000 yards of cloth. Neither of these companies became the success nor promoted the future of the area as much as two others originally conceived to serve the needs of farmers. These were the Oliver Chilled Plow Works and the Studebaker Wagon Works.

The Studebakers, Henry and Clement, migrated to Indiana from Pennsylvania, where their German Mennonite ancestors had come seeking religious toleration. Intending originally to be farmers, the Studebakers opened a blacksmith shop on the side. In common with other shops, the Studebakers built wagons to order. The first year they had two orders. Business increased dramatically when the Studebakers received a subcontract from the Mishawaka Wagon Works to supply 100 army wagons and when another brother, John, returned from the California gold fields in 1858 with both capital and energy to invest in the business. John had a talent for sales and began to build a sales network. When the Civil War came, the firm was ready for the flood of orders which soon engulfed it and, when the war was over, it already had 200 workers and a regional reputation.

James Oliver, a transplanted Scotsman, bought a quarter interest in a foundry in South Bend in 1855. Experimenting with various blends of steel, he finally developed a superior plow, the Oliver chilled steel plow. The plow could cut through the prairie sod more easily than cast-iron ones and scoured much better. Both Studebaker and Oliver presaged the development of farm machinery manufacturing which was to add to Indiana's postwar prosperity.

Regardless of their size or location, Indiana towns of the period were much alike. They were compact, with a commercial section in the center located around a courthouse square if the town were a county seat, or around an open square if it were not. The courthouse would be the largest building in town, often two stories high and constructed of brick or stone. The businesses would include the inevitable tavern, blacksmith shop, livery stable, and general store. The streets would be dirt which rutted badly in the spring and fall and which was stirred into dust by horses' hooves. Towns were unsanitary, dirty places. No Indiana town of this era had a central sewage system, or a garbage collection system, or a piped water supply. Residents threw garbage in the streets for hogs to eat, used outhouses, and relied on private or public water pumps.

Adding to urban problems was the absence of professional policemen and firemen. Indianapolis

New Albany, the largest city in Indiana, 1850.

The *Robert E. Lee* was built at the New Albany shipyards.

Cannelton, as seen from the south shore of the Ohio River, 1850. The Indiana Cotton Mills are in the center of the town.

Evansville on the Ohio River in the 1850s.

Courthouse and public square, Paoli, 1850s.

voted to establish a police force in 1854, but the department did not begin operation until 1857. This was two years prior to the beginning of the full-time, professional fire department in that city. Other towns trailed behind, still using an untrained watch or patrol at night to look for law violators or for signs of fire. In the day, town marshals or officers of the court, the sheriff and his deputies, carried out law enforcement. Fires were put out by volunteer companies which served without pay but used city equipment such as hand-drawn hose carts and pumpers housed in buildings supplied by the city.

The modernization of Indiana farms and towns continued during the 1860s. Hoosier attention, however, was diverted to the national arena because of the Civil War.

Time has eroded the passion of a century ago and the internal conflicts engendered by the war have vanished, leaving little evidence that the Civil War posed a real question as to whether the state could survive. The Civil War, in popular thought, has come to mean a war to free the slaves. It did not begin as a war for black liberation; it began as a war to preserve the Union. The abolition of slavery came later when national leaders such as Lincoln became convinced that such abolition would advance the possibility of victory.

In Indiana there was considerable opposition to the war, opposition based on two main principles. The first was the belief in a necessary connection with the South, fostered by families and by business, and the second was a strong belief in black inequality. Blacks in Indiana and throughout most of the North, prior to the Civil War, could not vote, attend public schools, marry whites, or testify in court if whites were party to the case. Article XIII of the Indiana Constitution of 1851 prohibited black immigration into the state. When submitted to the voters of Indiana, this section received more favorable votes than the constitution itself.

Adam Gimbel's store, Vincennes, 1842.

Herman Hulman, Terre Haute.

The division in the state was reflected in the complex political situation. Indiana was a Democratic state during most of the 1850s. Indeed, the most popular political figure of the decade was Joseph A. Wright, who served as governor from 1849 to 1857. The Republican party did not take its name and place in the state until 1858. It was preceded by a so-called People's party, which was created in 1854 and was a coalition of ex-Whigs, Know Nothings (who opposed foreigners and Catholics), temperance Democrats, Free Soilers, and Democrats against the Kansas-Nebraska Act, all tied together by one common bond, opposition to the extension of slavery into the territories. The Indiana People's party did send a delegation to the national Republican convention in 1856. Among the delegates were Henry S. Lane, Oliver P. Morton, and George W. Julian, all of whom were to become leaders in the Republican party.

A quick look at early Hoosier Republicans demonstrates the wide range of opinion in a party which had not yet achieved a sense of identity. Schuyler Colfax, who was originally from New York State, settled in Indiana to operate a newspaper, the *Saint Joseph Valley Register,* in 1845. Active in Indiana politics as a Whig, Colfax won election to Congress as a representative of the People's party. Having become a Republican, he continued to serve in Congress until 1869 when he became vice president of the United States. His companion in the Senate during the years of war and reconstruction was Henry Smith Lane, a Kentucky-born Hoosier, who was an antislave Whig. Lane was elected U.S. Senator in 1859 as a Republican, but the Democrats in the Indiana General Assembly blocked his seating, and he did not assume his seat until 1861 when the Republican-dominated legislature appointed him. Lane actually ran for governor of Indiana in 1860 with the tacit understanding that if he won he would resign in favor of his lieutenant governor and go to the U.S. Senate. His running

Hulman & Cox store, Terre Haute, 1867.

Market Street (now Main Street), Vincennes, about 1835.

Governor's house on the Circle, 1850. Drawing by Christian Schrader.

Market Square, Indianapolis. Drawing by Christian Schrader.

mate, who became governor, was Oliver P. Morton (Oliver Hazard Perry Throck Morton), who was a native-born Hoosier. Morton had been a Democrat until 1854 when he opposed the Kansas-Nebraska Act. Morton served as governor until 1867 when he replaced Lane in the U.S. Senate.

The Republicans elected their first governor in 1860 and controlled both houses of the General Assembly as they had in 1858. Immediately, however, they were faced with the problem of war. On April 15, 1861, Lincoln called for volunteers to put down rebellion in the seceding states. Governor Morton responded vigorously, as he was to do throughout the war, both to raise troops for federal service and for the creation of state regiments.

Volunteers were the heart of Indiana regiments in the Civil War for, although a national draft act did go into effect in 1862, the draft was primarily an incentive to encourage men to join. The process of unit formation varied from locality to locality, but the basic principle remained the same. Either an already established state militia unit would step forward for enrollment in federal service or an individual with authorization from Governor Morton would recruit a company, sixty-four men, or a regiment, ten companies. This individual would head the unit and the remaining officers would either be elected by the men or selected by the governor. The state would provide the necessary uniforms and equipment and then transport the unit to a mustering point. At the beginning of hostilities weapons were difficult to find and Morton dispatched private citizens, among them Calvin Fletcher, to search out stores of rifles.

Hoosiers rushed to enlist. Ten thousand men responded the first day Lincoln issued his call, even though Indiana's quota, as later set out, was only 4,683 men. Indiana originally mobilized six regiments of three-month volunteers; these were numbered six through eleven (Indiana's regiments in the Mexican War were the First through the Fifth).

View of Indianapolis, 1854.

Mr. and Mrs. Allen Hamilton, Fort Wayne.

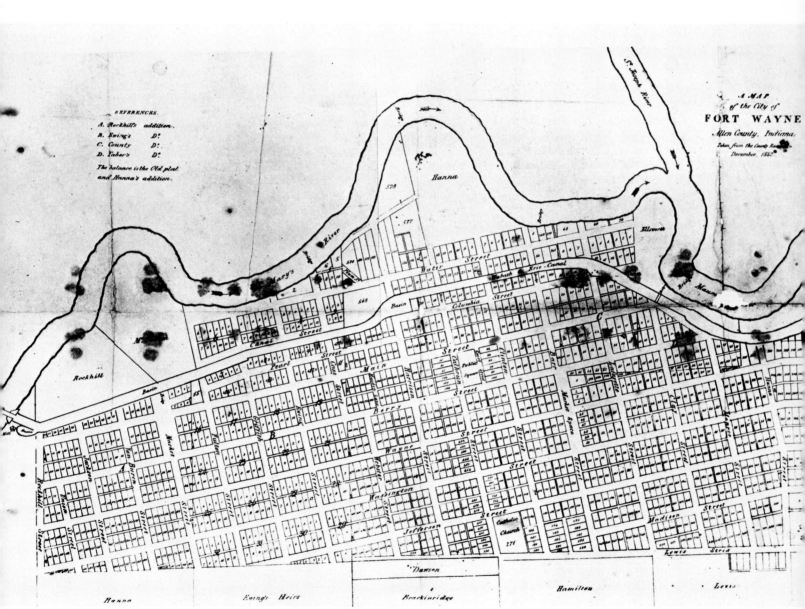

Map of Fort Wayne, Allen County, December 1842.

Oliver Chilled Steel Plow, manufactured in South Bend.

Covered wagon built by John Studebaker, 1830.

Perhaps the most famous of these regiments was the Eleventh (the Indiana Zouaves). By the end of 1861 the Fifty-Ninth Regiment was in the field along with twelve batteries of artillery and three regiments of cavalry. By war's end Indiana had contributed one hundred twenty-nine regiments, three companies of cavalry, plus 1,078 sailors and marines. Included in this total were ethnic regiments: the Thirty-Second (a German regiment), the Thirty-Fifth (the First Irish), the Sixty-First (the Second Irish), and most of the blacks who served in the Twenty-Eighth Regiment (U.S. Colored Troops) of the U.S. Army.

In addition to supplying many enlisted men, Indiana provided officers who achieved national prominence. Among these were Thomas A. Morris, a West Point graduate, who became a brigadier general; Benjamin Harrison, who received a brevet appointment as a brigadier general; Joseph J. Reynolds, a classmate of U.S. Grant at West Point, who became colonel of the Tenth Regiment and later a major general; and Lew Wallace, who commanded the Eleventh Indiana and achieved the rank of major general before losing favor with Grant for arriving late at the battle of Shiloh. One other Hoosier became a major general—Robert H. Milroy, who began as colonel of the Ninth Indiana.

Most Indiana regiments fought in the West. Five regiments—the Seventh, Thirteenth, Fourteenth, Nineteenth, and Twentieth—became part of the Army of the Potomac and fought at Second Bull Run, Antietam, Fredericksburg, Chancellorsville, and Gettysburg. Far more Indiana regiments went south with Grant to fight the epic battles of the Army of the Tennessee—Fort Henry, Fort Donelson, Shiloh, Perryville, Vicksburg, Chickamauga (more Hoosiers were killed in this battle than in any other), and Lookout Mountain. The Nineteenth Indiana, of the famous Iron Brigade, had the heaviest losses, 15.9 percent of its total enrollment, although the Twenty-Seventh was not far behind, losing 15.3 percent.

John Studebaker blacksmith shop and home, 1835.

The Celebrated Studebaker Wagon.

Captain Charles Euel Shrewsbury and Mrs. Shrewsbury, Madison.

Schenck house, Vevay.

Shrewsbury house interior, Madison.

The war took its tragic toll. Direct frontal assaults resulted in shocking casualty rates, sometimes reaching as high as 80 percent in certain regiments. The large caliber of the rifled musket, .58 being the most popular, and the low velocity of the "Minié ball" resulted in gaping wounds which, in the case of arms and legs, frequently led to amputation. Despite the awfulness of battle, more Hoosiers died in camp of the epidemics which swept those poorly constructed and badly drained sites. Altogether, Indiana suffered greater losses in the Civil War than in any war save World War II.

The war touched Indiana at home as well. The state was full of Democrats and southern sympathizers, not necessarily synonymous, but regarded as such by suspicious Republicans and Unionists. These suspicions were heightened when Democrats won control of the General Assembly in the election of 1862 and tried to divide control of the militia between Governor Morton and Democratic state officers. All but four Republican members of the General Assembly fled Indianapolis to Madison, thus effectively terminating the legislative session. This precipitate action, however, came before an appropriations bill was passed and left the state without funds.

Governor Morton was on the horns of a dilemma. In order to get an appropriations bill passed, he would have to call a special session of the legislature. If he did this, he ran the risk of losing control of Indiana's troops. If he did nothing, he would not have the state funds to pay the troops. Either way, Indiana's war effort would be hurt or even terminated.

Morton found a third way; he raised money outside the legislative process. He first asked the state auditor to release funds from the state treasury to pay the interest on the public debt. This action would maintain state credit and make further borrowing on that credit possible. The state auditor, a Democrat, refused, and his refusal was ruled legal by the Indiana Supreme Court, which was domi-

James F. D. Lanier, Madison.

The Lanier Mansion, Madison. It became the state's first Memorial in 1925.

Seventh Street.

Main Street.

nated by Democratic judges. Morton then turned to other sources—New York banks, the Secretary of War, Republican party officials, and private citizens. For instance, from 1863 to 1865 the governor was able to borrow $600,000 from James F.D. Lanier, a former Madison banker, through the banking firm of Winslow, Lanier & Company of New York. The governor could not place the money so collected in the hands of the Democratic state treasurer who would not pay it out again without approval of the General Assembly. The funds were put in a safe in the governor's office and were distributed by W.H.H. Terrell, his military secretary. All this was of questionable legality, but Morton justified his actions on the basis of wartime emergency.

Meanwhile, the state was invaded. In June 1863 a small force of rebel cavalry crossed the Ohio River and raided the area near Cannelton to try to obtain horses. The raid was easily dispersed. Not so Morgan's raid a month later. General John Hunt Morgan brought 2,000 mounted men into southern Indiana to seize horses and supplies. The Confederate force struck Corydon, Salem, Vernon, and Versailles before crossing into Ohio, where Morgan was captured. The invasion caused great consternation in the Hoosier state, leading to rumors that "Copperheads," or southern sympathizers, were trying to take over the state, aided by military action from the South.

Secret organizations such as the Knights of the Golden Circle, the American Knights, and the Sons of Liberty were believed to be plotting to attack the state arsenal to obtain weapons and to storm Camp Morton to free the Confederate prisoners. As a result, Governor Morton ordered members of the supposed conspiracy arrested in September 1864.

Among those arrested was Lambdin P. Milligan, a Huntington lawyer, who was a southern sympathizer and had been a candidate for the Democratic nomination for governor in 1864. All were tried for treason in Indianapolis by a military

Ice skaters near Richmond.

Fifth Street.

Episcopal Church.

commission and three of them, including Milligan, were given the death penalty. The war ended before the sentences were executed, and President Johnson commuted the death sentences to life imprisonment on May 30, 1865. Milligan carried his case to the U.S. Supreme Court, which ruled in *ex parte Milligan* in April 1866 that his trial was illegal since civilian courts were in operation in the state. Milligan and the others were released. The case had two consequences: a constitutional decision upholding civil over military justice and a belief by Indiana Democrats that Republicans had tried to railroad some of their leaders.

The notoriety of the supposed plot and the war fervor contributed to Republican victory in 1864, after which fears of invasion and subversion began to subside. In the 1864 campaign the Democrats denounced emancipation, Lincoln's amnesty proclamation, and the use of Negro troops. Early in 1864 the Indiana Republicans were demanding the end of slavery, saying that it was a moral necessity. Indiana's Democratic congressmen in Washington, however, refused to vote for the Thirteenth Amendment in 1865.

The passions aroused by the war remained after the war ended. The questions of Negro rights and treatment of the South were unanswered and became intertwined with other passions. After Lincoln's death, the Hoosier Republicans were sympathetic to President Johnson and were not radical. For example, Morton, the party leader, was opposed to Negro suffrage, and Colfax, Speaker of the U.S. House of Representatives, spoke favorably of Johnson. An exception was George W. Julian, an ex-Whig with a long antislavery record. He was a Radical Republican who continued to advocate racial equality, Negro suffrage, and women's rights.

By the middle of 1866 Indiana's Republicans were disillusioned with the situation in the South. Schuyler Colfax believed that Johnson had betrayed the country to the South, and Governor Morton,

Levi Coffin, an antislavery Quaker and a leader in the Underground Railroad.

soon to become a U.S. senator, urged Negro suffrage. Both played a part in the impeachment of President Johnson. Colfax appointed Julian to the House committee which drafted the articles of impeachment, and Morton voted to convict. The other Indiana senator, Thomas A. Hendricks, a Democrat elected in 1862, voted for acquittal.

As Radical Reconstruction changed the South, so also did it change Indiana. The passage of the Fourteenth Amendment, which gave Negroes civil rights, nullified the Indiana constitutional discrimination in courts. The Fifteenth Amendment, which said suffrage could not be denied for reasons of race, gave Negroes the right to vote. The latter amendment passed in Indiana only because Senator Morton, who had come from Washington to help in its passage, ruled that a quorum existed in the General Assembly despite the resignation of Democrats to prevent such a quorum. In the 1870 campaign the Democrats were still protesting the vote and declared their continued opposition to the ratification of the Fifteenth Amendment. The recognition of Negro rights proceeded slowly and grudgingly. In 1869 the General Assembly mandated school officials to organize all-black schools where justified by the number of prospective students, and not until 1877 did the legislature pass a law permitting a black child to attend a white school, and then only if no black school were available.

The war was over and Indiana survived, leaving as its heritage a party which was to dominate the state for a time and an issue—the "bloody shirt"—which asked citizens to vote as they had fought and which accused Democrats of being traitors, as well as promoted the political fortunes of Hoosiers such as Conrad Baker and Benjamin Harrison. It also left tangible evidence. In many Indiana towns today the courthouse square contains a memorial to those Hoosiers who fought in this great war. As long as the stone stands, memories of the "boys in blue" still linger.

Levi Coffin house, Fountain City, Wayne County, built in 1827.

Hotel at Indian Springs, Martin County.

Oliver P. Morton.

Schuyler Colfax.

George W. Julian.

The first air mail, Lafayette, 1859.

Hugh McCulloch, Fort Wayne.

General Lew Wallace, Eleventh
Indiana Volunteers.

Oliver H. Smith.

Calvin Fletcher.

Eleventh Indiana Volunteers, swearing to remember Buena Vista,
at Indianapolis, May 1861. *Harper's Weekly,* June 22, 1861.

Morgan's Raid into Indiana: Confederate guerrillas destroying
and pillaging the depot and stores at Salem, July 10, 1863. *Frank
Leslie's Illustrated Newspaper,* August 8, 1863.

Camp Morton, near Indianapolis, September 1862. *Harper's Weekly,* September 13, 1862.

Reception of the Ninth Indiana Volunteers at Danville, Kentucky, after they drove out the rebels, October 1862. *Harper's Weekly,* November 8, 1862.

Soldiers of the Fourteenth Indiana Regiment.

Soldiers line up in a village street.

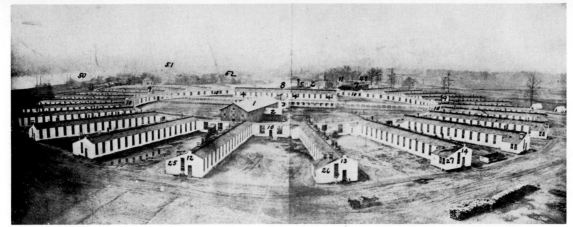

General Hospital in Jeffersonville during the Civil War.

Thirty-fifth Indiana Volunteers, First Irish Regiment, of the Army
of the Cumberland in the Atlanta Campaign.

Zouaves, probably the Eleventh Indiana Volunteers.

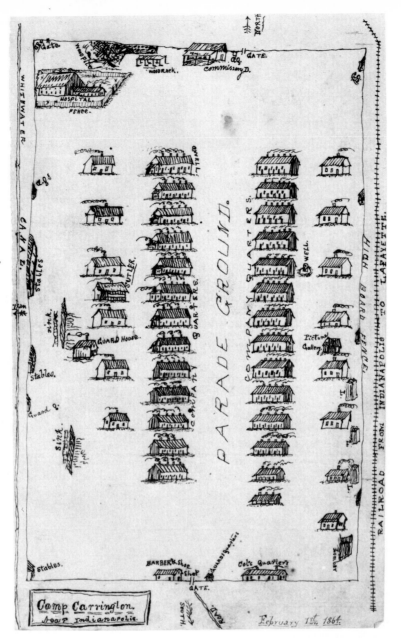

Map of Camp Carrington,
near Indianapolis,
February 1, 1864.

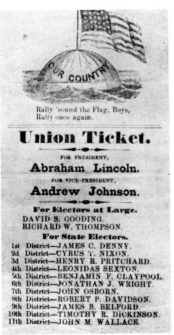

Indiana electors for Lincoln
and Johnson on the Union
(Republican) ticket, 1864.

A soldier's war record.

Five men were tried for treason by a military commission in Indianapolis during the Civil War. When Lambdin P. Milligan appealed the case, the U.S. Supreme Court set aside his conviction in *ex parte Milligan*.

The 1868 Republican ticket of Grant and Colfax was bannered outside the party's Fourth and Broadway clubrooms, Logansport.

Signs on the public square supporting Congressional Reconstruction and the Fourteenth Amendment, Delphi.

Politics and Social Change

The Indiana State Soldiers' and Sailors' Monument, Indianapolis, Memorial Day, 1894. "Victory," popularly known as "Miss Indiana," stands atop the monument. The cornerstone was laid on August 22, 1889, and the formal dedication ceremonies were held on May 15, 1902.

THE POLITICAL LIFE OF INDIANA FROM THE CIVIL WAR TO WORLD WAR I CAN BE DIVIDED INTO TWO PARTS. FROM 1865 TO 1896 Indiana was truly a two-party state with elections going first to the Republican candidate for President and then to the Democratic one. Indeed, Indiana was a swing state which, because of its early election date, was used to predict national trends. As Indiana went, so did the nation.

After 1896 the picture changed drastically as Indiana became a predominantly Republican state. From that year forward, Republican presidential candidates swept the state. Only Woodrow Wilson was able to crack the state in 1912 in his first campaign. The state was not to go for another Democratic candidate until Franklin D. Roosevelt in 1932. Despite this lack of success in the national arena, the Democratic party continued to be important on the state and local levels.

Indiana was a strong Republican state when the Civil War ended, but the Republican percentage of the total vote cast declined after 1872. The Democrats, however, could not take advantage of the decline, and the result was a political situation which Paul Kleppner, a noted historian of the period, has called one of protracted political stalemate.

The significant questions are why this stalemate occurred and why Indiana did not become a strong Republican state earlier. The answers lie in the issues of the day and the composition of the electorate in Indiana. The Republicans had several issues, and the major one was the Civil War. Indiana had contributed more soldiers to the Union cause in proportion to her population than any other state. Thirteen percent of those who joined the army died of wounds or disease. Almost every family in the state could point to a relative, sometimes far removed, who had been a victim.

Since the Confederates and the disloyal elements in the state were Democrats, the Republicans waved the "bloody shirt," blaming the Democratic party for beginning the war, for obstructing the peace, and for being responsible for atrocities in prison camps. This was succinctly put by a Hoosier Republican: "In short, the Democratic party may be described as a common sewer and loathsome receptacle, into which is emptied every element of treason North and South and every element of inhumanity and barbarianism which has dishonored the age."

Within the Republican party were at least two factions, one dedicated to party regularity and the other to reform and efficiency. The former was known as the Stalwart; the latter was called first the Mugwump and later the Progressive. The reform movement was supported largely by small-town businessmen and lawyers and, while never becoming a major issue, greatly influenced the lives of Hoosiers. The reform Republicans promoted, to a greater or lesser degree of enthusiasm, such movements as a professional civil service, prohibition, and women's suffrage.

The reform movements were calculated to improve the level of political life and to raise the standards of the participants. Civil service reform was designed to place the best-qualified persons into government employment and to use common business principles to run the government. As Lucius B. Swift, a leading Hoosier proponent of civil service reform, put it, in an address to students at Indiana University in 1888, the President must "take a scourge and drive the office changers out of his constitutional temple, and the road to resting government employment upon business principles will become smooth and straight."

Temperance would aid in uplifting the urban poor—usually of immigrant origin and often Catholic, and, hence, devoted to alcohol—out of their misery into the middle class. In part, the movement reflected anxiety about the shape of American society. Temperance reformers were middle-class Protestants who had exercised considerable control over local and state life but were now

The Boys in Blue: Soldiers' Reunion at Indianapolis, September 20–21, 1876. *Harper's Weekly,* October 14, 1876.

A mule named "Miss Fanny Huston" participated in a parade at Rising Sun.

94

Reunion of Civil War veterans at Indiana University, 1875.

German-American veterans of Civil War at the Atheneum in Indianapolis.

being eclipsed by the voters in industrial cities who were immigrants from Europe. Temperance, then, was a defense by the reformers against the onslaught of an urban order with values antithetical to those Protestant virtues of self-control, industry, discipline, and sobriety. Their crusade ended when the so-called Prohibition Amendment went into operation in January 1920.

The third reform urge was for women's rights. This movement had begun before the war and, like the temperance movement, was to culminate in a victorious constitutional amendment providing for woman suffrage in 1920. The impetus behind this movement was again one of uplifting society. If women voted, politics would be cleaner, less corrupt, and would more nearly approach the American ideal. The movement cut across party lines but was more closely connected with Republican reformers. George W. Julian, who had supported black rights, also sponsored a constitutional amendment to give women the right to vote after the Civil War. The reform element in the Republican party was never able to dominate and sometimes splintered away to assure Democratic victory. Still, most of the reformers refused to leave party ranks permanently.

Just as the Civil War confirmed Republicans in their party loyalty, so did it also for the Democrats. Those counties south of the National Road which went Democratic in 1860 were Democratic in 1870 and 1880. Both parties had a cadre of loyal voters who persisted in their support of the ticket, providing a basic irreducible foundation.

Starting with this base, each party desperately searched for voters who were not committed to either party. The major divisions between the parties at first did not seem to be class or economic ones, but ethnic and religious. Ways had to be devised to make these divisions appealing to the uncommitted voters, without overemphasizing issues which would be internally divisive.

Complicating the problem were the minority

parties which drew off committed voters on specific issues. The Greenback party which advocated inflationary policies cut into the Democratic vote in the 1870s; the Prohibition party drew votes from the Republicans during the latter part of the nineteenth and early part of the twentieth century; and the Populists took away from the Democrats in the 1890s.

This being the case, the appeal to independent voters had to be carefully couched. Ethnic and religious issues could backfire and injure the party. The major ethnic minority groups in Indiana were the Germans and the Irish; the influx of Southeastern Europeans was not to come until after 1900.

The Irish Catholic vote was then, as now, predominantly Democratic; the same held true for German Catholics, although this group was less firmly attached to the party. The German Protestants split almost equally between the two parties, with a slight edge for the Democrats. However, if German Protestants lived in close proximity to German Catholics, the advantage of the Democrats was reversed. This meant that, cleverly coaxed, German Protestants could be persuaded to join the GOP in great numbers.

Religious affiliation affected party preference of native-born voters also. Congregationalists, Quakers, Methodists, and Presbyterians more often than not were Republicans; Baptists and Disciples of Christ were Democrats. Republicans could attract defectors from the latter groups by emphasizing clean government, prohibition, and black rights. This would create problems for the Democrats who could not offend their wet supporters. Yet the issues that appealed to pious native-born Hoosiers, if carried to an extreme, would alienate German-born Protestants who would react against prohibition sentiments and clean government slogans which had anti-immigrant undertones.

By the 1890s, however, the economic issue had supplanted the "bloody shirt" and reform. A de-

May Wright Sewall, fifth from the left, front row, presiding at a session of the International Council of Women, 1888. Susan B. Anthony is at her right. Mrs. Sewall was an active leader in the woman's suffrage and woman's club movements in the state and nation.

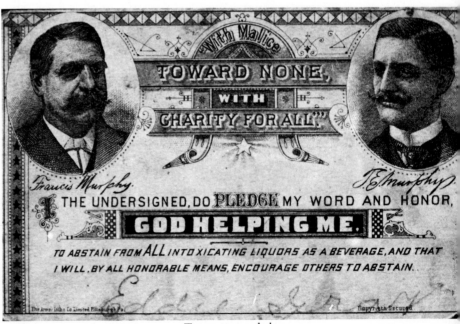

Temperance pledge.

A local option election was held at Muncie, April 27, 1909.

Marcus Mote cartoon, 1892: "Call at the Sign of the Old Gray Goose."

pression which began in 1893 and lasted until about 1900 gave the Democrats the reputation of being the party of economic disaster. Consequently, urban and rural voters alike began to move to the Republican party as the party of prosperity. This desertion was particularly true of farmers who began to accept the argument that the good farmers had much in common with businessmen. The movement toward Republicanism was not staunched by William Jennings Bryan, who, beginning in 1896, tried to unite farmers and workers together against the eastern economic interests which he claimed were exploiting them. At this point, Republicans de-emphasized their traditional cultural identification with native-born Hoosiers and such potentially divisive issues as prohibition and anti-Catholicism. Now, they campaigned as the party of prosperity and won.

That is the general pattern of Indiana politics to World War I; there are many specific examples. The loss of control by the Republicans in Indiana began in 1872. They had elected a governor and swept the General Assembly in 1868, but the corruptness of the Grant regime caused the Republican claims of superior political morality to seem hollow. By 1870 the Democrats had captured the General Assembly and—with the help of reform Republicans such as George W. Julian and David Kilgore, who supported the Democratic presidential candidate, Horace Greeley, and the Democratic gubernatorial candidate, Thomas Hendricks—won the governor's chair in 1872. The defeat of the Republican candidate for governor, Thomas M. Browne, was aided by the appearance in Indiana for the first time of a prohibition ticket. While the ticket attracted few voters, it took those voters from the Republicans.

The governor elected in 1872 had had a long career in both state and national politics. Thomas A. Hendricks was born in Zanesville, Ohio, but moved to Indiana to practice law and engage in

Daniel W. Voorhees.

Thomas A. Hendricks.

George W. Julian.

politics. He won a seat in the General Assembly in 1848, helped write the new state constitution in 1850–51, and went to the U.S. Congress in 1852. He was a U.S. senator from 1863 to 1869. After serving as governor, he was twice nominated for the office of vice president of the United States, once in 1876 and again in 1884. He was elected in 1884 but died after less than a year's service.

Hendricks's position as a U.S. senator represented the epitome of Democratic principles. He was against the draft, emancipation, the Thirteenth, Fourteenth, and Fifteenth Amendments, the Freedmen's Bureau, and the Civil Rights Act. He was originally opposed to the issuance of Greenbacks but voted to continue their use after the war.

Hendricks managed not to alienate too many voters while he was governor, although he had to deal with a Republican-dominated legislature. He did create consternation among German voters when he signed the "Baxter Bill," legislation allowing local option on liquor sales, a move regarded as a step toward total prohibition. He appealed to the moralists who might have been attracted to the Republicans by advocating a stricter divorce law (the law passed, ending Indiana's twenty-one-year stint as a quickie divorce state) and by also promoting state constitutional amendments to increase the time required for residency for voting and to hold state and federal elections at the same time.

During Hendricks's term, the Panic of 1873 occurred. This deflationary event stimulated the creation of another minority party, the Independent party, which advocated the "Indiana Plan" designed to inflate the currency with paper money. The next election, that of 1874, showed the splits in the Democratic party. Coalition with the Independent party appeared to be on the horizon, but the presidential ambitions of Hendricks, which made him support a hard-money candidate, ended that hope. Hendricks had to settle for the vice-presidential

Log rolling on Dr. Furnas' farm near Danville. The man indicated by the arrow is probably Governor James D. (Blue Jeans) Williams.

The *Brown County Democrat* reports the election results, November 7, 1884.

Theodore Roosevelt visited Muncie in 1904.

Albert J. Beveridge.

Charles W. Fairbanks.

nomination, and the Independent party became the Greenback party, which was now a national party.

The campaign of 1876 was a classic post-Civil War one which showed the self-conception and issues stance of both parties. The Democrats nominated James D. (Blue Jeans) Williams for governor. Williams was a self-made successful farmer who was an inflationist and who had won election to the U.S. Congress in 1874 with aid from the Grange and Independents. He had earned his name because of his habit of wearing a suit of denim and assuming the role of a backwoods farmer. The original Republican nominee, a man with the unlikely name of Godlove Orth, had to drop out of the race because of scandal connected with his service as minister to Venezuela. The substitute candidate was Benjamin Harrison.

Harrison, a grandson of William Henry Harrison, was born in North Bend, a community near Cincinnati, in 1833. He attended Miami University and read law in Cincinnati prior to moving to Indianapolis to practice law. Harrison was a political novice, but he had served with distinction in the Civil War, rising in rank from colonel to brigadier general. He thus fit the Republican political ideal of a war hero and a morally correct individual.

In the campaign of 1876 the Democrats attacked Republican corruption and advocated inflating the money supply. The Republicans waved the "bloody shirt" and pointed to the splendid war record of Harrison. The Greenback candidate for governor withdrew in favor of Harrison, but most of the Greenback votes went to the Democrats. The election showed divided results. The Democrats won the governor's seat and the upper house of the General Assembly; the Republicans won the lower house and 9 of 13 contested seats in the U.S. House of Representatives. The election showed the internal strife of both parties. The Democrats had problems with the issue of corruption.

The divisions were evident in the next presi-

William McKinley, speaking in Peru in 1892.

Benjamin Harrison,
twenty-third president of the
United States.

dential election, in 1880. The Democrats nominated a Hoosier, William Hayden English, for vice president. English was a hard-money Democrat who had served several terms in Congress prior to becoming a banker (he was responsible for the creation of the First National Bank in Indianapolis). The Republicans nominated James A. Garfield for president instead of James G. Blaine, who had a deserved reputation for being a spoilsman. The Republicans won most of the state and national political offices, but the major victor was Benjamin Harrison, who was selected by the legislature to go to the U.S. Senate. This step was to lead to the presidency.

Nothing succeeds like success; nothing fails like success either. Victory showed the divisions within Republican ranks. Problems were to arise from two different sources, women's rights and prohibition. In 1878 the Equal Suffrage Society, a women's rights group led by Zerelda G. Wallace and May Wright Sewall, was formed in Indianapolis. Wallace had been a national leader in the W.C.T.U. (Woman's Christian Temperance Union), and Sewall was to go on to become one of the founders of the International Council of Women and the General Federation of Woman's Clubs. The major goal of the Equal Suffrage Society was to amend Indiana's constitution to permit woman suffrage. In 1881 the goal was partially reached when a special session of the General Assembly struck out the word "male" from among the requirements for voting.

Coincident with this success was one for the prohibition wing of the Republicans, which also took the opportunity to get its amendment to prohibit both the distilling and sale of liquor in the state through the same session. Neither measure became law, however, as the next session of the General Assembly, which was dominated by Democrats, defeated the amendments in 1883.

By 1884 the tension in the Republican party proved to be too great. The Republicans picked

Celebrating Harrison's election to the presidency in Indianapolis. *Frank Leslie's Illustrated Newspaper,* November 17, 1888.

Benjamin Harrison, speaking in Peru in 1894.

Harrison's funeral was held in Indianapolis, October 17, 1917.

James G. Blaine as their candidate for the presidency, a move which alienated reformers in the party. This precipitated a crisis and resulted in the creation of an institutionalized reform group from among Indiana Republicans.

The leaders of this movement were Lucius B. Swift and William Dudley Foulke. Swift was a native New Yorker who had taught school and had been a principal and superintendent in LaPorte County prior to moving to Indianapolis in 1879 to practice law. Swift prospered in his law practice and in his real estate investments. Foulke was also born in New York but moved to Richmond to practice law. He was a Quaker who was interested in other reform movements, serving as president of the Indiana Woman Suffrage Association and later on the United States Civil Service Commission at the request of his friend Theodore Roosevelt.

In the campaign of 1884 Foulke sat out but Swift organized the Indiana Committee of One Hundred to support the Democratic nominees, Grover Cleveland and Thomas A. Hendricks. Following the election, the committee became the Indiana Civil Service Reform Association and Foulke, along with other independent Republicans, joined.

Nor was this the only dissident group. In the same election, another party, the Indiana Prohibition party, entered the arena under the leadership of Eli Ritter. While the party polled only 3,000 votes in the election, these votes came primarily from the Republicans.

As a result of all the defections, the Democratic candidate for the presidency won Indiana for the first time since the Civil War. The Democrats also swept the other contested offices in the state. The victory, however, was short-lived. It was soon apparent to reform-minded Hoosiers that the Democrats were as spoils minded as the Republicans. When the Democrats entered office, they used party affiliation as the basis for appointments.

The disillusion with Democratic practices led

to the election of the second president to come from Indiana, Benjamin Harrison, in 1888. Republicans such as Swift and Foulke returned to the fold because of Harrison's promise to support civil service reform. Harrison won a slight plurality in Indiana and, despite a smaller popular vote in the country as a whole, won the presidency.

Indiana residents still were interested in reform. The General Assembly, although dominated by Democrats, passed a secret-ballot act, the Indiana ballot, which mandated the use of a standard ballot to be marked in secret by Hoosier voters. This ballot served as a model for other states. In addition, Swift began to publish the *Civil Service Chronicle,* the only civil service reform journal in the Midwest.

During the early years of the 1890s agrarian problems came to dominate the political life. The People's party (the Populists) created by a coalition of Grange members, Greenbackers, and others, began to espouse the cause of cheap money, railroad regulation, and agricultural progress. The Populists were to create special trials for the Democrats, although these were not apparent in 1892 when the Democrats swept the state.

This was the high point of Democracy in the years after the Civil War as succeeding years reversed the trend and converted Indiana into a Republican state. By 1896 civil service reformers such as Foulke and Swift were supporting McKinley because of the fear that William Jennings Bryan would become president and would fill federal offices with common men. The Democrats had become identified with depression and radicalism.

Two years later Indiana was to send one of its most famous senators to Washington. This was Albert J. Beveridge. The other Republican senator, Charles W. Fairbanks, who was elected in 1896 and who was vice president under Theodore Roosevelt, never achieved the fame of Beveridge. Born in Ohio, Beveridge was a graduate of DePauw University and an Indianapolis lawyer. Noted for his

Tom Taggart's Gum Shoe Campaign: Front and rear views of Democratic Headquarters. John T. McCutcheon cartoon.

William Jennings Bryan speaking in Brookville in 1904.

Campaign poster for the Socialist party candidates, Eugene V. Debs and Ben Hanford, 1904.

speaking ability, Beveridge also was an excellent writer whose *The Life of John Marshall* (1919) was justly acclaimed.

Beveridge's career in the Senate illustrates the tensions in the Republican party as it moved away from an emphasis on the Civil War to the issues of imperialism and prosperity. Beveridge made his reputation as a hawk in the Spanish-American War and his fame continued as a progressive in the early years of the twentieth century.

The Republicans seemed in sure control of the state when Roosevelt succeeded to the White House in 1900. Roosevelt talked reform; he appointed Foulke to the Civil Service Commission and, in general, brought the party together.

The Democrats were in disarray. Not only did they have the Populists to contend with, but they also had to cope with another new party, the Socialist, whose national leader was Eugene V. Debs. Debs was born in Terre Haute in 1855 and had a long career as a union organizer and strike leader before combining the Social Democratic party and a faction of the Social Labor party into the Socialist party in 1901. Debs perennially ran for the presidency—in 1900, 1904, 1908, 1912, and 1920. The last time he ran he was in a federal prison for sedition. Ironically enough, this campaign netted him 919,000 votes, the most he ever attained. Though attracting few Hoosier votes, the ones he did get hurt the Democrats the most.

A minor party which created problems for the Republicans in the period was the Prohibition party. Begun in 1884 by Eli Ritter, the Prohibitionists lost strength when the Populists cut into their ranks in the 1890s. But their influence, along with the W.C.T.U. and the Anti-Saloon League, which had begun nationally in 1893 and which had an Indiana branch in 1898, helped dry up Indiana. In 1895 the Nicholson Act passed; this permitted local voters to file remonstrances against individual saloonkeepers in order to close them down.

The Prohibitionists tended to split the Republicans into a wet and a dry wing, and their polling of 23,000 votes in 1904 made them a force in the state. While the Republicans were united for that election, partly because the Republican vice-presidential candidate was Charles W. Fairbanks, a conservative, anti-imperialist Hoosier senator, the victory brought them problems in Indiana. The governor they elected was J. Frank Hanly, who exemplified the reform "dry" Republican. Hanly campaigned against liquor, gambling, and capital punishment and for railroad and bank regulation. He did succeed in getting a county option law passed in 1908; this enabled residents to vote themselves dry. Hanly left the Republican party after his term as governor and ran for president in 1916 as a Prohibitionist.

The election of 1904 also brought into prominence a Hoosier who became an almost stereotypical Democratic politician. This person was Thomas (Tom) Taggart, who was born in County Monaghan, Ireland, in 1856. Taggart came to Indianapolis in 1877 to run a restaurant in Union Station. He later moved south to operate the French Lick Springs Hotel (needless to say, he was not a prohibitionist). Entering politics, Taggart served as mayor of Indianapolis from 1895 to 1901 and became national chairman of the Democratic party in 1904. He continued to serve on the Democratic National Committee until 1916 when he was appointed to the U.S. Senate to fill the vacancy created by the death of Benjamin F. Shively. Taggart became a legendary figure in Indiana politics.

The reform policies of Hanly and the talent of Taggart combined to assure a Democratic victory in Indiana for the first time in the twentieth century in 1908. Thomas R. Marshall became governor, the Democrats won the majority of seats in the lower house of the General Assembly and in the U.S. House of Representatives. Marshall proved to be a popular governor, as he attempted limited reform measures, including a revised constitution for the state. The General Assembly passed the constitution

Evan B. Stotsenburg, New Albany, speaking at a political meeting.

Election day in Brookville, 1900.

Parke County float in the Indiana Centennial Parade, 1916.

New Harmony celebrated its centennial in 1914.

only to have the Indiana Supreme Court declare such action unconstitutional. Despite this defeat, Marshall achieved enough fame so that he became the vice-presidential candidate on the Democratic ticket with Woodrow Wilson in 1912. The Democratic victory which resulted from the Republican split on the national level was the high tide of Democracy in Indiana until the Great Depression.

The Republican party's comeback was aided by its position on women's suffrage. By 1911 interest in securing the right to vote by women had revived, as witnessed by the new life of the Indiana Woman Suffrage Association and the birth of the Woman's Franchise League midwifed by Dr. Amelia R. Keller and Grace Julian Clarke. The Republican-dominated General Assembly passed a state constitutional amendment assuring women the right to vote in 1917, following the Republican sweep of the state in 1916. Once again, the Indiana Supreme Court invalidated the action, but the good will gained among women paid off when the Nineteenth Amendment passed in 1920.

At the end of World War I, Indiana was safe in the Republican fold once more. The Democratic victories early in the twentieth century reflected less the Democratic strength than the Republican divisiveness. When Republicans joined hands, the Democrats lost. But the divisiveness showed that the party was transforming itself from one looking backward to the Civil War to one discussing the kind of society needed in the twentieth century.

Indiana capitol, Indianapolis, completed in 1888. It was one of the first large buildings to use Indiana limestone.

Down on the Farm

The farmer now gets the latest livestock report over the telephone.

BEFORE WORLD WAR I THE GOOD LIFE FOR MOST HOOSIERS WAS A RURAL ONE. FARMERS ENJOYED ENOUGH PROSPERITY SO THAT THE farm price / goods ratio had been enshrined as the ideal of parity. There were periods of agricultural stress, but they occurred in the deflationary episodes of the late nineteenth century, and the periods of prosperity that followed tended to cause the memories of distress to fade.

Rural voters outnumbered urban ones, giving the agricultural sector of the electorate considerable clout. In addition to political dominance, the farmers had even captured the language by holding a near monopoly on the metaphors of the day. The images of the rural landscape so impressed themselves upon the minds of Hoosier residents that they linger in recreations of the age of steam power on the farm. The rhetoric of the family farm still evokes powerful emotional feelings.

The physical aspect of Indiana farms changed noticeably during this period, and it is the changed landscape which is remembered. While both the number and size of farms remained relatively constant, the major change was in improvement of the land and buildings. Those areas in the state which were still forested were being cleared just as the swampy areas were being drained. The old log houses and their clapboard successors were being improved or replaced as rude homesteads evolved into well-kept farms.

The newer houses quite often were in the Carpenter Gothic style characterized by steep gables, perpendicular sheathing, and gingerbread carving. The houses, which also were common in towns, could be either one-and-a-half or two stories, depending upon the affluence of the owners. Whatever the size, the interior arrangement was always the same. There would be a kitchen which would be used extensively for other activities, a dining room which was used mainly for family gatherings, and a parlor which was rarely used at all. There might be a downstairs bedroom, but the majority of bedrooms were upstairs. There would rarely be a bathroom; instead, an outdoor privy could be found down by the garden and a dry sink could be found in the kitchen.

The rooms were poorly heated but stoves were replacing fireplaces, at least in kitchens and parlors. Base burners, often heavily decorated with chrome, became the center of the family group in the winter. The bedrooms were unheated and the cold inhabitants would huddle under layers of quilts, goose-down-filled comforters, and woven coverlets, either made by the women of the family or bought from an itinerant weaver. The rooms would be lighted by kerosene lamps which had been invented about the time of the Civil War and had supplanted lard- or tallow-burning lamps and candles.

Perhaps an even more important building for farmers was a new barn replacing the older log enclosures and reflecting the increased number of livestock. The barns might be long shed-type buildings; they might be round or octagonal. They would invariably be two-story, with the upper story being a haymow. The lower story would be divided into compartments, one for the horses which had supplanted the oxen and another for the cows which furnished milk for the family. The barn might contain a feed bin but would be unlikely to shelter sheep or pigs or chickens, which had buildings of their own. This was the era of the self-sufficient farmer who did not specialize.

While the farmers grew the necessary food for the family, they also were producing more food for sale. The principal cereal crop was still corn; the principal animal crops were hogs and cattle.

The sale of food had been made possible by improved technology. Roads were improved; bridges were built. Both facilitated the farmer's trip to the market. Down on the farm the availability of new fencing material enabled the farmer to keep his

A farm family.

Woman using the spinning wheel.

Woman spinning thread.

The Oppy family, near Crawfordsville, 1880s: Christopher Oppy and his third wife Elizabeth, his four sons, and the hired girl.

Fireplace and stove in kitchen of a house near Brookville, 1880s.

Man showing two children how to use the whetstone, 1912.

Woman pumping water.

Woman washing clothes with the help of a steam engine.

Woman washing clothes at the scrub board.

Log cabin with improvements added: porch, rain barrel, pump, barn, privy, fruit trees.

Cattle and hogs and rail fences.

Snake or rail fence, which preceded hedge and wire fences.

own animals within his fences and to keep out wild animals and other farmers' tame ones. These new fencing materials were of natural and manmade sources.

The first was Osage orange, a hedge with thorns which grew in dense clumps and which was cow- and hog-tight. European shrubs had proven to be weak or too susceptible to frost to use, but the Arkansas-native tree was not. Promoted by Jonathan Baldwin Turner of Illinois College, Osage orange fences replaced rail fences which were difficult to build and required continued upkeep. On the other hand, Osage orange trees had their own drawbacks. If not trimmed back, they shaded the land, diminishing both the available space and water. They also grew slowly and were ineffective for the first few years.

As a result, wire fencing replaced the natural barrier. Wire had been used for fences as early as 1840, but smooth wire did not hold livestock well, and until galvanizing was invented in 1851, the wire rusted out quickly. In 1868 Michael Kelly of New York patented a barbed wire, and by 1874 Joseph F. Glidden of Illinois had contrived a practical machine for making barbed wire. While barbed wire effectively restrained cattle and horses, it was less effective with hogs which rooted underneath. Not until the 1890s was the problem solved with the introduction of a loom to make woven wire which could restrain hogs. Indiana manufacturers such as Indiana Steel and Wire, a Muncie firm founded by the Kitzelman family, began to produce wire fencing for local customers and soon had a national market. Gradually, the rail fence disappeared; so too did the Osage orange fence. During the period of transition, farms had mixtures of two or three fence types, making for a varied landscape which reflected the agricultural frontier.

Not only had the spaces in the rural landscape been ordered by wire fences, but those spaces were tilled differently. Mechanization which had only begun at the time of the Civil War increased rapidly in the years following. Mechanization of agriculture went in stages: from man power to horse power, from horse power to steam power, and from steam power to gasoline power. The big explosion was in the availability of horse-drawn equipment. Although the reaper, mower, rake, and drill had been patented before the Civil War, their general use came later. In addition, new machines were being developed. John F. Appleby invented the grain binder in 1878; the binder received its name from the fact that it tied cut grain into bundles, unlike the reaper which only cut the grain. At approximately the same time, the spring tooth and the disk harrow were patented. Both improved the quality of the seed bed, making planting more often successful. Finally, A.S. Peck built a corn binder in 1890, which was soon followed by a corn picker. These speeded up the harvesting of corn considerably.

While horse-powered implements proliferated, steam-powered ones began to make their appearance. The earliest use of the steam engine was to power threshing machines. At first, the engines used were portable rather than self-propelled. Pulled by teams of horses, the engines, when put into place, drove the threshers by means of a belt on a pulley. By 1880 the U.S. Department of Agriculture estimated that 80 percent of the grain threshed went through steam-driven threshers.

The next major improvement was to devise a way for the steam engine to be self-propelled, to change from portable steam engine to a steam traction engine. By the end of the 1870s, the steam traction engine had been perfected. Despite the fact that it was self-propelled, the first models were steered by horses. Manufacturers were quick to exploit the market and to build both threshing machines and steam traction engines.

Several farm implement manufacturers began to prosper in Indiana. Among these were the Birdsell Manufacturing Company of South Bend,

Farmer standing beside the well and his barnyard, near Brookville.

Round barns were also used.

Corn picker, one of the first in Indiana, drawn by tractor driven by A.L. Henderson on his farm near Linden, November 1917. The mules were driven by Mrs. Henderson.

Husking corn on the farm of Frank Kantz, Romney.

Shredding fodder.

Digging potatoes near Hartford City. Both rail and barbed wire fences in the background.

Studebaker advertisement painted on the side of a barn, about 1900.

Filling hay loft, Purdue University.

Putting up silage, Purdue University farm,
August 30, 1911.

Feeding hogs on the farm of John F. Allen,
near Farmersburg.

Driving hogs to market, about 1915.

Taking hogs to market with one team and two wagons, Jennings County.

Gaar-Scott Company of Richmond, and M. Rumely Company of LaPorte. Oliver of South Bend continued to make and sell farm equipment. All illustrate the rapid growth of an infant industry in an expanding agricultural state.

Two companies will serve as examples of this growth: Gaar-Scott and M. Rumely. Abraham and Jonas Gaar lived during the transition period from the log cabin frontier to an industrial society. Born in a log cabin near Richmond, the Gaars became machinists in that Quaker community. By the 1850s they were building steam engines and threshing machines. By 1880 Gaar-Scott was the largest manufacturer of portable steam engines in the world. Not content with the market in Indiana or in the United States, Gaar-Scott aggressively sought to sell their machines in such faraway places as Sweden and Russia. The fortunes of the company declined in the early twentieth century as other manufacturers, notably J.I. Case, successfully challenged Gaar-Scott's leadership in steam engines, and the company lost out in the transition to gasoline engines.

One manufacturer who bridged the gap was Meinrad Rumely. After building his first threshing machine by hand, Rumely expanded into portable and steam traction engines. When the gasoline-powered tractor appeared (the Hart-Parr was first in 1902), M. Rumely shifted gradually to a different kind of tractor, developing one which ran on kerosene—"Kerosene Annie"—a prototype of the famous "Oil Pull" line. Later models utilized gasoline.

The technological improvement in harvesting grains had profound social consequences as well. The cost of the outfit—steam engine and thresher—far outstripped the resources of the average farmer. Instead, the equipment belonged to custom threshers or threshing societies, cooperative enterprises which shared expenses and profits, if any. Because of this fact, the isolation of rural life was relieved when the threshers came. Neighbors joined to help feed bundles into the maw of the machine and to haul the grain to the bin. Small boys carried water and did other service chores. Housewives vied with each other in preparing meals to feed the men, whose hunger added a new phrase to the rural vocabulary—to eat like a "threshing crew." At the end of the season when members of the threshing society gathered to determine the value of the year's work, they brought their families along for the picnic which accompanied the occasion.

The rapid increase in available tools stimulated another Indiana institution, the fair. Machinery manufacturers took their machines to county and state fairs to demonstrate and sell. But they were not the only ones there. Organizations designed to promote and improve breeds of livestock or the yield of crops also used the opportunity to educate farmers in the newest methods of husbandry and to reward those who had raised the best cow or sheep or the best apples or wheat. The fairs were also social occasions where families met relatives and shared lunches while watching and learning.

Other organizations tried to speak for the farmer, to improve his lot, to break down his social isolation. The first such group was the Order of Patrons of Husbandry, the Grange, a secret society set in a rural locale. Begun in Washington, D.C., in 1867, the Grange spread quickly to other states. By 1875 the Indiana Grange had 60,000 members. As the Grange, which had begun as a social and educational group, became more political, it gradually lost its appeal. Two later organizations proved to be more lasting. They were the Farmers' Educational and Cooperative Union (Farmers' Union) and the Farm Bureau. The Farmers' Union began in Texas and the Farm Bureau in New York. Both came to Indiana in the early years of the twentieth century. The former emphasized improving agriculture through education. The Farm Bureau became the

Taking hogs to market with a Model T and a wagon, 1916.

Unloading hogs from trucks at the Union stockyards, Indianapolis.

116

Taking milk to market in a buggy, 1917.

A mint still in Starke County, 1905.

Barns in Henry County.

A milk wagon, working out of Sheridan, 1916.

Empire steel plow, made by S. Horney & Co., Richmond, Indiana.

Picking up bundles of wheat, Blackford County, 1890s.

A single shovel plow.

Two-horse walking cultivator, the Buckeye corn cultivator or plow.

Making sorghum molasses on
the farm of Mrs. Ernest
Michael, near Bainbridge.

most successful because of its close connection with county extension agents, who were first appointed in 1914, and because of its more conservative reputation.

For many Hoosier farmers, however, life still consisted of trying to improve the old homestead, to fence those pieces of land not already enclosed, to buy a new binder, and to raise a family. Life was still lonely, but it had more creature comforts than life lived by an earlier generation. Better roads meant more trips to town; harvest time and fairs meant more social contact; and the new stove kept at least one room warm. If prices were low, they seemed to recover enough to allow most farmers to continue; and if the children kept moving away to town, the hope remained that they might one day return.

Corn shocks near farm buildings.

Farm families came to watch the cattle judging, about 1914.

Robinson traction engine and hand-fed separator on farm of
Stephen D. Lowe, near Burlington.

Threshing machine and crew traveled from farm to farm.

Farmers receiving their mailboxes at Delphi.

M. Rumely tractors, made at LaPorte.

Postman Daggett and his family. He delivered the mail on
Route No. 2, Crawfordsville.

Playing checkers in a country store.

Wheelwright-blacksmith at work.

Country store at Mickleyville.

Country store on Route No. 1, near Lafayette, 1899.

"Consumer's Guide for 1894":
Sears, Roebuck catalogue.

"Simple Rules for Ordering"
from the Spring 1906
catalogue.

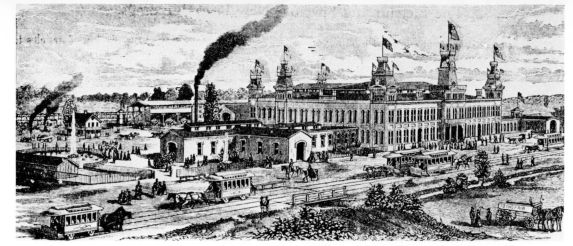

The Indiana State Fair, Indianapolis, 1873.

Studebaker and Birdsell exhibits at a fair.

Indiana State Fair poster, 1885.

Fence display at a fair at Muncie.

Advertisement for Birdsell Clover Thresher and Separator, made in South Bend.

Transformation of the Town

Starke County Courthouse, Knox: Wing and Mahurin, architects, 1897.

INDIANA TOWNS AND CITIES GREW SIGNIFICANTLY IN SIZE AND POPULATION FROM THE 1870s TO THE 1920s, AND THIS GROWTH TRANSFORMED them. The transformation shaped the urban environments into the familiar ones of today and fostered a sense of civic importance among urban residents which was demonstrated in the growing numbers of public and commercial buildings.

The public building which was the center of many Indiana towns was the courthouse. It is no accident that the courthouses which survive are monumental, massive, and overwhelming. They were meant to be so, to reflect the reach and strength of the county seat.

The structures built in the 1880s and the 1890s were usually the third or fourth generation of courthouses. The first had been simple log structures; these, in turn, were supplanted by more substantial brick buildings. Neither was very large, often consisting of two stories with a few rooms. The third generation was more often constructed of stone or contained stone elements. The buildings were multistoried and frequently had a tower or cupola above the top story.

The county courthouses of the period conveyed a sense of stability and a sense of control over space. They towered over other buildings; their very presence seemed to assure the continued survival of the town. Where these buildings still stand, the sense of their power remains. Where they are gone, their memory lingers.

Another symbol of growing power and complexity was the county orphans' home. Every progressive county had one after 1881 when the General Assembly permitted the county commissioners to create them. Prior to this time, children without parents were either apprenticed out to learn trades or were placed in county poor asylums. The building or buying of a home for the homeless showed the concern and charity of the community.

Public hospitals were slower in emerging. The

123

hospitals which did exist were usually private and paid for by religious benevolence. The first public hospital in Indiana was Indianapolis City Hospital, which had been a Civil War hospital before becoming a civilian one in 1866. The General Assembly finally permitted county commissioners to construct hospitals with tax funds in 1905. Both hospitals and orphanages made the town the center of the still simple, but becoming complex, social services of the time.

By far the most numerous buildings of the time were private ones designed to serve as commercial or industrial facilities. Changes in building technologies in the nineteenth century furthered changes in the urban landscape. Prominent among the changes were the passenger elevator and the steel-framed building, both of which made feasible the erection of buildings of over six floors. Prior to the first elevator put in use in New York City in 1857, persons had to climb the stairs to the top, the practical limit of which was five or six stories. In addition, these buildings which were constructed of stone or bricks had to use load-bearing walls; as a result, the buildings had extremely thick walls.

The steel-framed building of the late nineteenth century had been anticipated by the use of cast-iron buildings earlier in the period. The cast-iron front could be prefabricated and shipped to the site to be bolted together by unskilled laborers. It could be cast into different classical forms with columns and capitals. The cast-iron building became part of the Hoosier urban landscape. The steel-framed building was later in coming to Indiana; it was to be a phenomenon of the twentieth century. Instead, most Indiana cities and towns had a low skyline consisting of a mix of cast-iron and brick or masonry buildings without elevators and just beginning to get central heat (the steam radiator was invented in 1874).

What did change Indiana towns was an improved urban transit system. Inhabitants of pioneer

Parke County Courthouse, Rockville: T.J. Tolan and Son, 1878.

Wayne County Courthouse, Richmond: McLaughlin, 1889–92.

124

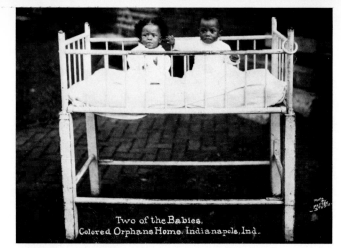

Two babies at the Colored Orphans Home, Indianapolis.

LaGrange County Courthouse, LaGrange: T.J. Tolan and Son, 1878–79.

Gibson County Orphans Home.

Clinton County Courthouse, Frankfort: C.W. Bunting, 1882.

Gibson County orphans. No longer were orphans apprenticed to work on the farms.

125

Chauncey Rose, wealthy Terre Haute businessman, was noted for his philanthropies.

Indiana House of Refuge, Plainfield, 1880.

Rose Orphans Home, Terre Haute, 1907.

Main building of the Indiana Soldiers' and Sailors' Orphans' Home, Knightstown, 1921.

Miss Hernley and children at the home, Knightstown, 1921.

Southern Hospital for the Insane, Evansville, opened in 1890.

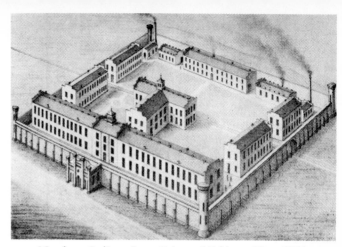
Northern Indiana State Prison, Michigan City, 1874.

Indiana Village of Epileptics, near New Castle, opened in 1907.

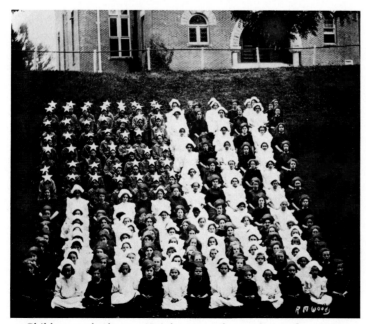
Children at the home, Knightstown, form a living flag, 1906.

settlements lived in towns which were compact and in which most travel was done on foot. Only the more affluent owned a horse or a carriage; horses or carriages were rented from livery stables when needed. This meant that workers had to live close to their work and that residential, commercial, and industrial sites were intermingled.

The first improvement which began the long process of urban decentralization was the street railway which first became practical in the early 1850s when a method of laying rails flush with the street was perfected. Because steam trains were so heavy and because they blocked other traffic, the first cars were drawn by horses or mules. The street railway reached Indiana during the Civil War. In 1864 the Citizens Company received an exclusive franchise to build and to operate a street railway in Indianapolis, contingent upon the successful completion of seven miles of track by July 4, 1866. The company did build the railway and start service by the deadline. Cars were drawn by mules at first.

Fort Wayne had streetcars by 1871. A resident of that city, Mrs. Sam R. Taylor, described the cars as lighted by an oil lamp with red lenses, as lacking heat but having straw on the floor to help keep passengers' feet warm, and as having two springless parallel seats on each side of the vehicle.

Despite the lack of creature comforts on the street railways, the transit system transformed the towns. Now workers could live a greater distance from their places of employment. Multifamily homes downtown began to be replaced by single-family homes in residential suburbs and the lateral growth of cities accelerated.

The streetcar was itself transformed by electrification. Frank Julian Sprague devised the technique of providing power to streetcars by overhead wires in the 1880s. Once begun, the electrification spread quickly. No sooner had Richmond, Virginia, instituted the first electric streetcars in 1888 than Indiana cities began to plan their systems. In

The first gall bladder operation was performed by Dr. John S. Bobbs in 1867 in Indianapolis.

1889 the Indianapolis City Council granted permission for the Citizens Company to begin the process, even going so far as to allow poles to be placed in the center of the streets between the double set of tracks. Fort Wayne began to electrify in 1892. Electrification added, however, to another problem. With the advent of the telephone, and with other electric expansion, cities began to resemble spider webs with wires going in all directions.

Electric streetcars speeded up suburbanization. In Indianapolis, Broad Ripple was connected to the city in 1894 by the Broad Ripple line; and, in Fort Wayne, the suburb of Lakeside, although platted in 1889, owed much of its growth to the coming of streetcars three years later. In addition, streetcar companies hit upon the idea of stimulating weekend business by opening parks and amusement centers to be served by their cars. In Fort Wayne, the electric railroad opened Robinson Park in 1906; in Muncie, the streetcar company developed West Side Park. When the cities built parks, as Indianapolis did in 1897 in areas such as Riverside, Brookside, Highland Square, streetcar lines were soon to follow.

The streetcar could also be adapted to longer runs, and beginning in 1900 it was, under the name of the interurban. Early electric cars ran between Indianapolis, Greenwood, and Franklin. With Indianapolis as a center, lines went to Dublin, Martinsville, Shelbyville, Muncie, and Lafayette. Indiana was to become the leader in the number of miles of interurban track and the Indianapolis Traction and Terminal Company's train shed was reputed to be the largest in the country. The interurban died before World War II, a victim of poor planning and of strong competition from automobiles, but its cheap fares and its convenience still linger in Hoosier memories.

Electrifying the town occurred about the same time. At the start, Indiana towns had little or no lighting at all. Gradually gas lighting had come in;

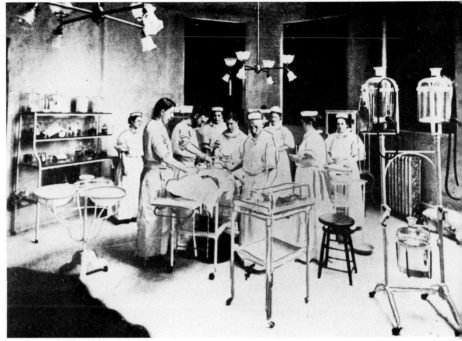

Surgery at Indianapolis City Hospital, 1906.

Doctor's saddlebag and early medical record, September 7, 1877.

128

Residence, beer garden, and brewery of C.L. Centlivre, Fort Wayne.

Horse-drawn vehicles on bridge near Lafayette, about 1900.

Grain office, warehouse, and residence of C.A. Gibson, Boggstown.

Residence and carriage factory of A.J. Taylor, Sheldon, Allen County.

Passengers in surrey-type vehicle, Bedford.

Delivering the milk, Fort Wayne.

Livery stable of P.J. Ryan, Terre Haute.

Electric Railways No. 70 leaving the baseball park at 25th and Wabash, Terre Haute. It was the only double-decker streetcar in Indiana in 1895.

Mule-drawn streetcar on Washington Street, Indianapolis.

Interurban station, Indianapolis. It was said to be the largest in the world in the 1920s.

Indianapolis Nature Study Club leaving the interurban car at Spiceland, 1921.

Madison was the first city in the state to install gas street lights in 1851. New Albany began to install gas lights the next year. The Indianapolis Gas Light and Coke Company received a corporate charter in 1851 to light that city, and the first gas lights were installed two years later. The gas was a manufactured gas, made either as a by-product of processing coal into coke or else specifically from coal. When the gas boom occurred, natural gas supplanted coal gas, at least until the supply was exhausted.

The successful rival to gas lighting was electric street lighting made possible by the invention of the carbon-arc lamp in 1879 by Charles F. Brush of Cleveland. Wabash paid Brush's company $100 to put four arc lamps on the Wabash County Courthouse dome and to test the lighting in that city on March 31, 1880. After the test the city could buy the equipment for $1,800, and it did. That equipment included a Brush Dynamo Machine that generated the current from its location in the courthouse basement and was connected to the lamps on the dome by ordinary telegraph wires. For the test it was driven by an old steam threshing engine on the courthouse lawn. The *Chicago Tribune* said that 10,000 people witnessed the event, and noted that "Wabash enjoys the distinction of being the first city in the world to be lighted by electricity."

In 1881 the Indiana Brush Electric and Light Company received a five-year franchise in Indianapolis and placed sample street lights on the Circle and at the intersections of Illinois and Pennsylvania with Washington and Ohio. A year later, Fort Wayne had its own electric plant.

Also connecting city streets with wire were the new telephone systems. Soon after Alexander Graham Bell demonstrated his invention at the Centennial Exposition at Philadelphia in 1876 telephones began to appear in Indiana. The first companies were small and served only a few customers. Apparently the first in Indianapolis was installed by Cobb and Branham, a coal supply company, to

Wabash River flood, Peru, 1913.

connect their yards at Christian Avenue and South Delaware Street with the office at Market and Delaware. By 1878 the Indiana District Telephone Company began operating by piggybacking on the telegraph poles of the Indianapolis Fire Department. In return for this use, the company furnished free telephones to the fire stations. The telephone was not an overnight success, but gradually it became less novel and less expensive and more used in Indiana cities. As telephones became more common, pressure to put the wires underground increased. As early as 1896, for example, Indianapolis mandated the Central Union Telephone Company to put its wire underground.

The wires were disappearing just as the streets were becoming decent. Early streets were dirt; then they were paved with a variety of materials—wood, brick, or cobblestone. Wooden streets were not uncommon. Miss Isabella Houghton, who came to Fort Wayne in 1881, claimed that the "best business street," Calhoun, was paved with cedar blocks. So also was Meridian Street from New York to Sixteenth streets in Indianapolis in 1882. Other materials were tried. In 1888 a section of Washington Street, from Senate Avenue to Alabama Street, was paved with vulcanite. The experiment failed because the vulcanite turned sticky in hot weather, earning the name, "Yucatan pavement" (after the chewing gum of the period).

The best surfaces were to be asphalt and concrete. The former was used first and was then partly supplanted by the latter. Both became common after the Indiana General Assembly passed the Barrett Law in 1899, which enabled city inhabitants wishing street improvements to pay for them in installments.

The paving of streets greatly improved the sanitary conditions of Hoosier towns, thus raising the general level of health. Other significant factors adding to this elevation were the provision of better water and sewage systems.

Unpaved street without curbs: Broadway, Peru, before 1900.

Main Street, Lafayette, 1915.

The Gimbel Corner, Vincennes, about 1900.

Horse-drawn sprinkler wagon, Bedford.

A cast-iron building in Indianapolis.

Office interior, Rockville, Parke County.

Pettis Dry Goods Store, Indianapolis.

The Bates House, a famous Indianapolis hotel.

DINNER.

TUESDAY, JANUARY 1, 1884.

—OLIVES—   —RAW OYSTERS—   —CELERY—

FISH.
Boiled Halibut, Oyster Sauce

SOUP.
Consomme   Mock Turtle

BOILED.
Chicken, Celery Sauce   Ham, Champagne Sauce

ROAST.
Sirloin of Beef
Loin of Pork, Apple Sauce   Turkey, Cranberry Sauce

COLD.
Corned Beef   Tongue   Roast Beef
Lobster Salad   Potato Salad   Italian Salad
Apple Jelly   Gallentine of Turkey   Currant Jelly

Punch, a la Roman   Champagne

ENTREES.
Chicken Croquettes, with Mushrooms
Pineapple Fritters, Brandy Sauce
Lamb Cutlets, Breaded Tomato Sauce

GAME.
Saddle of Rabbit, with Jelly   Broiled Quail, on Toast, Butter Sauce

VEGETABLES.
Green Peas   Mashed and Boiled Potatoes   Stewed Tomatoes
Asparagus, Cream Sauce   Lima Beans

PASTRY AND DESSERT.
Mince Pie   Peach Meringue Pie
Steamed Pound Pudding, Wine Sauce
Marble Cake   Chocolate Jumbles   Almond Kisses   Lady Fingers
Wine Jelly   Charlotte Russe
Tutti Frutti Ice Cream

ORANGES   BANANAS   APPLES   RAISINS
MALAGA GRAPES   MIXED NUTS   CRACKERS
EDAM, PINEAPPLE AND AMERICAN CHEESE

—COFFEE—

An extra charge will be made for dishes ordered not on bill of fare.

Dinner Menu, The Bates House,
New Year's Day, 1884.

Marion Park Hotel, Indianapolis.

Chas. Yorger Meat Co. Store, 1004 Virginia Avenue, Indianapolis, 1907.

The "New Center" lighting, South Michigan Street, South Bend, 1910.

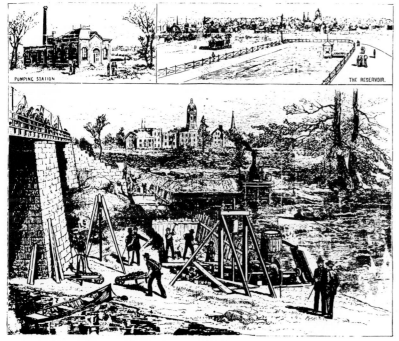

City water works under construction, Fort Wayne, 1880.

Men cleaning street light globes, Indianapolis.

In early Indiana towns water came from nearby streams or wells, but urban growth demanded a greater supply. Indianapolis was a typical example. Not until 1859 did an engineer, Daniel Marsh, recommend that the city utilize the abandoned canal to provide 1,000,000 gallons of water, though the recommendation went unheeded for ten years. In 1869 James O. Woodruff incorporated the Water Works Company of Indianapolis, obtained a franchise to supply water, and began pumping from two wells and the canal. Other cities had a similar history. The water was not always pure, however, and adequate means of filtration were not introduced until the twentieth century.

So also was the case with the treatment of sewage. The original outhouses in Indiana towns slowly gave way to indoor water closets, but the sewage systems often drained the waste into nearby streams and rivers, polluting them and rendering the water undrinkable. Modern sewage treatment facilities are a recent addition to most communities. The need to clean up towns did result in the employment of persons or firms to sweep the streets and collect the garbage. The problem was recognized, if not solved.

Another problem was how to make towns safer for their citizens, both from social and natural hazards. It was this era which saw the coming of the paid policeman and fireman. Most Hoosier towns had only a watch at night and county sheriffs and local constables for daytime law enforcement. If criminal actions became too flagrant, vigilantes formed gangs to punish the offenders. The social unrest which accompanied the Civil War seemed to breed crime and stimulated communities to create more professional police forces. Indianapolis had a regular police force, on paper at any rate, in 1854 and Fort Wayne had one in 1863. By the 1880s most Hoosier cities of any size had police forces.

Just as police forces were becoming more professional, so also were fire companies. Early fire

The first street lighting, Wabash, March 31, 1880.

Parade of wagons, New Harmony.

protection had come from volunteers who often had no equipment other than ladders and leather buckets. Although the volunteers, often representing different social clubs, worked hard, the system proved less than satisfactory. Paid, uniformed firemen stayed on duty 24 hours a day and were able to get to fires more quickly and with more foreknowledge because of a central alarm system. The equipment was still horse-drawn but it did the job, and nothing stirred the blood of a city dweller more than the sight of a steam pumper flying down the street behind a team of matched horses.

Because of the technological change and the urban growth, the era was a confident one. Prosperity was common and the quality of material life, at any rate, seemed to increase progressively. Although the twentieth century is coming to a close, memorials of the nineteenth-century Hoosier city can still be found in the county courthouses, the few patches of brick paving—some even with streetcar tracks—and in the occasional pump or privy. So the past lingers on.

Using a pumper at the Aveline Hotel fire, Fort Wayne, May 3, 1908.

Vigilance committee at the Floyd County Jail, New Albany, January 2, 1869.

136

Police bicycle squad, Indianapolis, 1913.

Indiana's first street fair, Peru, September 1894.

Exhibit at the 1894 Peru street fair.

Morris house, Maplewood, New Castle, 1920.

McAfee house, New Castle.

Two Victorian parlors.

Schoolchildren in Decoration Day parade, May 28, 1916, New Castle.

Culbertson Mansion, New Albany, built in 1868.

Business and Industry

Burton-Humphreys stills at Standard Oil of Indiana refinery, Whiting.

Optimistic hoosiers in the 1880s believed that they had discovered an unlimited supply of fuel in natural gas. Because of this belief, much gas was wasted as lights burned night and day. Pundits predicted the rapid industrialization of the "Gas Belt" which extended from Ohio into east-central Indiana. This prediction proved groundless as falling pressures in wells and dimming torches foretold the exhaustion of the gas.

Gas had been discovered as early as the 1860s in Indiana, but exploitation did not begin in earnest until the 1880s after a much publicized discovery in Ohio. The first wells producing gas were drilled in Eaton, Portland, and Kokomo in 1886. After a decade of frantic drilling, communities such as Muncie, Marion, Alexandria, Anderson, Hartford City, Montpelier, and New Castle not only used natural gas for lighting but also to attract industry. Pipelines had been built to nearby communities so that they too could enjoy the benefits of this cheap resource.

The existence of natural gas in Indiana became well known throughout the rest of the United States and, as a result, prompted a mini-boom in the area. Indiana attracted industries from areas where fuel sources were more remote and, hence, more expensive. Adding to the attraction was the fact that the area was rural and thus possessed a work force considered more reliable than the more recent immigrants who supplied the labor for eastern factories.

Three industries which relied heavily upon heat in their manufacturing process and which were attracted by the prospects of adequate natural gas were tinplate, glass, and strawboard. The first two were also connected with food processing so that a rural location was doubly advantageous.

Tinplate was the material used for canning foods. The technology of using a tin can with a soldered lid predated the Civil War. Among those

Dr. Robert E. Humphreys found a better way
to crack petroleum in 1912.

persons who became involved early was an Indianapolis grocer, Gilbert Van Camp. The Civil War greatly increased the business of what now is Stokely-Van Camp. So also did the discovery of Frank Van Camp, the son of Gilbert, that beans packed in tomato sauce had a ready market. By the 1890s the Van Camp Packing Company was one of the most successful suppliers of wholesale groceries in the country.

The increase in canned foods and the tariff on imported tinplate encouraged domestic producers to begin competing. In 1891 Elwood had a tinplate factory, soon to be followed by Atlanta, Gas City, Middletown, and Montpelier. Two Muncie men— Daniel G. Reid and William B. Leeds—along with a Chicagoan, William C. Moore, acquired control of American Tin Plate in 1894. The company acquired control of all of the tinplate factories in Indiana as well as some in the East, thus creating a near monopoly on that product.

The glass industry was also concentrated in the "Gas Belt" but it preceded the tinplate industry in Indiana. John Baptiste Ford, the first to make plate glass in the United States, began the first Indiana glass manufacturing company in New Albany in 1869. By 1872 he had lost control of the company to his banker cousin, Washington C. DePauw. Twenty years later DePauw moved the company, renamed the DePauw Glass Works, to Alexandria to take advantage of the supply of natural gas. By that time almost every village and hamlet in east-central Indiana had a glassworks turning out plate glass windows, insulators for telephone lines, and, most famous of all, fruit jars.

Most of the glass companies vanished with the natural gas. The hazards of fire did some in; the competition of larger companies did in others. A few—among them, Indiana Glass in Dunkirk, Sinclair Glass in Hartford City, and Ball Brothers of Muncie—remain in the area.

The story of Ball Brothers is the story of the

Oil well coming in.

Oil well near Monroeville, about 1916.

140

Oil well played out, near Madison.

NATURAL GAS DISPLAY IN THE INDIANA GAS FIELDS.

THE discovery of natural gas in Indiana was made first at the little town of Eaton, in Delaware County, about three years ago. From the date of that discovery prospecting and developing has been going steadily forward. Up to this date 380 gas wells have been sunk in the State, 75 per cent. of which have been gas bearing wells. The Indiana gas field embraces 3,500 square miles, or about two million square

Natural gas display in the Indiana gas fields, 1888.

From photograph of one of the gas wells supplying Indianapolis. Flame 105 ft. high out of 4 in. pipe. Output, 18,000,000 cubic feet per day.

Advertisement stressing the value of Indiana natural gas to manufacturers.

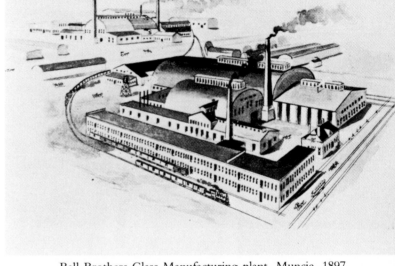

Ball Brothers Glass Manufacturing plant, Muncie, 1897.

Advertising gas fixtures and appliances.

Making Mason glass jars at Ball Brothers, Muncie.

Ball Brothers pose for their picture.

Mule power in an early underground mine, Indiana.

Orchard of fruit trees, Clay County, 1918. It marked the first reclamation of surface-mined land in Indiana and the nation.

glass industry in Indiana in microcosm. The company originated in Buffalo as a manufacturer of wood-jacketed cans in 1880. Ball Brothers turned to the manufacture of glass containers five years later and, after the factory burned for the second time, decided to move to the "Gas Belt." Muncie induced the Balls to move there by giving them $7,500 in cash, seven acres of land, and as much free natural gas as was needed for the first five years of operation.

Ball Brothers began glass production in Muncie on March 1, 1888, and was almost immediately successful. The company expanded in a variety of directions; by 1894 it had a unit constructing wooden boxes in which to pack the jars as well as the strawboard with which to wrap the jars. By skillful management which developed a sales department, which other companies failed to develop, Ball Brothers outstripped its competitors by capturing 65 percent of the market. It was so successful that twenty other companies relied upon Ball Brothers to sell their jars.

By 1900 Indiana was second in the nation in the value of glass products produced from 110 factories in the state. When the gas supply failed, the glass factories had several options. They could close down, move to another area, or search out alternative supplies of fuel. Ball Brothers, for example, remained in Muncie by switching to coal which was supplied by rail from the coalfields of western Indiana.

The third industry promoted by cheap gas and a rural setting was the strawboard industry. Strawboard was a cardboard made from straw which had a variety of uses for packing in the tinplate and glass industries. It could be fashioned into boxes to ship canned goods or glass jars; it could be used as industrial paper to wrap jars or cans. As a result, the strawboard plants were found in the "Gas Belt"—Albany, Anderson, Muncie, Gas City, Hartford City, Marion, Kokomo, and Eaton. The straw-

Blue Hole Stone Mill, Bedford, in the early 1900s.

board industry underwent the same pattern of consolidation which characterized the tinplate and glass industries. The smaller, less efficient operators were squeezed out by the larger ones. The major producer of strawboard in the state became the Fort Wayne Corrugated Paper Company which dominated the field.

The gas wells are only a memory for most Hoosiers, although an infrequent advertisement for a house in Muncie, Alexandria, or Dunkirk may include a note that the property has its own gas well, or a casual conversation with a resident may elicit the same information. A few scattered pumps still working slowly in the area attest to the presence of oil, and as energy resources become scarcer, drillers talk of sinking new holes to tap what remains of the oil and gas. So far this remains speculation.

By an odd quirk of history, just as Indiana petroleum reserves were being exhausted, a transplanted Hoosier, Dr. Robert E. Humphreys, discovered a better way to "crack" crude oil into gasoline. As a result, Whiting became an important refinery center for Standard Oil of Indiana and its skyline symbolic of the rapidly industrializing northwestern corner of the state.

Other mineral resources in Indiana became more important because of the overall demands of a modernizing United States. The coalfields around Terre Haute began to supply the nascent steel industries of the state and region. The clay and limestone deposits, when exploited, provided the brick and stone to build factories as well as houses and streets. Both industries increased during this period.

The completion of the railway network by the end of the nineteenth century meant that Indiana products could be shipped to almost any point in the state or nation. The base for an industrial commonwealth was in place.

Nor had the railways completely eliminated the traffic on the rivers which had early been the

Limestone quarries, near Bloomington.

Pyramid of toy wagons made for Studebaker by the South Bend Toy Company, about 1912.

"A trip around the world" in a Studebaker junior wagon, 1910.

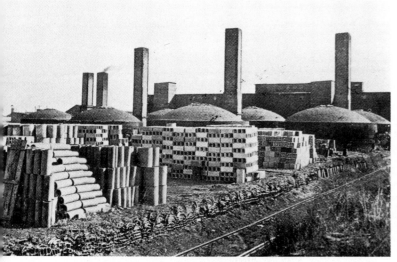

Terra Cotta factory, Brook.

C.L. Centlivre Brewing Company, Fort Wayne, 1906.

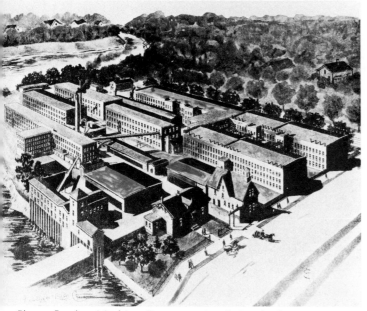

Singer Sewing Machine Company, South Bend, about 1902.

20-Mule Borax Team "from Death Valley" at the Studebaker factory, South Bend, about 1890.

Big Four train at New Castle station, 1920.

Packet boat, *Catherine Davis,* leaving Aurora, 1918.

The famous railroad cut, near Madison.

Building steamboats, Madison shipyards, late 1880s.

Unloading mail sacks, Spencer, 1900s.

Rail and water terminal, near Madison.

Advertisement for Van Camp's Pork and Beans, 1890.

Madame Walker, businesswoman, driving her car, 1910.

Delaware County National Bank, interior, 1897.

major transportation links. Shipyards at Madison and New Albany continued to turn out paddle wheelers which plied the Ohio and the Mississippi. While river traffic no longer had a monopoly on freight, it still was important enough to justify continued capital investment.

The growth of an industrial commonwealth required an infrastructure which provided the financial and administrative services necessary for business expansion. Hoosier cities, as a result, saw a proliferation of banks and credit institutions as well as offices. These institutions reflected the pride of ownership and a new sense of economic prosperity. They also offered career opportunities for women in secretarial and clerical roles which, humble though they were, made self-support possible.

Other industries came and went. Singer Sewing Machine had a cabinet factory in South Bend, so located because of the abundant timber in the region. But when the region was cut over by 1902, the company moved out. Another industry which was in Indiana for a short time was a cosmetic firm aimed at the black woman. Madame C.J. Walker, a poor black orphan from Louisiana, had developed a cosmetic business in St. Louis but decided to move to Indianapolis to build her factory. She lived in Indianapolis for five years prior to moving to New York, where she became one of the first women millionaires.

Not all Hoosier industries came from other states or left or died. One native Hoosier business which portended the future was Eli Lilly and Company, a pharmaceutical company founded by Colonel Eli Lilly, a Civil War veteran, in 1876. Specializing in prescription drugs, the company became one of the major manufacturers of those items in the country.

By 1920 Indiana's hopes for becoming the major industrial state in the nation had been dashed because of the exhaustion of natural gas. On the other hand, Hoosiers could console themselves with the knowledge that the loss of gas had not caused a reversion to a completely rural economy. Indiana had firms making glass, tinplate, and drugs which were among the largest and most significant ones in the country. These businesses portended increasing commercial development and increasing wealth.

Colonel Eli Lilly founded his company on Pearl Street, Indianapolis, in 1876.

Lilly electric delivery wagon, about 1900.

Lilly's *Bulletin*, 1893.

Man mixing ingredients for ointment, 1890.

Women working with staphylococcus albus vaccine, Biologicals Finishing Department, about 1919.

Iron and Automobiles

Pouring iron, Gary Works, U.S. Steel, about 1914.

INDIANA WAS A PIONEER IN THE DEVELOPMENT OF TWO INDUSTRIES WHICH BECAME SYNONYMOUS WITH AMERICAN MANUFACTURING — iron and automobiles. The first was to modify drastically the northwestern Indiana landscape and to create a city which symbolized the making of steel; the second proved to be a lasting economic influence.

Small blast furnaces dotted the land in Indiana as early as the Civil War. These furnaces could be found where there was cheap fuel such as in the coal-mining area around Terre Haute. Most of these small furnaces for the refining of iron ore did not survive into the twentieth century. In addition to the blast furnace, plants fabricating steel were common in small cities such as Muncie, Anderson, Elwood, and Kokomo. The plants were competitive until large-scale producers put them out of business.

The large-scale producers chose The Region, in northwestern Indiana, to create a planned city designed to support a giant iron and steel manufacturing center. The planned city was Gary, Indiana. The reasons for the choice of the Calumet Region were obvious. The land was swampy and sandy, hence undeveloped, and unoccupied and cheap. Further, the location near Chicago meant that an available pool of workers, both native and foreign, could be drawn upon to build and work in the mills. Transportation connections made the site even more advantageous. The Lake Michigan beachfront provided a connection with the Mesabi iron range and the railroads leading into and out of Chicago could carry the finished iron and steel anywhere in the country.

First to exploit the advantages of the Calumet Region was the Standard Oil Company of Indiana, which set up a refinery in Whiting in 1889; twelve years later Inland Steel Company built open-hearth furnaces and rolling mills there after an East Chicago land company donated fifty acres of land

149

Leveling sand on site of Gary Works, 1906.

for industrial purposes. The most significant addition, however, was the United States Steel Corporation, which acquired nine thousand acres of land in 1906 in Lake County to build what at the time would be the world's largest steel-making facility.

At the same time the mills were being constructed, U.S. Steel directed the Gary Land Company to plan for a community of 100,000 to be named Gary after Judge Elbert H. Gary, chairman of the board of U.S. Steel. The company arranged for private contractors to build houses for workers which were sold with generous and lengthy credit arrangements. Despite enlightened plans, the company had great difficulty in creating a city overnight. A temporary housing facility consisting of tents and jerry-built houses constructed of scrap material became an instant slum. When the construction workers for whom the temporary housing was intended left, unskilled workers in the steel mills replaced them. Two other areas became blighted almost as soon as the first timbers went up. One was a housing area designed by U.S. Steel for unmarried workers; it became known as "Hunkeyville" after the immigrants who settled there. Another was "The Patch," a low-quality housing development, built by private contractors and designed for the unskilled workers after they left their tents. Rapid, uncontrolled growth demolished the dream of the planned city. The whole region soon became part of the urban conglomeration which is Chicago.

The major part of the population growth came from Europe. The immigration to the region changed the character of the state's population. While Indiana as a whole remained one of the states with few foreign-born residents, Gary had a population which was about 50 percent foreign born. Workers from eastern and southern Europe boosted Gary's population so that by 1920 Gary was the sixth largest city in the state.

Although there had been blacks in Gary almost

Nineteenth and Broadway, facing north, Gary, 1907.

The last of the shacks on Euclid Avenue, Gary.

Judge Elbert H. Gary, chairman of the board, U.S. Steel.

Going to work in the steel mills, Gary.

Board of Works meeting, Gary, about 1917.

from the beginning, the boom of the First World War began the tide of black migration to supplement the foreign one. From making up 10 percent of Gary's population in 1920, blacks would predominate by 1970. By that time Gary was one of sixteen cities over 25,000 in population in the United States with a majority of black residents.

The growth of Gary's population made the city into a kind of Pittsburgh and helped catapult Indiana into third place as an iron- and steel-producing state. No longer could the bucolic images of James Whitcomb Riley be applied uniformly to the Hoosier state.

If Gary became Pittsburgh, Indianapolis did not become Detroit. Yet it almost became the hub of the automobile industry; only by chance and circumstance did Michigan become the home of the Ford and Chevrolet.

The automobile was not an American invention. The name is French and the operable gasoline-powered engine is German, patented first by Nicholas Otto in 1877. Another German, Karl Benz, put Otto's four-cycle, internal-combustion engine on to a chassis and thus built the first automobile in 1886.

Other forms of propulsion competed with gasoline power. Steam cars appealed to some manufacturers and customers. They had a longer technological history and had had greater experimental use. Two very successful steam cars were the White and the Stanley Steamers. Another competitor was the electric car. Powered with batteries, the electric car was reliable and simple to operate, although both its speed and range were limited. By 1900 the electric car appeared to be the car of the future, with the steam-powered and gasoline-powered automobiles fighting for second place.

The early technology of automobile manufacturing was such that companies building buggies, wagons, or bicycles could easily begin making cars by buying engines to put on their vehicles. Conversely, engine companies could readily buy vehicles on which to attach their engines. The early history of the automobile is replete with examples. In Indiana, the Studebaker Company shifted easily from wagons to electric and gasoline cars. The Nordyke and Marmon Company originally built flour mill machinery. In 1903 it built the Marmon car. David Parry built wagons in Indianapolis. He built a car there called the Parry. He took over the Overland Car Company, which originated in Terre Haute as a product of the Standard Wheel Company in 1902, and moved it to Indianapolis. It later moved to Toledo to become Willys-Overland.

During the first twenty years of automobile manufacturing (1900–20), almost every Indiana town of any pretensions had a plant. The United States in that period had over 2,200 makes of cars, and Indiana had more than 200 of them. Most of the names are long forgotten except by the antique automobile collector, but they reflect the energy and the enterprise of Hoosiers. A few representative models were: Apperson and Haynes, Kokomo; De-Soto and Auburn, Auburn; Lexington Minute Man 6, Connersville; Interstate, Muncie; Premier, The American, and Cole, Indianapolis; Octoauto, Columbus; Amplex (which had an engine without valves), Mishawaka; Lambert, Anderson; Model, Peru; and the Maxwell (Jack Benny's car), New Castle.

The automobile companies grew quickly and then died. Many produced only a few models, not enough to insure customer recognition. Others succumbed because of inadequate financing or were bought out by entrepreneurs who merged smaller units into larger ones. Indiana car manufacturers, with the exception of Studebaker, were never able to raise enough capital to become serious competitors. The result is best typified by the fate of the Interstate, which became part of the General Motors complex.

A good example of the rise and fall of a

Children and teachers at Neighborhood House, Gary, 1917.

A night class for adults in the Gary schools, about 1913.

Elwood Haynes in his automobile.

Haynes-Apperson factory, Kokomo, about 1899.

Hoosier automobile company is the history of the Haynes Company. Elwood Haynes was an American original, a man of talent and genius who was a genuine contributor to the development of the automobile. He built the world's third gasoline-powered automobile and the second operable vehicle in America, which he successfully test drove down Pumpkinvine Pike near Kokomo on July 4, 1894. The next year he began to manufacture cars; by the time of his death thirty years later, the company was bankrupt.

Elwood Haynes was born October 14, 1857. He early showed an interest in chemistry and metallurgy. Growing up on a farm near Portland, Indiana, he built a railway car of threshing machine parts which he successfully ran until chased off the tracks by an irate railroad official. Haynes left Indiana to attend the Worcester County Free Institute of Industrial Science in Massachusetts, but returned to teach high school in 1881. In 1886 he became superintendent of the Portland Natural Gas Company during the gas boom. As the gas began to fail, Haynes supervised the laying of pipelines to more remote wells. This experience convinced him of the need for a mode of transportation beyond the horse.

While working as superintendent of the Indiana Natural Gas and Oil Company's plant in Kokomo, Haynes built his pioneering automobile. He bought a one-horsepower marine engine from the Sintz Company of Grand Rapids in 1893. He then attached it to a chain-driven vehicle built in a machine shop owned by the Apperson brothers. The automobile was advanced for its day, having a steel frame and rubber tires. When Haynes built his second car, he added pneumatic tires, another first for the noted Hoosier.

Haynes and the Appersons formed a partnership in 1895 to build automobiles. By 1898 the company was producing five cars per year. In 1899 Haynes and Edgar Apperson drove one of their cars

The First Quarter Century of Automobiles

1893

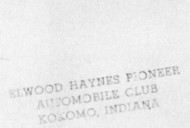

The first car was years ahead in one respect—it had wire wheels.

1896

More passenger room, not speed, was the object in a lengthened wheelbase on the third Haynes ever built. The gasoline tank made an excellent dash.

1899

A door in the rear provided access to the "innards" of this "horseless carriage." Tubes through water tanks along each side cooled the engine.

1900

The first runabouts well might be termed "horseless buggies." Graceful lines were sought even then—hence the "plowshare" radiator.

1902

A matchless equipage for the fashionable folk two decades ago. The coil radiator was a big mechanical improvement. Rear tires suffered terribly, if the brakes were ever used.

1903

In 1902 Haynes began designating its models by letter. This is the model A surrey. After much technical argument, the lever control was discontinued in favor of the steering wheel.

1903

If you bought a two-passenger phaeton-surrey, model H, attachments could be obtained to accommodate six. The door to the rear compartment is in the back and it was a long climb up there.

The first quarter century of Haynes automobiles.

1904

The rear entrance "tonneau" was all the rage in 1904. Manufacturers began putting the engine in front, and the automobile assumed in general the form it was to retain. This is a model F, Haynes "tonneau."

This view of the model F shows why backing had to be attended with care if passengers intended to enter or alight.

1905

1906

The seat-over-the-radiator idea died hard. It was revived in this model L Haynes, which to all appearances was a two-passenger runabout until Presto! the hood gave forth another seat.

This type Haynes was a great favorite with those sporty motorists of 1906 who admired racy lines and "class." Wide, flaring front fenders kept down mud when you "opened 'er up."

1911

1907

Wheel-conforming fenders, front entrance handles, and a spare tire carrier on the running board were introduced in the model S. A tank of compressed gas took the place of the acetylene generator which formerly supplied gas for the lamps.

Then came doors for the front compartment. The 1911 catalog says this is a *closed body* on a model 20 chassis. Windshield was regular equipment. Control levers were soon put inside.

1918

The Haynes "Fourdore" speaks volumes for the motor car of 1918. It is a worthy expression of the experience which the Haynes organization has been accumulating since Elwood Haynes invented America's first successful automobile in 1893.

Waverley Electric Car, made in Indianapolis.

Waverley Company office. Waverley made bicycles before making cars.

The Reeves Motocycle with its inventor Milton O. Reeves at the lever, Columbus, September 26, 1896.

Advertisement for "The Reeves" Octoauto in the *Horseless Age,* August 9, 1911.

"THE REEVES" OCTOAUTO

THIS TYPE AND GRADE 40 H. P., FOUR-PASSENGER, $3,200

THE EASIEST RIDING CAR IN THE WORLD

Built on the principle of a Pullman Parlor Car. A truck in front, a truck in the rear. An old and accepted principle accomplish easy riding applied to the automobile. The Octoauto rides more like a boat than an automobile. Ultimate tire expe reduced more than one-half according to tire authorities, while blowouts are practically eliminated. Safety to passengers gre increased. Demonstration car has been driven some 3,000 miles, including a trip to Toledo, Detroit, Cleveland, Akron, Canton Columbus, Ohio; has been seen by and demonstrated to thousands of persons. Is now in constant use and can be seen and ridde any time in Columbus, Indiana.

I claim the Octoauto rides with less shock and vibration and is more safe than any car of any make or price, and I st ready to prove these claims by competitive demonstration in Indianapolis, Indiana, bearing all expenses thereof of com titors if found untrue. The eight wheeled idea is applicable to any kind of automobile, and privilege to use same may be Therefore, if interested, write your automobile manufacturer or myself.

FOR FURTHER INFORMATION OR CIRCULAR, ADDRESS
M. O. REEVES, Columbus, Ind.
Pres. Peoples Savings & Trust
V. P. Reeves Pulley Company

Speed sign in Brookston, 1915. Automobiles frightened horses in those days.

Studebakers in Studebakers, South Bend, October 25, 1908: Vice President of U.S. Charles W. Fairbanks and J.M. Studebaker (first car); Mrs. J.M. Studebaker, Col. and Mrs. George M. Studebaker, and J. M. Studebaker, Jr. (second car); Mrs. J.M. Studebaker, Jr. (third car); Mr. and Mrs. Clement Studebaker, Jr. (fourth car).

Thomas A. Edison in his Studebaker electric phaeton, with George Meister at the tiller, 1909.

to Brooklyn for delivery to a prospective customer. This was the first time a car had been driven one thousand miles, and gained the company considerable attention.

As production grew, so did tension between partners. The Appersons and Haynes dissolved the company in 1901; the Appersons began the Apperson Brothers Company while Haynes began the Haynes Company. Haynes, never fond of management, persuaded his brother Calvin to abandon his grocery business in 1905 and take over the management of the business. With his time freed for experiments, Elwood Haynes continued his search for an alloy which would withstand high heats. In 1907 he succeeded in alloying cobalt and chromium into a material he called stellite. He also experimented with stainless steel, once again successfully. However, he encountered patent difficulty and had to fight two years to get his claims recognized. By 1915 the Haynes Stellite Company joined the Haynes Automobile Company, just in time to share the general prosperity brought on by World War I.

The prosperity of the Haynes Automobile Company was short-lived. It expanded in 1919 and then encountered the first general slump in the industry in 1920. The inherent weaknesses of management—the lack of adequate sales organization, inaccurate estimates of costs, and overspending—helped push the company over the brink. It staggered along for four more years before finally going bankrupt. The Haynes Stellite Company became a division of the Union Carbide and Carbon Corporation in 1920, but with a profit instead of a loss for Haynes. The founder of the automobile industry in the state had failed to exploit successfully his initial advantage. He had produced an excellent automobile. It was, however, too expensive and the sound engineering did not overcome the poor management. The future belonged to the manager, not the engineer.

One large Indiana automaker survived the

157

1920s crisis; the company was Studebaker. The biggest manufacturer of wagons in the United States in 1900, Studebaker had even at that early date become involved in the automobile industry by supplying bodies to other builders. By 1902 Studebaker had produced its first car, an electric one. Two years later the company had a gasoline-powered automobile, and in 1908 the management decided upon a major entry into the market. The decision was not, however, to build cars but to use the company's sales network to sell a car, the E-M-F, for the Everett-Metzger-Flanders Company. The business arrangement failed to satisfy either side, and by 1910 Studebaker bought out its erstwhile partner and went into car building seriously.

Studebaker looked like a winner. Unlike other producers of automobiles, the company had adequate financing, a dealer network, and a well-trained work force, both on the floor and in the office. The early record seemed to reflect those strengths. In its first year Studebaker sold 22,555 cars; three years later, it sold 114,000. When World War I ended, Studebaker was the largest automaker in Indiana and the fifth largest in the United States, following Ford, General Motors, Dodge, and Willys-Overland.

While Studebaker survived the crisis of 1920, it did have problems. Its models were expensive and the market of the 1920s was for inexpensive and medium-priced cars. Studebaker had an entry in the latter arena in 1927, a six-cylinder car called the Erskine. It was not a great success. The company was the largest independent by 1930, but its profits had declined steadily after 1923. In 1932 it lost money and went into receivership in 1933. Bailed out in 1935, Studebaker remained in operation for another thirty-odd years before going under for the last time, a victim of competition with the Big Three.

If an Indiana automobile company would have

Automobiles pause at Union City on their way to Richmond in the gasoline test run sponsored by White Steamer Company, June 13, 1910.

Driving on a country road in the 1900s.

Lomer Armored Tire Company, New Castle.

Hybrid bridge, Gosport.

Tire stands, Lomer Armored Tire factory, New Castle.

"Cross this Bridge at a Walk": Covered bridge built by J.J. Daniels, 1873.

Leveling a roadbed, still using teams of horses and mules.

Founders of the Indianapolis Motor
Speedway Corporation, with Henry
Ford (left), Arthur C. Newby, Frank
H. Wheeler, Carl G. Fisher, and
James A. Allison, about 1911.

Ray Harroun, winner of first 500-mile race, 1911.

Ralph De Palma, winner of the race, 1915.

King road drag.

Stuck in the mud, 1914.

Eddie Rickenbacker in his race car, 1914.

One of the early 500-mile races.

succeeded, it should have been named Studebaker. It had the resources, the know-how, and the reputation for quality. Studebaker's failure shows how competitive the business was.

Although no Indiana company assembles automobiles in the Hoosier state, involvement in the industry is still heavy. Many of the components for automobiles built in the United States and abroad are made in Indiana. Warner Gear of Muncie builds transmissions; it began in 1900 when Thomas W. and Harry Warner began making differentials. Delco-Remy of Anderson produces electrical products; it began in 1901 as the Remy Electric Company to sell the dynamos developed by its creators Frank L. and B. Perry Remy in 1895. Finally, the Prest-O-Lite Company of Indianapolis, founded by Carl G. Fisher, still manufactures batteries and other parts for cars, just as it did in 1904.

Fisher was responsible for another automobile enterprise which still is important to Hoosiers. In the early days of the motor car, racing was the premier means of advertising. Every carmaker tried to earn the reputation of having the fastest car around. Fisher realized that a commercial raceway had considerable potential so he, along with James A. Allison, Frank H. Wheeling, and Arthur C. Newby, built the Indianapolis Speedway in 1909. The proprietors experimented with different kinds of races at different times of the year before deciding that a 500-mile race in May was the best. The first race occurred in 1911, and the "Indianapolis 500" became an annual Hoosier event.

As the reader drives through Gary or Kokomo or attends the race at the "brickyard," he ought to reflect on the times gone by when Gary was to be the best planned city in the country, when Elwood Haynes drove slowly down Pumpkinvine Pike, and when Ray Harroun won the "Indy 500" in a Marmon "Wasp" made in Indianapolis. America has come a long way and part of the trip has been on Gary-made iron and Indiana-made wheels.

Starting lineup of the first race, 1911.

Orville Wright and his sister came to Memorial Park, New Castle, April 15, 1923, to dedicate the Wilbur Wright stone. Biplanes flew overhead to honor Wilbur Wright, who was born at Millville, Henry County, April 16, 1867.

Arthur Ray Smith, Fort Wayne, built his own plane at the age of 16.

Pilot and plane up a tree.

Aviation Day at Stuart Field, Purdue University, June 13, 1911.

The World of Work

Noon at the Singer Manufacturing Company factory, South Bend, 1908. The company made wooden cabinets for sewing machines. Lewis Hine, the photographer, took this picture for the Congressional committee investigating child labor in the United States.

THE FORCES OF URBANIZATION AND INDUS-TRIALIZATION CREATED A SELF-CONSCIOUS WORK FORCE, ONE WHICH BEGAN TO SEE itself as a group apart from farmers and small merchants with whom it had earlier identified. The industrialists of the late nineteenth century had little social conscience and extracted as much labor as possible for as low a wage as possible. The average workday was ten hours and the average workweek was six days. In some industries the work load was even heavier. Typically, iron- and steelworkers had an eighty-four-hour week, or twelve hours a day for seven days. Coal miners were luckier; by the turn of the century they had achieved an eight-hour day and a forty-eight-hour workweek. By the 1920s the forty-eight-hour week was more nearly the average, although approximately one in six still worked a sixty-hour week.

Wages were low and workers were paid irregularly. Unskilled laborers could expect little more than $1 a day while the most skilled earned a maximum of $4.50 a day. Steelworkers in Gary as late as 1910 were earning only 17 cents an hour. Other workers were even less fortunate. Coal miners, for example, were paid piece rate for each ton they mined. They were also subject to frequent layoffs because of market conditions.

As was the case in other industrializing areas, women and children were among the first to be employed in factories. In Indiana women were most often found in such industries as bookbinding, clothing, packing plants and other food-processing operations, and in such occupations as salesgirls, clerks, secretaries, and telephone operators. They worked almost as long hours as men and for less wages. A study in 1894 showed that women in Indiana worked an average of 56.3 hours per week for an average weekly wage of $5.66. This meant a rate of about 10 cents per hour.

Children played an important part in Indiana industries down to World War I. Boys labored in

Brotherhood of Railroad Trainmen at their meeting in Central School yard, Bedford, Labor Day, 1908.

such industries as glass, coal mining, furniture making, and food packing. Girls were more often found in the textile trade: tending looms in cotton or wool mills, cutting and sewing clothes in clothing factories, or washing clothes in laundries. Despite continuing attempts to legislate against child labor (an 1867 law prohibited the work of children under the age of 16 for more than 10 hours; an 1885 law prohibited any child under the age of 12 from working in selected industries—iron, steel, nails, machinery, and tobacco; and an 1893 law raised the minimum age to 14), child labor persisted in factories. Indeed, Indiana was third in the proportion of children to adults in the work force in the northern states in 1910. Only during World War I was there a decrease in child labor.

Industrialization also brought health hazards, both physical and mental, to the workers. Machines driven by unguarded long belts often ensnared the unwary worker who tended them. Factories were dirty and smoky from coal; the idea of air pollution as a hazard had not yet come into its own. Smoke meant prosperity, owners said and workers agreed. Workers who were injured on the job often received no compensation; not until 1915 was a workman's compensation law passed and even this was voluntary. In addition to the danger of being physically injured, workers suffered boredom from the repetitive work and a sense of loss of craftsmanship from the routinized assembly line.

All these factors led to the growth of labor unrest and of labor organizations designed to alleviate these conditions. Those unions which predate the Civil War most typically were craft unions such as the Shoemakers Union, the Blacksmiths and Machinists Union, and the Typographical Union. They had the same goals and used the same tactics as the industrial unions which later supplanted them. In 1863, for example, the Typographical Union struck the Indianapolis *Sentinel,* and a year

Coal miners in Greene Valley mine, Jasonville.

Workers at Clark and Bros. Sewer Pipe and Stoneware Factory, Cannelton. Each man holds tools of his trade or a finished product.

Workers at Sibley Machine and Foundry, South Bend, 1920s.

Workers at Perkins Windmill Factory, Mishawaka, about 1912.

later the Blacksmiths and Machinists Union called a strike against local iron companies.

These nascent unions were faced with the problem of using political means to accomplish their objectives or concentrating upon direct economic pressures. Early on, one union took the political road. At the conclusion of the Civil War, a group of Hoosier workers led by a member of the Blacksmiths and Machinists Union, John Fehrenbatch of Indianapolis, called a Workingmen's Convention to push for an eight-hour day. The result was the formation of the Eight Hour League, an organization which supported candidates for political office who were committed to the eight-hour day. The Eight Hour League spawned successors, including the Workingmen's National party, which had Indiana affiliates, but none of these proved attractive enough to gain much support.

Another tactic was to form industrial rather than craft unions. One of the first to appear in Indiana was the Ancient Order of United Workmen, a branch of which was functioning in Terre Haute in 1873. A rival group, the Independent Order of the Mechanics, came into existence shortly thereafter. Neither of these was successful in Indiana as the Knights of Labor, which had twenty-three locals by the mid-1880s. The goals of the Knights of Labor were not dissimilar from those of other industrial unions: an eight-hour day, workman's compensation, a tax on income, postal savings banks, and the expropriation of the unearned increments from the increase in the value of land.

The Knights of Labor were not immune to the controversies which rent other unions. The argument over which kind of means—political or direct action—to use continued. Direct action proved stronger and involved the union in several unsuccessful strikes. These, combined with the Haymarket Riot in Chicago and a rival, the American Federation of Labor, begun in 1881 by the Knights of

Industry and the Amalgamated Labor Union, caused a gradual decline in membership.

The A.F.L. was primarily composed of craft unions, although it did include such industrial ones as the United Mine Workers and the International Union of Brewery Workers. It also eschewed political programs and opted for direct action.

One group of labor unions, the railroad brotherhoods, antedated both the Knights of Labor and the American Federation of Labor. The first was the Brotherhood of Locomotive Engineers, which had locals in the state in 1864. Next was the Brotherhood of Locomotive Firemen, which had a Grand Lodge in Indianapolis in 1876. The Grand Lodge moved to Terre Haute in 1880; it was here that Indiana's most famous labor leader, Eugene V. Debs, learned his trade.

The unions lost ground in the 1870s because of the panic of 1873 and the unsuccessful strikes. Only 18 percent of the unions founded before 1870 survived the decade. The remaining ones barely held on to their organization.

The first strikes of the 70s came in the coalfields of Vigo, Fountain, and Clay counties. Miners in Clay County struck in 1871 and again in 1872. The reason for the strikes was the failure of the operators to carry out their agreement to pay 20 cents more per ton and to pay bimonthly instead of monthly. The owners of the mines successfully broke the strikes with the importation of black strikebreakers. This did not end the disturbances but subsequent strikes were no more productive than the earlier ones.

The unrest in Clay County was overshadowed by that in Fountain County in 1877 and 1878. Miners in Coal Creek struck in 1877 when a non-union worker was hired. The company responded by bringing in black strikebreakers and arming them. Once again, the operators succeeded in breaking the strike. A local militia consisting partly of miners on strike exchanged shots with the blacks.

Workers engaged in various activities in the Studebaker Spring Vehicle Department.

Workers at the Mitchell Printing Company.

Telephone exchange, Cannelton, 1908.

Office workers, early 1900s.

Women hand dipping chocolate candy at the Indianapolis Candy Company, early 1900s.

Four blacks were killed in the violence. Order was finally restored when Governor "Blue Jeans" Williams ordered state troops into the area to disarm the white militia.

Even more serious strikes occurred on the railroads. Unlike the unrest in the coalfields, these strikes were not localized ones. Like them, they were unsuccessful. The first serious one, in 1873, involved the Pennsylvania Railroad and the Brotherhood of Locomotive Engineers and, later, the Brotherhood of Firemen. The issue was the reduction of wages because of the panic of 1873. The railroad brought in strikebreakers with resultant violence; the worst was in Logansport, where state troops were dispatched. In 1876 the Ohio and Mississippi Railroad, which had connections at Seymour, North Vernon, and Vincennes, reduced wages, an action which precipitated a strike. The same tactics were employed and violence ensued, but Governor Hendricks refused to dispatch troops.

These two strikes were dwarfed by those in 1877 against most of the railways in the state. Extremely vulnerable to the economic instability of the times, these railways—the Pittsburgh, Fort Wayne, and Chicago; the Vandalia Line; the Bee Line; the Indianapolis and Peru; the Indianapolis and Vincennes; the Jefferson, Madison, and Indianapolis Line; and the Ohio and Mississippi—tried to cut wages. The owners obtained a federal injunction, and used strikebreakers and the threat of federal troops to end the strike. Fifteen strikers were convicted of contempt of court for not obeying the injunction and other strikers were blacklisted.

While the railroad brotherhoods survived the disastrous strikes, their members became more conservative. An exception to this trend was Indiana-born Eugene V. Debs, who was to become the outstanding labor leader of his time.

Born in Terre Haute in 1855, Debs began to work at the age of 15 by scraping paint off railway cars. He joined the Brotherhood of Locomotive

Eugene V. Debs, of Terre Haute.

Firemen when it was organized in Terre Haute in 1875 and soon became the secretary of Vigo Lodge No. 16. Despite his opposition to the strikes of 1877, he was elected national secretary-treasurer soon thereafter. Disillusioned by the failure of the Brotherhood of Locomotive Engineers to continue a strike against the C.B.&Q., Debs tried to resign from the Brotherhood of Locomotive Firemen in 1892 in order to establish a federation of all railroad workers. When his resignation was not accepted, Debs began the American Railway Union in 1893, while working for the brotherhood.

One year later, 1894, the Pullman strike in Chicago occurred. Debs opposed the strike but fought when his union, A.R.U., was drawn into the dispute. As a result, Debs was charged with violating a federal injunction and with conspiracy to obstruct the mails. He received a six-month sentence and, while in jail, became a convert to socialism. After his release he helped found the Social Democratic party of America, later the Socialist party of America, in 1897. As its nominee for president, Debs ran in every succeeding election year from 1900, with the sole exception of 1916, until 1920. Debs continued his union activities, helping to establish the Industrial Workers of the World, a giant industrial union, in 1905. He opposed American entry into World War I; as a result, he was convicted of violating the Espionage Act of 1918 and sent to the penitentiary in Moundsville, West Virginia. Released in 1921, he lived five more years, highly regarded for his personal integrity.

In the decades preceding the First World War, Hoosier workers remained dormant and conservative. The American Federation of Labor had two periods of rapid growth, from 1898 to 1904 and during World War I, but grew slowly in other eras. The United Mine Workers also attracted its share of adherents, but no large industrial union, such as the Industrial Workers of the World, sparked the imagination of the workers in Indiana.

Girls working at the Lincoln Cotton Mills, Evansville, 1908.

Boys working at midnight at the Glass Works, Dunkirk, 1908.

168

Men and boys leave for lunch at the Indianapolis Meat Packing Company, 1908.

The growth of unionism fostered by the First World War ended abruptly in 1919. Three strikes in Indiana—the Home Telephone Company in Linton, the Standard Steel Car Company in Hammond, and the steel strike in Gary and East Chicago—resulted in the calling out of the state militia to restore order and to protect strikebreakers. The steel strike even brought out federal troops, as requested by William F. Hodges, mayor of Gary. The unfavorable atmosphere for unions in Indiana and the United States caused a decline in membership in the 1920s. It was not until the decade of the 1930s, with a favorable national administration and a push from auto workers, that unionization once again flourished. It was in this decade that labor unrest again showed in renewed worker militancy and strikes.

Steelworkers going to work, Gary.

Federal troops at the Gary Commercial Club during the steel strike in 1919.

169

Painters of Terre Haute & Indianapolis Railroad, 1870: the 15-year-old Debs is at the left in the front row.

The Red Special, campaign train for Debs, presidential candidate for the Socialist party.

Grocery store, Terre Haute, with living quarters on second floor, rear, where Debs grew up.

Debs campaigning beside the train, Waterbury, Connecticut, 1908.

Signing petitions to "Bring Debs Home for Xmas." President Harding ordered his release from federal prison on Christmas Day 1921.

Toward a Better Life

Schoolchildren of Millgrove march in a parade.

ONE OF THE GREATEST TRANSFORMATIONS OF HOOSIER LIFE WAS THE CHANGE FROM A STATE WITH A HIGH PERCENTAGE OF ILliterates to one with a high culture—to a society consisting of an educated audience for nationally acclaimed authors. Furthermore, the change was accomplished in a few generations.

Meredith Nicholson in *The Hoosiers* (1900) correctly said that, "Nearly half a century after the organization of the first territorial government, no system of common schools had been perfected in Indiana." The Constitution of 1816 had said that free schools should be created "as soon as circumstances will permit." The legislature never found the right circumstances. The Constitution of 1851 allowed the establishment of common schools supported by state funds; but in a famous suit, the Greencastle Case, just three years later, the State Supreme Court ruled that no township tax could be levied to supplement state funds. Not until 1867 did the General Assembly pass a law allowing local funding. It is from this date that the growth of public schools should be traced.

The growth in the tax funds for public high schools meant these institutions could successfully challenge the county seminary and the private academy, both of which predated the Civil War. The county seminary was a school whose land, buildings, or maintenance was financed by fines collected for law violations or exemptions from military duties. Attendance required the payment of fees for instruction. In 1852 an Indiana law permitted the closing of county seminaries and the sale of their assets, the proceeds of which went into the public school fund. Many were purchased and turned into private academies.

Private academies were schools which required fees for attendance and which taught common subjects—mathematics, English, history, geography, and science—as well as the Latin and Greek prerequisite for college admission. They were sec-

Eleutherian College, Lancaster, Jefferson County.

Graduating class of 1898, Central Academy, Plainfield.

ondary schools, although sometimes they included the elementary grades on one end of the spectrum and college-level classes on the other. The most substantial academies were those sponsored by religious groups such as the Quakers and the Catholics. Often, because of the dearth of public high schools, colleges maintained their own academies in order to provide qualified students for their institutions.

The peak of the academy movement was in 1860; from that time on, the number of academies shrank until, by 1890, fully as many high schools existed as academies. The end of the private academy seemed near. By World War II less than fifty such schools continued to operate. However, the decades of the 1960s and 1970s witnessed a resurgence of private schools, particularly those with religious connections. Although the academy has passed from the scene, the Christian school remains.

For most Hoosiers, however, education meant a one-room rural schoolhouse supported by local taxes and supervised by township trustees overseen by a county board of education. The buildings were frame and lacked running water, indoor sanitary facilities, or adequate lighting. The school term rarely lasted beyond six months and attendance was indifferent; students attended as parents and work permitted. Not until 1895 were these schools required to have eight grades and not until 1897 was attendance mandated (all children between 8 years and 14 years of age had to go to school for a minimum of 12 weeks per year).

The one-room schoolhouse, inadequate as it was educationally, provided a welcome social outlet for its patrons. On Christmas and other holidays, the students presented dramatic and musical productions in the festival mood; and, on the last day of school, a picnic often was the order of the day. The school was, next to the voting place, the symbol of local community.

Central Academy, Plainfield, 1880s.

Borden Institute in Clark County began in 1884.

172

Fresh-air school, for healthier children, Indianapolis.

Black drill team, Crawfordsville.

School wagons at Wea High School, Montgomery County.

Children playing in schoolyard, Mitchell, Lawrence County.

In the twentieth century, however, the desire for educational improvement began to be manifest in the desire for larger, supposedly better schools. As early as 1899, school districts had the authority, granted by the General Assembly, to provide free transportation of students within their districts. Obviously designed to encourage the demise of very small schools, the law had little effect. As a result, in 1907 the legislature required the closing of all township schools with less than twelve pupils. By 1920 about half of them had been closed, but the movement did not fully succeed until the Second World War. Ironically, the methods used in the 1970s—the ungraded class, the open concept, and the use of older students to teach younger ones—were practiced in the one-room school.

Public high schools lagged behind elementary schools, mainly because they were located in town and because they were identified with college and so-called elitism. Most communities preferred to invest their scarce resources in elementary education which was mandated by the state. Not until 1913 was the age of leaving school raised to 16. Gradually communities began to build public high schools, but as late as 1920, according to Clifton J. Phillips, "nearly three fourths of the state's four-year high schools enrolled less than one hundred pupils."

As high schools became more common, they also diversified their offerings from the purely academic. Manual training, designed to improve students' moral fiber as well as their vocational chances, came to Shortridge High School in Indianapolis in 1888 and Indianapolis Manual Training School opened its doors in 1895. Gradually, attendance increased so that, by the 1930s, one-half of the eligible school-age population was enrolled.

But just as the trend to consolidation occurred some twenty years after the completion of the system of elementary school, so also did the trend to the consolidation of high schools occur some

173

Teachers in schoolroom, Brown County, 1918.

Evansville High School.

twenty years after the completion of that system. After World War II, the push to eliminate the small-town and rural high school began in earnest and, by the 1970s, the large consolidated high school, often an island of cement, brick, or stone set in a grassy plot and surrounded by cornfields, became a recognizable part of the landscape.

No doubt the facilities are better and the class offerings more varied. But the price has been high. The small town in Indiana survived because of community loyalty; in part this loyalty centered on the high school, particularly at basketball tourney time. Now the center of the community seems lost, the empty or converted high school a reminder of what once had been.

Indiana schools changed in other ways as well. One of the more obvious ways was in racial composition. Prior to the Civil War, according to Emma Lou Thornbrough, "colored children were denied any public education facilities whatsoever." Black students did attend private schools, especially those established by Quakers. These schools were either integrated, as in Hamilton County, or all black, such as the ones in Beech Settlement in Rush County and in the town of New Albany.

After the Civil War, when other northern states had provided public support for the education of blacks, Indiana and Illinois lagged behind. Not until 1869 did the Indiana General Assembly allow trustees to arrange for black education, either by creating separate schools or by a variety of other means, and a law requiring black admission to white schools if no separate facilities existed was not passed until 1877.

The result was that all-black schools were built in Richmond, Logansport, Evansville, Fort Wayne, Mount Vernon, Jeffersonville, Madison, and Indianapolis. As a rule, just as in the deep South, these black schools were inferior to white ones in equipment, buildings, and financial support. Despite these handicaps, blacks began to attend and

One-room schoolhouse, Brown County, 1918.

Valparaiso Public Graded School.

174

Ovid Butler, Indianapolis philanthropist.

Washington C. DePauw, industrialist. The name of Indiana Asbury University was changed to DePauw University in his honor in 1884.

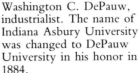

Center Hall, Wabash College.

Indiana Asbury University students and friends in front of the first building, which burned February 12, 1879.

graduate from school. The first black graduate of an Indiana high school was Mary Rann, who received her diploma from Indianapolis High School (now Shortridge) in 1876.

The racial barriers in education continued into the first part of the twentieth century. Indeed, the most famous black high school in Indiana, Crispus Attucks of Indianapolis, was built in the 1920s. It was not until 1949 that the General Assembly mandated the end of separate schools in Indiana. The history of the thirty years since 1949 has been replete with attempts to rectify eighty years of legal separation of the races and fifty years of neglect prior to that.

The transformation of the homogeneous rural school to the racially mixed urban one has been no less dramatic than the transformation of Hoosier colleges and universities. New institutions continued to be founded as churches felt the need to compete with older, more established ones. Old institutions often changed name or location, reflecting the pressures of the times.

The need to supply teachers as Indiana developed elementary and high schools was a primary one as the history of the post-Civil War era shows. In 1884 Tri-State College opened its doors at Angola as a teacher-training institution under private, nondenominational sponsorship. Manchester College began as North Manchester College in 1889, the heir of the United Brethren Seminary at Roanoke, for the purpose of preparing public school teachers; it was purchased by the Dunkers (now Church of the Brethren) in 1895. The Baptists incorporated Oakland City College in 1885 and began operating the institution in 1891 for the same purpose. The Catholics, not to be outdone, founded St. Joseph's College in Rensselaer in 1891. The Mennonites sponsored Goshen College, which began as Elkhart Institution in Elkhart in 1894; the college received its new name and location in 1903.

Nor did college founding cease with the end of

Women students at Hanover College, about 1903.

Hanover College students, 1903.

the nineteenth century. The United Brethren opened Indiana Central to students in 1905. Anderson Bible School was founded in 1917 by the Church of God, became a seminary in 1925, and became Anderson College and Theological Seminary in 1929. Finally, Marion College in Marion, Indiana, which opened its doors in 1920, was the successor of Marion Normal College and Marion Normal Institute. The Wesleyan Methodist Church became the sponsor of the latest effort.

Not only did these new institutions spring from the ashes of old institutes and schools; older ones changed names and/or functions. North Western Christian University moved to Irvington, a suburb of Indianapolis in 1875 and took the name of Butler University, after its benefactor Ovid Butler, two years later. Valparaiso Male and Female College, a Methodist school, expired in 1869, was reopened as the Northern Indiana Normal School and Business Institute in 1873, and ended up as Valparaiso University in 1907. Eighteen years later the Evangelical Lutheran Synodical Conference took control. Indiana Asbury College became DePauw University in 1884, named after Washington C. DePauw, a benefactor. Finally, Fort Wayne Female College, founded in 1846, became Fort Wayne Episcopal College in 1852, and Taylor University in 1890. It moved to Upland in 1893 under the aegis of the National Association of Local Preachers of the Methodist Episcopal Church. Moores Hill College, founded in 1854 as a Methodist institution, moved to Evansville to become Evansville College in 1919.

As the twentieth century wore on, the differences between the older and the newer colleges diminished. The original impulse of the founders waned, the religious orientation became less strong, but the academic quality of instructors improved.

The need for teachers led to the establishment of a State Normal School in Terre Haute in 1870. The school offered courses but did not offer a

"The Point" House, Hanover College, 1897.

Wabash College cadets drilling in front of South and Center Halls, about 1857.

Actors in a play at Notre Dame, 1876.

Laboratory class, University of Notre Dame, 1880.

St. Joseph's College, Rensselaer.

The first YMCA on a college campus, Hanover College, 1883.

college-level class until 1907 and did not grant a bachelor's degree until the following year. A branch of the State Normal School was soon located in Muncie. Its history is instructive. Begun as the Normal and Classical Institute in 1891, the Eastern Division of Indiana State Normal School came to life in 1918 after the Ball Brothers had bought the defunct Muncie National Institute, one of the successors of the original school, and donated the land to the state.

In 1929 the two schools divided, becoming Indiana State Teachers College at Terre Haute and Ball State Teachers College at Muncie. The Depression hurt enrollments, but the postwar baby boom meant demand for elementary teachers skyrocketed. Both institutions grew enormously and so did their aspirations. They became, in the parlance of the day, emerging universities in 1965 by legislative enactment. By this time the state of Indiana had four state-supported universities.

The original one, Indiana University, had changed a great deal as well. At the beginning of the era, the university had two buildings and ten professors. It had admitted its first woman student (1867) and had just closed its preparatory department—high school (1871). It had a one-room library and a part-time librarian. Despite these weaknesses, it offered postgraduate work in English, philology, public speaking, history, languages, and the physical sciences in 1874.

Indiana University took a great step forward in 1885 when it moved to a new site in Bloomington and chose a new president, David Starr Jordan. The university began to expand, creating a Law School in 1889 (the original had been discontinued in 1877), a School of Medicine in 1903 (with clinical facilities in Indianapolis after 1908 and a teaching hospital there in 1914), a School of Commerce in 1919, a School of Music in 1921, and a School of Dentistry in 1925. By this time Indiana University was a university in fact as well as in name. When Herman B

John Herron Art School, Indianapolis.

Mr. and Mrs. John Herron, about 1890. In 1895 Herron left $200,000 to the Indianapolis Art Institute.

Wells became president in 1937, the base was laid for him to lead the school to higher levels of excellence.

The university at Bloomington had acquired a rival in this era in the northern part of the state. That rival was, of course, Purdue University, which came into being as a result of the Morrill Act of 1862 establishing land-grant colleges to teach agriculture and the mechanical arts. Putting the endowment funds from the federal land-grant sale (over $200,000) together with $100,000 given by John Purdue and another $100,000 pledged by a group of citizens and 100 acres of land at Lafayette, the General Assembly created Purdue in 1869.

Opened in 1874, the school grew slowly. Five years after opening, two separate schools, agriculture and engineering, were organized. In the 1880s, the single school of engineering split into three: mechanical engineering (1882), civil engineering (1882), and electrical engineering (1888). The School of Agriculture expanded its domain by moving into adult education in the same period, largely through the use of experimental farms and agricultural bulletins. An agricultural experiment station came later, in 1905, and this promoted the effort.

When Winthrop Stone of the chemistry department became president in 1900, he expanded the scope of the university by successfully encouraging the creation of a department of home economics and a department of education. Purdue even tried for a medical school in 1905, with an attempted merger of the Indiana College of Medicine and the Fort Wayne Medical School. Though unsuccessful, the attempt revealed the extent of the ambition.

The twentieth century, however, did see tremendous growth for Purdue. The requirement for military training meant Purdue had an important role to play in two world wars. The technological demands of the automotive, construction, computer, and aerospace industries caused engineers to be eagerly sought. In addition Purdue had expanded

St. Meinrad Archabbey, 1874.

Henry Harrison Culver, a St. Louis stove manufacturer, founded Culver Military Academy on the shores of Lake Maxinkuckee in Marshall County in 1894.

Vincennes University, about 1895.

North Western Christian University changed its name to Butler College in 1877.

into graduate education in such traditional fields as sociology and English, making it a multipurpose university.

The growth of formal educational institutions helped raise the literacy of Hoosiers. The rise in literacy, in turn, helped make Indianapolis a center of culture, particularly in the world of publishing. One of the most famous publishing houses of that era, Bobbs-Merrill, still exists. Begun in the 1850s by a stationery store owner named Merrill, the company through expansion and merger took its present name in 1903. Originally specializing in legal publishing, the company ventured successfully into other areas, beginning with the poetry of James Whitcomb Riley in the 1880s. Encouraged by sales, the company entered the field of fiction. This provided a ready outlet for local writers who now seemed to sprout from every field.

The writers celebrated the joys of nature, the pleasures of rural life, and the virtues of pioneer settlers. The literature recalled a way of life which either had never existed or was about to vanish. Romance was its mood.

How else can you explain the career of James Whitcomb Riley (1849–1916), who began his working life as a sign painter and then wrote poetry for the Indianapolis *Journal* as "Benj. F. Johnson of Boone"? When his poems were collected and printed under the titles of *The Old Swimmin'-Hole* and *'Leven More Poems* (1883), Riley became the Hoosier poet. His poetry evoked images of the hired man, of harvest festivals, and of simple pleasures. This is evident in the titles of books such as *Green Fields and Running Brooks* (1892), *Farm-Rhymes* (1901), *Out to Old Aunt Mary's* (1904), *While the Heart Beats Young* (1906), *The Raggedy Man* (1907), and *Orphant Annie Book* (1908).

Another celebrant of unabashed sentimentality who also attained both regional and national attention was Gene Stratton Porter (1863–1924). Born in Wabash County, Porter moved to Geneva in

Earlham College, Richmond, 1855.

179

Jake Gimbel, Vincennes businessman and philanthropist, with Oscar Beesley, one of the students he sponsored at Vincennes University, 1911.

Evansville College: Moores Hill College founded in 1854–56 moved to Evansville and adopted a new name in 1919.

Adams County, where, with her husband and child, she explored the yet undrained Limberlost Swamp. Out of this experience came books of nature and romance such as *The Song of the Cardinal* (1902), *Freckles* (1904), and *A Girl of the Limberlost* (1909). When the Limberlost was drained in 1913, Porter moved to Sylvan Lake and continued to write, still in a romantic vein but now using both local and foreign settings, such books as *Michael O'Halloran* (1915), *Friends in Feathers* (1917), *The White Flag* (1923), *Jesus of the Emerald* (1923), and *The Keeper of the Bees* (1925). The last book was published posthumously for Porter, who moved to California in 1923, was killed by a streetcar the following year.

The most famous Hoosier novelist of the era had preceded Porter. He was Lew Wallace (1827–1905), who had been a lawyer, soldier, and diplomat. Born in Brookville, Wallace fought in the Civil War and, as a good Republican, was appointed the governor of New Mexico Territory in 1878 and served until 1881; he then became U.S. minister to Turkey from 1881 to 1885.

Wallace's first book, *The Fair God* (1873), reflected his interest in Mexico and was a story of the Spanish conquest of Mexico. It was not a success. His next novel was. It was *Ben-Hur: A Tale of the Christ* (1880). Not noticeably religious and never a communicant in any church, Wallace wrote the story to refute the atheistic ideas of Robert G. Ingersoll, whom he had met on a train. Filled with action and drama, the book became a best seller and movies based on it are made anew each generation. Wallace's next novel, *The Prince of India: or, Why Constantinople Fell* (1893), did not match the success of *Ben-Hur*. Wallace died at Crawfordsville before he completed his autobiography.

Wallace never wrote about Indiana life, but another, almost equally successful, lawyer turned novelist did. This was Charles Major (1856–1913), who was born in Indianapolis; his family soon

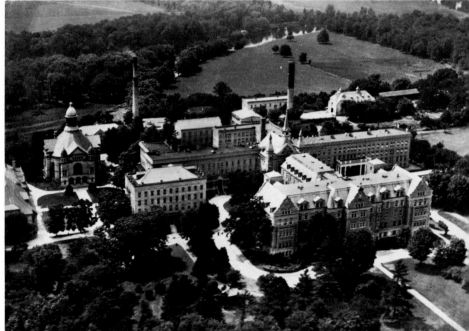

St. Mary's College, South Bend.

University of Notre Dame campus, South Bend, 1900.

180

The first building of the Eastern Division of the Indiana State Normal School, Muncie, 1918. The name was changed to Ball State Teachers College in 1929.

John Purdue, Lafayette and New York City merchant, gave $100,000 so that the federal land-grant college might be located in Tippecanoe County.

Purdue University, about 1880.

The first building of Indiana State Normal School, Terre Haute, 1870.

moved to Shelbyville, where Major spent the rest of his life. He began his literary career with *When Knighthood Was in Flower* (1898), a historical romance about the young sister of Henry VIII of England, and it was an immediate success. He wrote three others in this genre—*Dorothy Vernon of Haddon Hall* (1902), *Yolanda, Maid of Burgundy* (1905), and *A Gentle Knight of Old Brandenburg* (1909). These books have been forgotten but his novels with an Indiana setting—*The Bears of Blue River* (1901), *A Forest Hearth: A Romance of Indiana in the Thirties* (1903), and *Uncle Tom Andy Bill* (1908)—are still read, for they tell of Indiana in the early days of settlement, portraying pioneer life as difficult but exciting.

Another novel with an Indiana setting was written by Maurice Thompson (1844–1901). He was born in Fairfield, Indiana, but his family moved to northern Georgia in the early 1850s. After serving in the Confederate army during the Civil War, he and his younger brother, Will, both of them civil engineers, decided to go north to Crawfordsville, where they eventually became lawyers. Maurice Thompson's first writings were essays on nature study and the outdoor life. In 1900 he achieved his ambition to write a successful novel, *Alice of Old Vincennes*, a story of George Rogers Clark and the conquest of the Old Northwest.

Another famous novelist of the period, who also used the Hoosier past in his work, was Meredith Nicholson, who was born in Crawfordsville in 1866 and died in Indianapolis in 1947. Like Lew Wallace, he had a diplomatic career, in the Democratic party, however, as U.S. minister to Paraguay (1933–34), Venezuela (1935–38), and Nicaragua (1938–41). Two of his novels have Hoosier themes—*The House of a Thousand Candles* (1905) and *A Hoosier Chronicle* (1912), which treated contemporary politics. Nicholson also wrote essays which were collected in *The Hoosiers* (1900), *The Provincial American* (1912), *The Valley of Democracy*

ROTC class at Purdue University, about 1880.

(1918), and *The Man in the Street* (1921). These celebrated life in the Midwest and expressed faith in the strength of American institutions.

Not all Hoosier writers remained in Indiana. Among the transplanted ones were two brothers, Edward and George Cary Eggleston. Born in Vevay, they went separate ways as teenagers, but by coincidence both lived for a time in New York City. George (1839–1911) chose to write about the South, where he had lived and fought as a Confederate soldier, in *A Rebel's Recollections* (1874) and in novels such as *A Carolina Cavalier* (1901) and *A Daughter of the South* (1905). Edward (1837–1902), who lived for thirteen months in Virginia in 1854 and thereafter supported the antislavery cause, drew on his Indiana boyhood to produce his first and most famous book, *The Hoosier School-Master* (1871). He wrote other novels about Indiana frontier life, such as *The Circuit Rider* (1874) and *The Hoosier School-Boy* (1883), but none of them achieved the success that his first book did.

Another writer who did not remain in Indiana was George Barr McCutcheon. He was born on a farm in Tippecanoe County in 1866 and died in New York City in 1928. In 1882 George entered Purdue University, which during that period was to have as students the McCutcheon brothers, Bruce Rogers, George Ade, and Booth Tarkington. McCutcheon left Purdue after one year to become a reporter for the Lafayette *Journal*. His first successful novel was in the realm of romance, *Graustark* (1901), which was followed a year later by *Brewster's Millions,* another best seller. The success of *Graustark* led him to write a popular series about that mythical kingdom.

His brother, John T. McCutcheon (1870–1949), achieved fame in a different form of creativity. After graduating from Purdue in 1889, he worked for several newspapers in Chicago and after 1903 for the *Chicago Tribune*. He is still remembered for his political cartoons, for which he won the Pulitzer prize.

Women students potting houseplants in the Purdue greenhouse, 1890s.

Women students in domestic science class, Purdue University, 1890s.

Professor John J. Flather and his Purdue engineering class.

Indiana University campus, Dunn's Woods, 1898.

First women students at Indiana University, 1868. Sarah Parke Morrison, from Washington County (front row, fourth from left), enrolled in 1867.

A fellow student of John T. McCutcheon at Purdue University was Bruce Rogers (1870–1957), who was born in Lafayette and walked the three miles from his home to his college classes. He and McCutcheon were the only boys in the Art School at that time. His first job was as a newspaper illustrator for the Indianapolis *News* in 1890. He was the book designer for the Riverside Press at Cambridge, Massachusetts, and later for the printer William Edwin Rudge at Mt. Vernon, New York; he was also printing adviser to the Cambridge University Press and to Harvard University Press. Bruce Rogers is the finest book designer that America has produced, and he is famous for his Centaur type design and the two-volume folio Oxford Lectern Bible (1935).

George Ade (1866–1944), who was born at Kentland and died at Brook, both in Newton County, Indiana, was also a student at Purdue University at the same time as Rogers and John McCutcheon. In 1890 Ade began writing a daily column for the *Chicago Record* entitled "Stories of the Streets and of the Town." Stories from the column began to be collected and published as books after 1894. His first book of fables from the column—*Fables in Slang*—was a best seller as soon as it was published in 1900. Ade became a successful playwright; some of his better-known plays were *The Sultan of Sulu* (1902), *The County Chairman* (1903) about a politician in a small Indiana town, and *The College Widow* (1904).

The most famous of the Hoosier authors in the early twentieth century are Booth Tarkington and Theodore Dreiser. Both tried to picture American life as they saw it, Tarkington using a middle-class Indiana setting and Dreiser a more national and urban one.

Newton Booth Tarkington, who was born in Indianapolis in 1869, and attended Purdue for one year and Princeton for two years, began his literary career with the publication of *The Gentleman from Indiana* (1899), a tale of happenings in a small In-

David Starr Jordan, professor of Anatomy, Botany, and Zoology, 1875–79; president of Indiana University, 1885–91.

Mitchell Hall was the center of cultural arts at Indiana University for many years.

diana town. It was followed by *Monsieur Beaucaire* (1900), a historical romance set in eighteenth-century England. His next book, *The Two Vanrevels* (1902), was a story of Indiana in the Mexican War. In 1903 he served as a Republican member of the Indiana House of Representatives, an experience which gave him ideas for his books.

After a personal crisis, Tarkington embarked on two projects which marked his maturity as a writer. The first was *Penrod* (1914), the story of a boy growing up. He wrote other books in this genre, including *Penrod and Sam* (1916), *Seventeen* (1916), and *Little Orvie* (1934). His more serious project was a trilogy about the effects of industrialism on Indianapolis families. The books were *The Turmoil* (1915), *The Magnificent Ambersons* (1918), and *The Midlander* (1924). The three novels make up the contents of *Growth* (1927), although the title of *The Midlander* was changed to *National Avenue*. Two of his books—*The Magnificent Ambersons* and *Alice Adams* (1921)—won Pulitzer prizes. Tarkington continued to write until his death in Indianapolis in 1946, but these writings never attained the critical acclaim that his earlier books had received.

A contemporary of Tarkington was Theodore Dreiser, who was born in Terre Haute in 1871 and died in Hollywood, California, in 1945. Dreiser, a child of a poor family, grew up in Terre Haute, Vincennes, Sullivan, Evansville, and Warsaw. He managed to attend Indiana University for one year (1889–90) before going to Chicago, where he worked at various jobs before becoming a reporter there and in St. Louis, Toledo, and Pittsburgh. Dreiser eventually landed in New York City at the urging of his brother, Paul Dresser, who was a popular songwriter of the day. (Paul Dresser was to gain lasting fame, at least in Indiana, as the composer of the state song, "On the Banks of the Wabash, Far Away.")

In New York Dreiser wrote his first novel, *Sis-*

Indiana University School of Medicine, Indianapolis, 1910.

A law class in the old Science Building, Indiana University, 1876.

A country church.

Old Cathedral, Vincennes.

Market Street Temple, Indianapolis.
Sketch by Leslie E. Ayres.

Fort Wayne Temple.

ter Carrie (1900). The book was not a success because of the frankness of its story; the publisher refused to promote it and finally even removed it from sale. The naturalism that permeated his first novel continued in his second, *Jennie Gerhardt* (1911), which had descriptions of poverty gleaned from his Indiana boyhood. Dreiser next wrote a trilogy based on the life of Charles T. Yerkes, the traction magnate. The three novels were *The Financier* (1912), *The Titan* (1914), and *The Genius* (1915). He explored his Hoosier past in three books: *A Traveler at Forty* (1913), *A Hoosier Holiday* (1916), and *Twelve Men* (1919). He returned to fiction to write *An American Tragedy* (1925), his greatest success and his most famous book. During the Depression, he published several nonfiction books advocating isolation and greater social justice. Two novels of a projected trilogy about a Quaker businessman—*The Bulwark* (1946) and *The Stoic* (1947)—were published posthumously.

No account of Indiana-born intellectuals is complete without the name of Charles A. Beard, a writer who was perhaps the most influential American historian of the twentieth century. He was born near Knightstown in 1874 and graduated from DePauw University in 1898 before taking his Ph.D. at Columbia in 1904, where he was to teach until World War I. In his books—*An Economic Interpretation of the Constitution of the United States* (1913), *The Economic Origins of Jeffersonian Democracy* (1915), and *The Economic Basis of Politics* (1922)—Beard argued that commercial interests had subverted agrarian ones and that the revitalization of American civil government could be accomplished by controlling big business. Beard became skeptical of the foreign policy of Franklin D. Roosevelt during the 1930s and urged promotion of the American national interest. After the Second World War Beard attacked Roosevelt in *American Foreign Policy in the Making, 1932–1940* (1946) and *President Roosevelt and the Coming of the War, 1941* (1947). His influence waned

185

Birthplace of Edward Eggleston, Vevay.

Edward Eggleston.

after his death in 1948, but he was a giant in his time.

The distance from a backward frontier state to a center of culture in the United States was short for the Hoosier state. Hardly had the state developed a full set of educational institutions before it was able to boast of the nation's leading writers. The crop needed only watering before springing up and early coming to flower.

George Ade.

Gene Stratton Porter.

Lew Wallace statue and study, Crawfordsville.

Hoosiers earned a reputation for writing books: John T. McCutcheon cartoon.

Frank McKinney (Kin) Hubbard.

Lew Wallace.

Booth Tarkington.

Caricature of Charles Major.

Caricature of Meredith Nicholson.

James Whitcomb Riley.

"Abe Martin," cartoon creation of Kin Hubbard.

Bruce Rogers, the world-famous designer of books, was born at Linnwood, now a part of Lafayette. He signed his works "Bruce Rogers of Indiana."

Indiana Day at the St. Louis World's Fair: John T. McCutcheon cartoon.

Birthplace of Paul Dresser and his brother Theodore Dreiser, Terre Haute.

Theodore Dreiser.

Charles A. Beard, 1910.

Recreation and Leisure

Summertime, 1898, near Madison.

Tⁿ HE LAST YEARS OF THE NINETEENTH CEN-
TURY AND THE FIRST YEARS OF THE TWEN-
TIETH WITNESSED A PROFOUND CHANGE IN
the patterns of Hoosier behavior. Instead of a life
centered entirely upon work, there was interest in
finding and using leisure time. There were an
awakening of enthusiasm for amateur sports and
the beginning of professional sports; there was an
appreciation of nature as something to be enjoyed
rather than exploited. These new interests covered a
broad spectrum of the population—young and old,
male and female.

Frontier society had had its rough games, but
life was perilous enough so that little energy remained for recreation. Further, those pursuits now
regarded as private sports—hunting and fishing
—were means of sustenance and taken very seriously indeed. There were some public amusements.
Horse racing was one, although its connection with
gambling aroused the apprehensions of religious
groups. Still, the temptation of racing your
neighbor in a light buggy while on your way to
church or meeting often proved too strong to resist.
Jessamyn West's description of just such a race run
by the Quaker father in *Friendly Persuasion* rings
true and must have occurred among Baptists and
Methodists as well.

Other rough sports such as cock- or dogfights
were common on the frontier, although these
earned the censure of most of the respectable citizens. Reputable public sports came later. Among
the groups which contributed to the respectability
of sports were the Germans who brought the gymnasium to America. The gymnasium was the mark
of the Turnverein, an association dedicated to political discussion and physical exercise.

The unsuccessful revolutions of 1848–49
brought Germans into such Hoosier towns as
Evansville, Fort Wayne, and Indianapolis, where
their enthusiasm for sports could find free rein. The
Indianapolis Turngemeinde began in 1851; it later

189

Dan Patch from Pike County, a famous standard-bred harness racer.

became the Social Turnverein of Indianapolis. Among its founders were August Hoffmeister, Jacob and Alex Metzger, Clement Vonnegut, Karl Hill, and John Ott. Lacking facilities, the group placed a horizontal bar in the front yard of a furniture store owned by Ott which was located across the street from the statehouse. A rival club also emerged; this was the Socialistic Turnverein, which had older and more settled members. Both clubs became centers of culture as well as centers for political discussion and physical training. By 1872, however, the two merged into the Indianapolis Socialer Turnverein.

The Turnverein did permit physical education for those enrolled in the nearby schools, but organized sports were almost totally nonexistent. Indiana colleges and universities lacked both the facilities and the inclination. Nor were the public schools much better. About the only sport played at recess or after school was shinny, a variation of lacrosse or field hockey. It was played by pickup teams who used wooden clubs to hit a small, hard ball made of wood or rubber across an opponent's line or into his goal. The game resulted in a mass melee where players hit each other almost as often as they hit the ball and where broken bones, missing teeth, and scattered bruises were common.

The public sport that first engaged Hoosier attention was baseball. Originally known as rounders, baseball became particularly popular after the Civil War. In 1867, for example, an Indianapolis team played the touring Washington Nationals. By the 1870s, baseball clubs representing either the community or a local business had been formed in many Hoosier towns. Practicing or playing on Saturday afternoon, these clubs gave participants their first taste of organized sports.

The sport spread to colleges as well. M.A. McDonald, the first baseball coach and the father of that sport at Indiana University, recorded that on his arrival in 1866, "Home base was a piece of flat

Harness racing in the early 1900s at Beech Grove.

A game of billiards, Traveler's Protective Association, Terre Haute, 1895.

190

Baseball team on the field, Fort Wayne.

Turnverein Turnfest, Indianapolis, 1905.

Baseball team, Indiana University, 1894.

Mordecai (Three Finger) Brown, Chicago Cubs pitcher, 1903–16.

Oakland City Walk-Overs, 1911.

Football team, Indiana
University, 1893, was the first
to have a black
player—halfback Preston
Eagleson (third row, fifth
from left).

Football team, Bloomingdale Friends Academy, Parke County.

Hanover College athletes.

Waiting for the results of the Notre Dame-Army football game before
the days of radio, South Bend.

The Purdue train wreck at 18th Street, Indianapolis, October 31, 1903. Purdue and Indiana were to play for the state football championship and four special trains were to haul about 1,000 students from each university to Indianapolis for the game. Fourteen players, their trainer, and one fan were killed, and 41 others were injured.

Football game at Purdue University, Stuart Field, 1918.

iron thrown on the ground, and the bases were bags stuffed with straw." The players had to furnish their own bats and gloves. Formally organized in 1867, the university club first played other teams in the school. The first extramural game seems to have been played with a team representing the town of Spencer in 1873. Indiana University played its first intercollegiate game ten years later. In that encounter, Indiana Asbury University (now De-Pauw) beat Indiana by a score of 23–6. Not only was this the first intercollegiate baseball game for Indiana; it was one of the first intercollegiate athletic contests of any kind.

Sports grew slowly in Hoosier colleges. Indiana, for example, permitted its baseball team to play only home games until the 1880s. The university had no gymnasium until 1892, when one was erected for men. Women had to content themselves with an exercise room in Wylie Hall.

Although baseball was the first organized sport, it was soon surpassed by football, which came to typify both college and the strenuous life. By the 1880s, Indiana colleges were fielding teams. Indiana University, for example, had its first football team in 1886. The team, curiously enough, was an amalgam of athletes as it played both baseball and football games on road trips. Limited to playing other institutions in the state, Indiana faced Wabash (which beat Indiana 40–2 in 1889), Franklin, DePauw, Rose Polytechnic, and Earlham, in addition to the now traditional rival Purdue. Despite charges, some of them true, that schools had hired players, the colleges and universities were more evenly matched then than at any time since. Because of the charges, the Indiana Intercollegiate Association and the Indiana High School Athletic Association were created in the 1890s to make and enforce rules governing sports contests.

Not until 1895 did interstate football competition become authorized for Purdue when six institutions—Wisconsin, Chicago, Minnesota, Northwestern, Michigan, and Purdue—founded the Western Conference; it was soon to be known as the Big Ten. Indiana joined in 1899; Notre Dame was also a member for a time.

Football had its critics; fights were common and, because of the primitive equipment, fatalities were not unknown. Even getting to the games could prove hazardous. In 1903 on their way to play a football game with Indiana 14 members of the Purdue team and the trainer were killed in a train wreck on 18th Street in Indianapolis. The tragedy had a profound effect upon both schools, Purdue because of the loss of so many players, Indiana because it had counted on the gate receipts to pay off the debts of the Indiana University Athletic Association, which managed sports at Indiana University.

Despite these and related problems, collegiate football survived in the era before World War I and, with a brief disruption caused by the war itself, became a fixed part of the sports scene. By this time, income from student fees, stricter rules governing play, and improved equipment—leather helmets and pads—had made the sport more stable and safe.

A younger rival was soon to surpass football even as it had surpassed baseball in Indiana. This was basketball. Invented by Dr. James Naismith of Springfield College and the Y.M.C.A. in 1892, basketball was intended to attract participation in indoor sports in the winter months. Growth of the sport was slow at the start, but gradually more and more persons became interested. Unlike football, which began in colleges and trickled down to high schools, basketball began in high schools and moved up to colleges. By the early 1890s the game was being played in Y.M.C.A.s and high schools, but Indiana University did not even have intramural games until 1899. The first games often had high school teams playing against college players; Indiana University, for example, began its 1903 season by

The first gymnasium, Indiana University.

Basketball team, Indiana University, 1910.

Men bicyclists at Madison.

Bicyclists pause to eat apples, sitting beside their penny farthings or boneshakers.

Women bicyclists at Crawfordsville.

The Crawfordsville Athenians became the first Indiana state high school basketball champions at Indiana University, March 11, 1911. Dave Glascock was the coach.

Hiking Club, Indiana University, 1890.
Theodore Dreiser is seated on the right in the
second row.

Chautauqua visitors relaxing in front of a tent, Jefferson County.

Women and children wading, while on a
nature hike.

Columbia Park, Lafayette, about 1915.

Learning basketweaving.

Women display their catch, about 1905.

playing Salem High School. Gradually, however, the sport became more popular in high schools and colleges, although it was a distant third to football and baseball until after World War I.

Although team sports such as baseball, football, and basketball occupied the attention of many participants at the turn of the century, the most popular participant sport was bicycling. The older boneshaker bicycle with a high front wheel and small back wheel had been supplanted by the safety bicycle which had two wheels of equal size. Bicycling became a social pastime with people riding for recreation rather than to work. The bicycle was one of the first recreational vehicles which women could use, and one noted historian has suggested that the bicycle helped transform the Victorian Woman into the New Woman, an energetic, athletic individual who played hard and began to think in terms of greater equality. The explosion of bicycles was impressive. In 1890 less than one million were on the road, but by 1900 over ten million were being used.

Cyclists formed wheel clubs which met regularly to discuss the merits of new models, to display their wheels, and to plan for group trips. Clubs sprang up in such towns as Indianapolis, Fort Wayne, and South Bend. Local factories also began to supply the seemingly insatiable demand for the two-wheelers. One, the Indiana Bicycle Company of Indianapolis, became a model factory with a plant reputed to be the most perfect in the world (the bicycle it produced was the Waverly; later the company was to develop and sell an electric car with the same name).

The cycling mania died almost as rapidly as it had grown. Rich people bought cars, the electric trolley competed with the bicycle for weekend excursions, and, increasingly, the bicycle assumed the role of a children's toy. The cycle clubs closed their doors and only the memory remained.

The bicycle helped people to get back to na-

Bobsledders, near Madison.

Small boy pulling small girl in a toy sleigh, about 1912.

ture. A new interest in hiking, camping, hunting, and fishing evolved. Combined with a flood of books on nature study and the preservation of the American wilderness, this interest inspired Hoosiers to develop areas in the state which would be unspoiled and would help urban residents to discover the beauties of nature and to heal the wounds of city life.

In 1915 Governor Samuel M. Ralston created a State Park Memorial Committee, Richard Lieber became chairman in 1916, and within two years the state acquired its first two parks, McCormick's Creek and Turkey Run. Both were made possible by private effort. The idea of making a state park at Turkey Run in Parke County occurred to Richard Lieber, Juliet Strauss, Dr. Frank B. Wynn, Sol S. Kiser, and Leo Rappaport when a large estate in the area became available for sale in the spring of 1916. They then hoped to raise enough money to buy the estate from a lumber company which had outbid them at the auction. Fortunately, Carl Fisher and Arthur Newby, two of the founders of the Indianapolis Motor Speedway, came to the rescue, first with funds and then with a promise of a percentage of the receipts from the 1917 500-mile race. This money, along with that already subscribed and a state appropriation, enabled the park committee to buy 288 acres and donate it to the state.

The opportunity to buy a similar area on McCormick's Creek came while the negotiations for the Turkey Run tract were still under way. Residents of Owen County, in conjunction with the state, bought the estate of Dr. Frederick Denkewalter in May 1916 and gave it to the state. McCormick's Creek thus became the first Indiana state park.

The father of the Indiana state park system was Richard Lieber, who became the first director of the Indiana Department of Conservation in 1919. He pressed for the acquisition of other areas to be designated as state parks, and the 1920s witnessed the

Ice skaters, near Brookville.

Richard Lieber,
conservationist, the father of
the Indiana state parks system,
at Turkey Run State Park.

Beechwood Shelter House at McCormick's Creek State Park, the first
Indiana state park, 1916.

Visitors to a waterfall at the Shades,
Montgomery County, about 1900.

A high dive, near Brookville.

The Richey family playing croquet, Muncie, about 1900.

199

Backyard in Indianapolis, about 1900.

Taffy pulling, a favorite pastime in the early 1900s.

Visitors to the Constitution Elm, Corydon.

Women with horses.

A class picnic, Hanover College, 1903.

Friends Sunday School picnic, Marshall, August 21, 1913.

Boarding cruise boats at a northern Indiana lake, 1909.

Wonderland Park, Indianapolis, early 1900s.

Children playing at Island Park, Elkhart.

great growth of the system. The parks established were Clifty Falls (1920), Muscatatuck (1921), Indiana Dunes (1925), Pokagon (1925), Spring Mill (1927), Shakamak (1929), Brown County (1929), and Mounds (1929). In 1916 an effort to create a national park in the Indiana Dunes area failed when Congress did not act; Richard Lieber was more successful in raising funds to create a state park in the area. The Mounds had been developed privately by an interurban company which donated it to the state when business slacked off. These facilities became the backbone of Indiana's recreational and tourist system and remain so to this day.

For the ordinary Hoosier, leisure offered other possibilities not connected with the rise of team sports, the bicycle, or the state parks. Much of the leisure time was spent in family activities, a picnic in the backyard or at the city park or fairgrounds, a game of croquet at home, or just relaxing and talking. Parties with friends might be spent in parlor games, pulling taffy, or amateur dramatics. Clubs which reflected common interests proliferated. Some of these organizations were devoted to improvement; others were frankly for fun. Most combined the two.

Recognizing the market for recreational activities, promoters began to develop facilities for just that purpose. Almost every town of any size had an opera house where touring companies put on plays and entertainments. In the summer, traveling shows put up tents for their circus and carnival acts. Starved for the strange and exotic, Hoosier audiences flocked to these attractions and insured their survival.

Other amusements were less transient. Typical were the amusement parks of the period, either built by or connected to the streetcar companies, which became popular. Much like the ones of today, these parks had rides, thrills, and sideshows. Indeed, almost all of the standard items of today's theme parks existed in the older ones.

Indian performers, Al G.
Barnes Circus, New Castle.

Life became healthier and richer, at least in experience, for Hoosiers as the hard work of farm and factory was relieved by occasional holidays. Play was no longer entirely the monopoly of the children; adults now felt less guilty about having fun and sought more recreational activities to enjoy.

Getting ready to raise the big tent, New Castle.

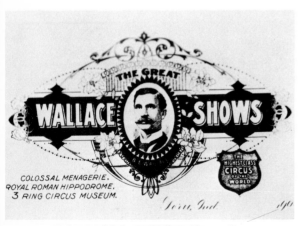

Ticket to the Great Wallace Shows, Peru.

Horses in Hagenbeck-Wallace circus parade, Peru.

Elephants in the circus parade, Peru.

The tent is up, New Castle.

The Payne family at the circus, New Castle.

Theater audience, Hartford City.

Winter headquarters of the circus, Peru.

Lake James Hotel, Angola, about 1915.

West Side Hotel, Rochester, about 1910.

English Hotel and Opera House on the Circle, Indianapolis, about 1915.

West Baden Springs Hotel lobby, in the early 1900s.

New Albany Opera House, 1893.

Surreys in front of hotel.

Over There and Back Home

Exhorting the men to enlist. Patriotic parades were a part of the recruiting efforts of the First World War.

O F ALL THE AMERICAN WARS, WITH THE POSSIBLE EXCEPTION OF THE CIVIL WAR, THE FIRST WORLD WAR HAD THE PROfoundest effect on Hoosier lives, dividing the populace, raising old ethnic antagonisms, and creating political problems for both parties. The war changed attitudes, turning the gaze of Hoosiers toward the overseas world.

The attitude of most Hoosiers in 1914 was best summed up by Wilson's idea of neutrality. The Germans and Irish who settled in Indiana in the nineteenth century had a tradition of Anglophobia or support for countries opposed to Great Britain. In addition, a prevailing strain of pacifism from the early Quaker settlement also damped enthusiasm for a European involvement. Despite their neutral position, however, according to Cedric C. Cummins's *Indiana Public Opinion and the World War,* somewhere between two-thirds and three-fourths of the Hoosiers favored the Allied side.

Neither political party had a clear position on the war. The Democrats had won Indiana in 1914; two days prior to the election, William Jennings Bryan had stumped the state with a speech declaring the Democratic party to be the party of peace. The Republican party had taken no stand, primarily because of the problem the war posed to the reconciliation of the Progressive element, which was returning to the party. One segment of the Progressives, which included individuals such as Lucius B. Swift and William Dudley Foulke, was anti-German and pro-intervention. Another segment composed of Albert J. Beveridge and others was as adamantly opposed to any involvement.

Nor were other leaders in the Hoosier state of one mind. By 1915 Indiana had become a battleground of differing opinions on the war. Two against the war were former Indiana University president David Starr Jordan, now at Stanford University, and May Wright Sewall, a leader in the women's suffrage movement, who took time off to

38th Infantry band, First World War.

oppose the war and even sailed on Henry Ford's ill-fated peace ship in 1915. On the other side were even more well-known Hoosiers, including Booth Tarkington and Meredith Nicholson, who contrasted English parliamentarianism with German totalitarianism.

Despite the rhetoric, Indiana moved closer to the threshold of involvement as America became the supplier for the Allies. Demand for foodstuffs and for industrial products—steel, cars, and trucks—increased Hoosiers' prosperity. Along with the increased prosperity came great pressure to prepare for war. One of the means of preparation was conscription, which was being vigorously promoted. Despite the promotion of military training, an attempt to recruit five hundred Hoosiers for officer training at Fort Sheridan, Illinois, in the summer of 1915 barely succeeded. Nor did an attempt by some faculty members at Indiana University to establish a company of the Indiana National Guard on campus—an attempt motivated in part by a desire to obtain an armory which might also serve as a gymnasium—meet with an enthusiastic reception. Military training at the university did not commence until March 1917, when a Reserve Officer Training Corps was created at Bloomington.

The presidential campaign of 1916 offered no clear-cut choice. Neither party argued for intervention, though the Republicans did sound more hawkish on occasion to attract the anti-German vote. Wilson did not stump the state, but Hoosier-born Thomas Marshall, the vice-presidential candidate, did, pointing to the record and repeating the campaign slogan promoting Wilson, "He kept us out of the war." The Republicans won the state but not the nation.

Shortly after the election, war came to the United States. When the declaration of war came before the House and to the Senate, no Hoosier representative voted against it. Public opinion then was rallied so as to create the illusion that the decision

Cavalry unit, Fort Benjamin Harrison, Indianapolis.

Staff of the American Red Cross Teaching Center, Indianapolis.

Battery F, organized at Indiana University in April 1917, went to France in 1918.

Cash register for the 1918 War Savings drive, Meridian and Washington streets, Indianapolis.

was unanimous. The German-American community in Indiana took pains to assure other citizens that it loyally supported the war effort. The leading spokesman for this position was Richard Lieber, who became military secretary for Governor Goodrich and who traveled over the state reassuring those who lumped all Germans with Germany.

The drive for conformity in World War I exceeded that of later wars, where more protest was allowed. Debs was imprisoned, as we have seen, for his antiwar views. Two college professors—one at Indiana University and the other at the Indiana State Normal School—were fired for their statements questioning the propaganda of the period. Much social pressure was exerted to insure support of the war. This support could be proved in two ways, by contributing money to bond drives or by enlisting in the service.

Indiana had four Liberty Loan campaigns and one Victory Loan Campaign. Prominent figures, either from the state or nation, vied with each other to promote the sale of bonds, usually by emotionally charged speeches in major urban centers. Displays of the money collected spurred other contributors to participate, even those who had been reluctant to become involved.

Indiana gave much more than money to the war effort. Ninety thousand Hoosiers were drafted, and forty thousand volunteered. The Indiana National Guard was mobilized. The guard went to Mississippi for a year's training before being sent overseas as the 38th Division in September 1918. The First Regiment, Indiana Field Artillery, had preceded the 38th Division; it became the 150th Field Artillery, an integral part of the Rainbow Division, commanded by Douglas MacArthur, and it was one of the first elements to go into combat in February 1918.

For most Hoosier servicemen, the war was a short one. Unlike the Civil War, the period when most saw action was less than a year. Like the Civil

War, the majority of casualties resulted from disease rather than wounds.

Hoosiers at home shared the sacrifice of relatives in the service. The influenza epidemic of 1918–19 killed many with a virulent strain. Women entered the labor force in great numbers to replace the men who had gone to war. Many residents, in addition, voluntarily observed "meatless" and "wheatless" days in order that these foodstuffs could be exported overseas.

The war was also brought home to Hoosiers by the presence of a training camp in the state. Fort Benjamin Harrison was one of the important infantry training camps for the United States Army. Here, trainees from all over the country, except for the black soldiers who were sent to Fort Des Moines, learned the rudiments of combat under the tutelage of strong-voiced corporals and sergeants. Fort Benjamin Harrison served as a constant reminder to Hoosiers that a war was being waged; the sight of khaki-clad soldiers on Indianapolis streets did that.

The First World War ended November 11, 1918, for most Americans, but not all the troops returned home that year. Among those units which served as part of the Army of Occupation in Germany was the First Regiment, Indiana Field Artillery, which did not return to Indiana until 1919. Public displays of solidarity and patriotism continued for the next several years as visiting dignitaries —a company of Belgian soldiers and Marshal Ferdinand Foch, the supreme commander of all Allied forces in France—made Indianapolis one of their stops.

The memory of the war lingered on even after the celebrations ended as the ideological divisions created by the push to involvement remained. German-Americans did not forget what they considered to be President Wilson's betrayal of his campaign promise of neutrality in 1916; they returned to the Republican party in large numbers.

Alpha Hall, women's dormitory, Indiana University, was occupied by the military in 1918.

Hoosiers in Indianapolis say hello to doughboys in France. They were filmed marching toward the camera in a parade 14 blocks long.

Women working at Standard Oil Company of Indiana Whiting plant. They were forerunners of the women who worked in factories during the Second World War.

The sixth day of the War Chest drive, Monument Circle, May 25, 1918.

Those persons who had opposed the war as a political mistake remained convinced of the correctness of their position and, in the 1930s, argued for nonintervention again.

The campaign for militancy, on the other hand, was institutionalized in the American Legion, which became as important in Hoosier political life after the First World War as the G.A.R. had been after the Civil War. The Legion emerged as an organization devoted to the welfare of the veterans of the war, one which lobbied for veterans' benefits, for aid to dependents, and for an ideological program of Americanism dedicated to fighting communism and fascism. Critics found the latter a prolongation of the drive for a homogeneous society which had characterized the wartime years.

The Legion flourished in Indiana for a variety of reasons, not the least of which was the successful bid of Hoosiers to obtain the national headquarters in 1919. A special session of the General Assembly met the following year and voted funds to carry out the promise to the Legionnaires for a home built at taxpayers' expense. Aided by county and city appropriations, in addition to state funds, the builders completed War Memorial Plaza in 1929. The plaza contained both a memorial to those who had fallen in war and the national headquarters of the American Legion.

The Legion proved to be a ladder of success for would-be politicians. Unlike the G.A.R., Legion membership cut across party lines, with both Republicans and Democrats striving for posts in the organization. The list of persons who went from State or National Legion Commander to political office is long; it includes two governors—Ralph Gates, a Republican, and Paul V. McNutt, a Democrat—two congressmen—Forest A. Harness and Raymond Springer, both Republicans—and one state political boss, Frank McHale, Democratic National Committeeman and a power in Democratic politics for over twenty years.

Armistice Day parade, Cannelton, November 11, 1918.

Part of the alleged conservatism of Hoosiers may be attributed to the influence of both the First World War and the American Legion. Yet one must still remember that participation in the war was regarded by many as folly before 1917 and even those sympathetic to the Allies hesitated to take the step toward actual hostilities. The war went against the grain of these Hoosiers, against the force of their tradition, against their values. The seeming cohesion that the war's outbreak brought was only a surface phenomenon concealing unresolved tensions underneath.

Vice President Thomas Riley Marshall, a former Indiana governor, speaking at Flag Day services, Washington Monument, June 17, 1919.

Women's Overseas League in parade celebrating the end of the war, Bloomington.

Marshal Ferdinand Foch of France visited Indianapolis and was made a Crow Indian chief, November 4, 1921.

Military band, 150th Field Artillery, at the Victory Arch, Indianapolis, May 7, 1919.

A living red cross formed to honor Marshal Foch, Indianapolis, 1921.

The Twenties

Miss Melville and the Girl Scouts, Decoration Day, New Castle, May 30, 1924.

THE 1920S HAVE BEEN DESCRIBED AS A DEC-
ADE OF RAPID SOCIAL CHANGE, WHERE
FLAMING YOUTH LISTENED TO JAZZ, DRANK
bathtub gin, and petted in the back seats of Model
T's. According to this view, the era was one in
which old values had been completely overthrown
by the new, and "modern" life had replaced traditional life.

The evidence is that there was less change in
values than this view assumes. For the majority of
Hoosiers, life went on pretty much as it had before;
people were born, grew up, got married, went to
work, went to church, lived quietly, and died.
Only the visible minority, promoted by the radio,
the movies, and sensational journalism, displayed
the behavior which was taken to be typical. For
more conventional individuals, this behavior was as
foreign as any seen by the soldiers in the A.E.F. in
Paris or London. Indeed, there was resistance to
change and an attempt to hold on to older values.
These attempts were most noticeable in the political
arena.

Republicans controlled Indiana during the
1920s, gaining back the ground lost by the defection
of the Progressives in 1912, adding votes gained
from German-Americans who had deserted the
Democratic party because of its close identification
with an aggressive internationalist foreign policy.
The addition of women's suffrage did not diminish
Republican strength; indeed, the women who voted
did so on the basis of socioeconomic class rather
than sex. The Republican hegemony in Indiana
lasted down to the Depression and was dissolved
only by the charismatic appeal of Franklin D.
Roosevelt.

Within the dominant party, however, there
were battles that showed deeper social divisions.
The most noticeable battle was over the Ku Klux
Klan. The Klan movement of the 1920s was, unlike
the earlier Klan, northern as well as southern, urban, and more anti-Catholic and anti-Jew than

anti-Negro. It was especially powerful in Indiana. Kenneth J. Jackson estimates that Indiana had the largest membership, 240,000, of any state, North or South, and that Indianapolis had 38,000 members, Gary-Hammond had 10,000 members, while Fort Wayne had 3,000.

The Klan espoused "one hundred percent Americanism" and was composed mainly of lower middle-class factory workers who were not at the time union members. They were religious, belonging to such pietistic churches as the Baptists, Methodists, and Christians (Disciples of Christ). They lived in urban areas undergoing considerable growth and instability, though they themselves were settled residents. If they were middle class, they were salesmen, clerks, small businessmen, lawyers, and dentists. They had joined the Klan because of fear of "alien communism" and of a society where moral controls had loosened and where sexual behavior was less restricted. Like the prohibitionists, the Klansmen had a vision of an older America, more Protestant and more puritanical. They feared the Catholic immigrants and southern blacks coming into the city, competing for housing and for jobs. These fears increased with the periodic economic fluctuations of the 1920s, of recession followed by recovery.

The Klavern offered a refuge for the frightened, and a social club for persons of like mind. It held marches, had meetings, and conducted funerals. It had spectacles such as mass meetings for initiation and church visits when Klansmen, dressed in robes, unexpectedly dropped into services. But, above all, the Klan relied upon political action, particularly in local elections. While the Klan was often believed to be Republican, it supported Democratic candidates if their positions paralleled the Klan's.

The Klan came to Indiana in 1920. The first Klavern was in Evansville and the organizer was Joe M. Huffington. Indianapolis got its Klavern, and the Grand Goblin of the Indiana Ku Klux Klan ob-

American Legion marching in parade, New Castle, May 30, 1921.

Ladies in flag-bedecked car, ready for the parade.

214

California-style bungalow.

Workers attend Eli Lilly & Company 50th anniversary ceremonies, May 1926.

Indianapolis police with stills seized during Prohibition days.

Silver Flash filling station, Muncie.

Ku Klux Klan marches in Muncie.

Billy Sunday and his family, Winona Lake.

H. Brokkage dry goods store, Vincennes.

Moore Grocery Company store, Illinois and Ohio streets, Indianapolis.

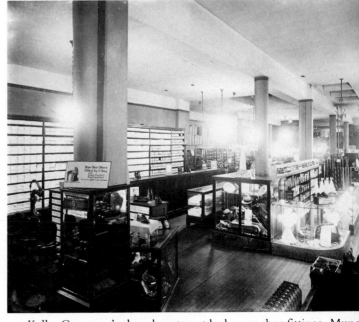

Keller Company's shoe department had x-ray shoe fittings, Munc

E.B. Steck & Son Coal truck decorated for a parade, Muncie.

Mo-Ton Herb Medicine show, Muncie, 1922.

Billy Burton, 125-hour driver, in Muncie, 1926.

tained a state charter in 1921. Early members of the Klan included such prominent individuals as the president of the Commercial National Bank. The most notorious, however, was an Evansville resident, D. (David) C. Stephenson.

D.C. Stephenson was born in Texas and lived in Oklahoma before serving in World War I. Twice married and divorced, Stephenson moved to Evansville in 1920 to enter the coal business with a man named L.G. Julian. Originally a wet Democrat, Stephenson became a Republican prohibitionist. He joined the Klan in 1921 and became the Grand Dragon the following year. Stephenson furthered his Klan career by helping to take control of the Horse Thief Detective Association, a volunteer organization whose members were empowered by state law to act as constables in apprehending suspected criminals. This gave the Klan quasi-police power. Stephenson also added the power of the purse, becoming director of Klan recruiting for the eastern half of the United States.

The Indiana Klan grew rapidly under Stephenson's leadership, establishing Klaverns in such towns as Kokomo, Shelbyville, and Muncie. The state headquarters was in Indianapolis at the Cadle Tabernacle, a center of fundamentalist religion founded by E. Howard Cadle. Other Indianapolis churches which supported the Klan were the Wesley Chapel, Calvary Baptist Church, Riverside Baptist Church, Wesleyan Methodist Church, Windfall Christian Church, Hall Place Methodist Church, Garfield Christian Church, and Brightwood Congregational Church.

By 1924 the Klan was at the height of its political power in the state. In the Republican Party contest for the gubernatorial nomination the Klan supported Ed Jackson over Indianapolis Mayor Samuel Lewis Shank, who had taken a strong anti-Klan position. Although only 500 of the 1,300 delegates to the Republican State Convention were sympathetic to the Klan, the state chairman, Clyde

Small boy at an outside facility, Muncie.

Walb, was a Stephenson man. Consequently, Jackson won the nomination and, later, the election.

Disaster struck the Klan in 1925. Stephenson was charged with the murder of Madge Oberholtzer, a twenty-eight-year-old employee of the office of the State Superintendent of Public Instruction. Stephenson's emotion-charged trial took place in Noblesville and resulted in his conviction of second-degree murder and a sentence of life imprisonment. Stephenson did not take the stand in his own defense, though he did claim privately that he had been framed by the Imperial Wizard. He believed that his friend, Governor Jackson, would pardon him. When Jackson did not, Stephenson disclosed enough information about him and the mayor of Indianapolis, John Duvall, who also was a Klansman, that Jackson was indicted and Mayor Duvall imprisoned. These scandals effectively ended the Klan's popular support in Indiana. By 1928 it had fewer than 7,000 members.

Another attempt to perpetuate older values can be discerned in the prohibition movement. By 1920 the long-sought end of the sale of liquor had been accomplished by an amendment to the United States Constitution. The prohibition issue split Americans. Those who were of older American stock supported it, while those of recent vintage—German, Irish, and Italian—opposed it. Because Indiana did not have as many of the second group as other states, opposition to prohibition was not as pronounced.

In their classic study of Muncie, *Middletown* (1929), Robert S. and Helen Merrell Lynd did not even consider the impact of prohibition upon drinking habits, a failure they themselves admit. Apparently the issue was not a pressing one and information on the question can only be derived incidentally. The Lynds did interview an ex-saloon owner who believed that the saloon business had been severely damaged by the movies before prohibition had become the law of the land. They also

Soapbox derby, Fort Wayne, about 1920.

Trolley cars, Lafayette.

Traffic in winter, state road 37, 1926.

Truck accident, 1928.

Members of the General Assembly traveled to Purdue
University on interurban cars, 1921.

Indiana State Highway Commission vehicle No. 3 used in
road building, 1927.

Laying gravel during road building.

Country store in southern Indiana.

Giant sycamore near Worthington, Greene County, February 20, 1928.

The need for roads and state parks. Gaar Williams cartoon, *Indianapolis News*, January 25, 1921.

AFTER WORKIN' UP TO A CAR — THE NEXT THINGS NEEDED ARE ROADS AND — PLACES TO GO TO.

Deciding which state park to visit. Charles Kuhn cartoon, *Indianapolis News*, April 18, 1925.

NOW YOU SAID ALL ALONG WE WERE GOING TO TURKEY RUN THIS TIME!!

TOM WAS DOWN T' CLIFTY FALLS ONLY LAS' WEEK, AN' HE SAYS TH' ROADS 'R' GREAT, AN' WE HAVEN'T BEEN THERE FOR A LONG TIME, AN' ANYWAY. I WANTA STOP IN AN' SEE A FELLOW WHO LIVES ON STATE ROAD 26, AN'—

AW, GEE, THE CAR IS ALL PACKED, AN' EVERYTHING. LET'S GO!!

Library bookmobile, Logansport, Cass County, 1929.

Schoolchildren at Horace Mann School, Gary, about 1923.

Consolidated grade school, near Mitchell.

seemed to believe that the money previously spent on liquor was being spent on automobiles. Despite these indications, Indiana did have its share of bootleggers and of moonshiners.

A third expression of older values was the growth of the revival tradition, especially in fundamentalist churches. Aided by the news media, revival ministers attempted to fight new social trends with a return to Bible Christianity. One of the most famous evangelists of the time was Billy Sunday, an ex-baseball player turned Presbyterian minister. Sunday built a tabernacle, named after himself, at Winona Lake in Kosciusko County, in addition to having a lake cottage there. Here he preached or vacationed, making this little resort community, for a time, the center of American revivalism. Sunday was not alone; less well-known ministers traveled over the state attempting to fan the fires of revival and stop the tide of modernism.

However successful they were in retaining older values, they could not change the technological innovations of the 1920s which exposed Hoosiers to new ideas, and experiences. Nor could they stop the growth of cities. By 1920 the United States and Indiana were, for the first time, more urban than rural. While the movement to cities had been characteristic of the period since the Civil War, the eventual tipping of the balance did cause concern.

The fear of cities as unhealthy places, both physically and morally, remained. It was partly assuaged by the growth of automobile ownership. The automobile, it was believed, would relieve some of the pressure on rural youths to move to the city. With it, they could go to town on Saturday night and taste urban delights. Conversely, the automobile would enable urban workers to escape the unwholesome atmosphere of the city by trips into the country on weekends.

So the 1920s became the age of the automobile. The newly developed advertising business pushed car ownership and buyers responded. The extent of

221

this response can be seen in *Middletown,* where the place of the automobile is a topic occupying considerable space. In 1923 Muncie, a town of 38,000, had 6,221 automobiles, one for each six persons and two for every three families. One-half of the working-class families had a car; car ownership was so pervasive in the business class that nonpossessors were as apologetic about the lack as their fathers had been about not having telephones. So important had automobiles become in one generation that one wife in Muncie said that, if offered a choice between decent clothing for herself and her nine children and an automobile, she would take the automobile. Another stated that the automobile was more important than food on the table; and a third, when queried about the fact that the family had no bathroom but did have a car, responded that you couldn't go to town in a bathtub.

Despite its attractions, the automobile aroused anxieties, particularly about the sexual activities of the young. Ministers attacked cars as pits of iniquity and even the Lynds detected a correlation between sex crimes and the use of the automobile.

Other factors also made the automobile more of a novelty and less a necessity than in present practice. The automobile existed in an uneasy balance with public transit systems—the train, streetcar, and interurban. People who owned automobiles often followed the common European practice of using them for weekend recreation while relying on other means for getting to work. The phenomenon of the commuting worker was not yet all-encompassing. The Lynds found that 55 percent of the employees of the three largest Muncie industries lived within one mile of work and, hence, could walk, while only part of the remaining 45 percent were commuting by car.

Another limitation was the lack of a modern highway system. Nor were there adequate support services—gasoline stations, auto repair services, and auto parts stores—let alone adequate garages for

Women's rifle team in Armory, Purdue University, 1925.

May Day program, Purdue University, May 12, 1928.

222

Knute Rockne, Notre Dame football coach, 1918–31. His record: 105–12, 5 tied.

Football game at the University of Notre Dame, South Bend.

Washing machine demonstration at Farmer's Short Course, Purdue University, 1921.

The Old Oaken Bucket was the victory trophy at the Indiana-Purdue football game in November 1926, which ended in a 0–0 tie. George Ade is holding his hat and Harry Kurrie holds the bucket.

housing new vehicles. Much of the prosperity of the 1920s came from the construction of highways and buildings for supporting the use of automobiles.

The first requisite was adequate highways and streets, replacing the mud roads which became bottomless in spring and winter. For the first time since the early nineteenth century, the federal government became involved in road building. The Federal Highway Act of 1916 stipulated that each state would receive matching federal dollars for building rural toll-free roads, providing the state create a highway department to plan, supervise, construct, and maintain roads. The Indiana Highway Commission, as a result, came into being in 1917. Not only did the commission begin to plan a network of roads but it also had to plan how these roads should connect to those of other states, according to another highway act in 1921, and to number them according to the acts of 1925 and 1926. Thus did "Lincoln Highway" become U.S. 30 and the "Old National Road" become U.S. 40.

Not to be outdone by the building of state and federal highways, Hoosier cities speeded up the process of paving city streets. No longer could the towns afford dirt roads or streets covered with crushed rock. Instead, they had to have modern cement streets and sidewalks. Much of the local political discussion of the time centered upon the needs and upon the graft available to the local "paving trusts."

But public enterprise was not the only sector of the economy stimulated by the automobile boom. Owners wanted to house their cars in order to protect the flimsy cloth tops characteristic of the age. Some of the more affluent citizens in towns had sheds or other outbuildings used for their horses and/or carriages. These, like their counterparts on the farm, could be converted into garages. This conversion was not without hazards, as is evident in this segment of a column written by Ernie

L.S. Ayres style show at the Indiana State Fair, 1926.

Percheron power on the farm of B.S. Washburn and Son, Benton County.

The oldest man attending a fair, Muncie, September 1922.

Ira Fisher, Brooksburg,
husking corn from the shock.

Pyle for the Scripps-Howard newspapers reflecting on events some twenty years earlier on the family farm near Dana:

> We got our first automobile in 1914. We kept it up in the north end of the wagon shed, right behind the wagon. At the south end of the wagon shed there was a big gravel pit. One day we came home from town, my mother and I got out at the house, and father went to put the car away. We saw him make the circle in the barn lot, and then drive into the north end of the shed. The next instant, the south end of the shed simply burst open, a wagon came leaping out, and with one great bound was over the cliff and down in the gravel pit. My father said he never did know exactly what happened.

The need for a garage influenced the homes constructed during the 1920s. These houses are still identifiable, though they are no longer in the suburbs but are in the older sections of town. Built in a bungalow-style popularized in California, the houses had detached garages which faced or were parallel to alleys and which had to be entered from the alley. Occasionally, the driveway led from the street to the garage fronting the street. The houses themselves were on narrow lots, 40 to 50 feet wide and 100 feet deep, were a story-and-a-half tall, containing a living room, dining room, bathroom, kitchen, and one bedroom on the first floor and one or two on the half floor. Still oriented to the sidewalks in front, the houses had small front porches which could hold chairs or a swing for family members who, on warm summer nights, could watch and talk with passing pedestrians. The architecture of these houses reveals that the automobile had not yet moved into the house and was still relegated to the back lot.

Related structures appearing on the Indiana landscape housed filling stations and garages which were springing up on the main-traveled streets and highways. They were being joined by the first

225

motels, which originated in the 1920s. Detached cottages, each self-contained, began to appeal to motorists who dared the primitive highways of the time. While the day of the solitary gas pump in front of the general store had not yet passed (and was to return in the gas-starved 70s in a different form), it was waning.

The automobile and the general prosperity, except among farmers, made Indiana downtowns booming places. Saturday night became the well-established shopping time for farmers and city dwellers alike. The streets were crowded; the shoppers marveled at the electric lights and the advertising. It was still the heyday of the big department stores, for although these stores had originally been built near the termini of streetcar and interurban systems, they had not yet been challenged by the shopping center or mall and could compete successfully for auto-driven customers.

The main attraction, however, was entertainment. This was available in several forms, in the drugstore soda fountain, in the pool hall, or at the band concerts frequently scheduled. More popular than any of these were the movies which entered their golden age in the 1920s. It was here that Hoosiers learned of the wider world beyond their borders and of cultural practices strange to their settled ways.

The movies had been around as long as the automobile; Edison exhibited a commercial motion-picture machine at the Columbian Exposition in Chicago in 1893. At first, movies were aimed at working-class audiences, with storefronts in neighborhoods being converted to nickelodeons, so-called because of the price of admission. Evansville had an unsuccessful movie house in 1905 and Indianapolis obtained its first, The Bijou, in 1906.

Indiana cities had been well supplied with opera houses and theaters, often built in the 1870s and 1880s, in a conscious attempt to bring culture to budding metropolises. Among these were the

Parade of horses, Wabash, 1928.

Unloading limestone, Linton Township, Vigo County, 1929. Using limestone was an extension service project for the boys clubs.

Country store of W.A. McKee, Clay City, 1926.

Chas. Rogers Cash Store, a traveling store.

Grand Opera House (1875) and English's Opera House (1880) in Indianapolis and Naylor's Opera House (1870) in Terre Haute. These theaters, however, were quite large, located in the best parts of town (English's was on the Circle), and appealed to high culture.

The movie houses soon began to move out of low-rent districts into higher-rent areas to compete with opera houses both in terms of opulence and audiences. The number of movie houses grew rapidly, outstripping their more elegant, expensive, middle-class competitors. The first theater built specifically to show movies was the Regent, built in 1914 in New York City. The idea spread rapidly to other states, including Indiana. By 1920 Indianapolis had fifty-five movie theaters, some of them qualifying for the title of movie palace.

The movie palace, the crumbling remains of which can still be seen in Indianapolis, Fort Wayne, South Bend, and other large towns, had to be seen to be believed. Designed to overawe the patron and to create a sense of splendor, the movie palaces often had exotic motifs, Near Eastern or Chinese, reinforced with murals on the walls, carvings on the ceiling, and fountains in the foyer. Commonly, they had large staffs; for example, the Palace in Fort Wayne had, in addition to the usual manager, assistant manager, and others, three ushers, six usherettes, and a matron whose sole function was to act as a chaperone. Once inside, the patron would not only see a movie but would be entertained by an orchestra or by an organ solo from the mighty Wurlitzer. A few of the organs still remain in such palaces as the Paramount in Anderson, but the sense of awe and magnificence which was a part of the program is gone forever.

The very success of the movies proved frightening to many Americans. Made by immigrant Americans and sometimes overtly sexual, the movies seemed to be perverting the morals of the younger generation. The industry, in order to coun-

Children in wagon hitched to a Guernsey calf.

teract this image, hired a Hoosier to impose a kind of self-censorship. That Hoosier was Will H. Hays.

Hays became president of the Motion Picture Producers and Distributors Association on January 14, 1923, and proceeded to develop codes to which member companies were expected to conform. At first glance, Hays seems an unlikely choice for chief censor of the movies. Born in Sullivan County, Hays had become a lawyer and a power in the Republican party, working his way up to chairman of the Republican National Committee during Warren G. Harding's successful campaign for president in 1920. As a reward, Hays became postmaster general in Harding's cabinet, a position he left for his $100,000 movie job. Yet, on second glance, the choice was a wise one. Hays was an able administrator as well as a consummate politician. He brought the sensibilities of a midwestern Protestant (he was an elder in his hometown Presbyterian Church) and of a conservative small-town Republican to an industry dominated by immigrants from eastern urban centers. He helped make the movies respectable to Middle America.

Small wonder that few heeded the warnings about the evils of the movies and that the building of larger and larger movie palaces proceeded apace during the 1920s. Yet, in a sense, the critics were right. The movies, like the automobile, were subversive, providing an angle of vision and a system of values foreign to most Hoosiers, encouraging the materialism characteristic of the time and downplaying the religious values which were still strongly held by a large segment of the population. On the positive side, they made Hoosiers less provincial and more cosmopolitan and helped end the cultural isolation of rural life.

Contest to find out who can drink soda pop the fastest through a nipple at the boys and girls club picnic, near Covington, Fountain County, June 21, 1921.

Mrs. E.E. Brown, Veedersburg, using her pressure cooker, 1924.

Lyric Theater, Indianapolis, 1929.

Palace Theater, Hartford City.

Foyer of the Indiana Theater, Terre Haute.

The Browns listen to the radio, Veedersburg, 1924.

A sewing class in the 1920s.

The Lean Years

Waiting for Franklin D. Roosevelt. The President's campaign train was on its way to Gary, August 1936.

THE STOCK MARKET CRASH OF 1929 DID NOT APPEAR TO BE A SERIOUS THREAT TO HOOSIER SOCIETY. NOT TOO MANY Hoosiers were investors in the market and business was good. For industrial Indiana, the 1920s had been prosperous because of the demand for durable goods such as steel, automobiles, and automobile parts, and consumer goods such as glass jars. Indiana farmers had suffered along with the rest of agricultural America, but they had survived. However, as time went on, the Depression began to have a serious impact.

By 1930 approximately one of every four factory workers had lost his job and the same proportion was on relief in 1932. By 1935, the heart of the Depression, the number of factory workers was about half what it was at the start of the decade. Bread lines and relief projects became common.

The Depression instituted a political change in Indiana, as in the United States in general. President Franklin D. Roosevelt with his charm and persuasiveness put together a national coalition which swept him into office four times. He helped the Democratic party to control the Hoosier state during the decade. Hoosier politics reflected the shift in population from farm to city, the attraction of the Democratic party to ethnic groups, and the support for Roosevelt by unionized labor.

Indiana Democrats won in 1932 under the leadership of Paul V. McNutt, who received more votes than Roosevelt in the state. McNutt, who was born in Franklin, was the dean of Indiana University's Law School when tapped to run for governor. Identified as a New Deal Democrat, McNutt seemed destined for higher elective office but never made it. After leaving the governor's chair, he became an administrator of the Farm Security Agency in 1939, chairman of the War Manpower Commission in 1942, and U.S. High Commissioner to the Philippines after World War II. McNutt was followed by another Democratic governor, Clifford

Thomas D. Taggart and C.C Pettijohn, Hoosier delegates to the Democratic National Convention, Chicago, June 1932.

Townsend, who continued his New Deal policies.

Indiana, therefore, cooperated with the policies of the Roosevelt Administration. In the "first hundred days" Congress enacted three pieces of legislation which had profound effect upon the Hoosier landscape, both rural and urban. The first created a Civilian Conservation Corps which employed young men between the ages of 17 and 25 to plant trees, beautify parks, and build dams. The purpose was dual, to improve the natural landscape and to give unemployed young men a sense of what outdoor living was like.

The second was the Agricultural Adjustment Act, the purpose of which was to raise farm prices to parity, a level achieved in the period from 1909 to 1914. The means to accomplish this was by the limitation of production, at the start by plowing up corn and slaughtering pigs and later by restricting acreage and numbers of producing sows. While farm income had doubled by 1936, many Hoosiers found the limitation of food production reprehensible.

The crop limitation program of the New Deal helped accelerate a process already begun in Indiana, the reduction in the number of farmers making a living from agriculture. This was not immediately evident as Hoosiers moved back to farms and small towns during the Depression in order to survive. But marginal farmers were hard hit. Unable even to make a subsistence living with full production, they were in no position to cut back their corn and hogs even with the addition of subsidy payments. This was especially true of tenant farmers.

The New Deal recognized the existence of the problem. In 1935 Roosevelt created the Resettlement Administration by executive order; the agency tried to move farmers from poor areas to those of greater fertility. It operated for the most part in southern Indiana, in Brown County and others, and was succeeded by the Farm Security Administration in 1937.

Governor Paul V. McNutt, dedicating the Education Building, Indiana State Fair, September 9, 1936.

Reading newspapers in the library, Fort Wayne, 1936.

WPA workers building Fall Creek Parkway, Indianapolis, 1935.

Sign painters, Vincennes, late 1930s: The Eighteenth Amendment was repealed on December 5, 1933.

A breadline in Peru during the Depression.

The first U.S. sitdown strike at Bendix Automotive Products plant, South Bend, early 1930s.

233

Prospective clients for rural resettlement in southern Indiana: a mother and her three children.

Buttermilk Junction, Martin County.

Crossroads community, Martin County.

Enjoying the sunshine in front of a theater, late 1930s.

234

Prospective clients for rural resettlement in southern Indiana: an elderly couple.

Claude R. Wickard of Carroll County, Secretary of Agriculture, 1940–45, and fourth administrator of Rural Electrification Administration, July 1945.

Before REA: woman adjusting a coal oil lamp.

After REA: woman with electric stove and refrigerator.

For those farmers who remained on the land, two technological developments improved their lives. One was the beginning of rural electrification; the other was the virtual end of horse-powered cultivation. One was the result of federal programs; the other was not.

In 1935 Congress created the Rural Electrification Administration (REA), which was to lend money to locally owned rural electric cooperatives to build power lines to farms and to purchase or generate power for farm use. By 1940, 3 in 10 farms had electricity, as compared to 1 in 10 at the beginning of the decade. The process continued during the years so that eventually almost all Hoosier farms were electrified.

The coming of electricity affected both the economics of agriculture and the quality of rural life. The farmer could specialize; he could, for example, buy an electric milking machine to milk his cows. In order to make the electric machine economically useful, however, he would have to buy more cows, thus cutting back on the capital he had to buy hogs. The whole process encouraged the end of the general-purpose farm. Cash was necessary every month to pay the bills.

For the farm family, the change was even greater. No longer did the members have to feel inferior to members of city families. Now they had electric lights, refrigerators, stoves, irons, and toasters; they had running water and an indoor bathroom. The memory which haunted Ernie Pyle when he returned to Dana, Indiana, in 1939 need no longer haunt them:

> People who have been around say Dana is a medium-good town. I really don't know whether it is or not. I never felt completely at ease in Dana. I suppose it was an inferiority hangover from childhood. I was a farm boy and town kids can make you feel awfully backward when you're young and a farm boy. I never got over it.

Farm of Albert Ball, near Muncie.

As the Depression eased, farmers increased their mechanized farming as gasoline-powered tractors replaced horses. By the 1930s, the basic form had evolved, a four-wheel vehicle with the front two wheels either set close together to fit between two corn rows or else set out to straddle them. The original steel, spade-lugged back wheels were giving way to rubber, pneumatic tires which, although they packed the soil, did not tear it up as much. With the tractor came a whole line of implements fitted to the power source. Horses served in auxiliary ways, to pull wagons to the combine, to pull in hay wagons, or to pull in loads of corn; but as teams grew older, they were not replaced. The horse population dropped as horse auctions sold horses to slaughterhouses to process into animal food.

The face of the farms changed but so too did the face of cities. One of the ways in which change came was through the creation of public works to provide work for the unemployed. Three agencies did the bulk of this work. They were the Civil Works Administration, begun in 1933, and administered by Harry Hopkins; the Public Works Administration, which was slower in getting started and did not have an impact until 1934, was administered by Harold Ickes; and the Works Progress Administration, begun in 1935, was also administered by Hopkins. The work done by these three agencies was similar; the reason for the overlap was Roosevelt's penchant for agency proliferation and competition. In general, the PWA undertook the largest projects, bridges, post offices, and other public buildings; the CWA did smaller ones, streets, schoolhouses, airports, parks, and sewers. The WPA tried to find employment to match the skills of the workers. Any attempt to sort out which agency did what is bound to be confusing. In Muncie the CWA workers removed trolley tracks from the streets in 1933; in Indianapolis WPA workers built Fall Creek Parkway in 1935.

Outdoor privy in the snow.

Making apple butter.

236

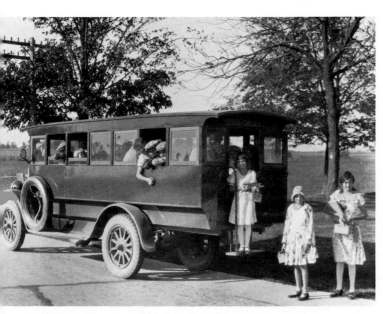

Ira Eby's children boarding the school bus, Wakarusa, 1930.

Drilling for coal, using an old Canadian spring pole method.

Harvesting potatoes on John Workman's farm, near Lafayette.

Butchering on the farm.

Regardless of the confusion, New Deal projects changed the Hoosier landscape. New post offices, bridges, and parks improved the general appearance of towns and became part of the accepted services provided by those towns. Only now are some of these edifices crumbling and having to be replaced.

Not all WPA projects were construction ones. Anxious to end unemployment among all sectors of the economy, the WPA embarked upon a program to aid out-of-work authors, painters, and other creative persons. In Indiana the program's most notable project was *Indiana: A Guide to the Hoosier State* (1941), which was a part of the American Guide Series to all the states. Under the editorial guidance of the Department of Public Relations of Indiana State Teachers College, the book was published by Oxford University Press and remains one of the best guides to the natural and cultural features of the state. The persons working on the guide were the best Hoosierdom had to offer. Among them was Ross Lockridge, director of the New Harmony Memorial Commission and state supervisor of the Indiana Writers Project. His son, Ross Lockridge, Jr., was to become a famous writer with the publication of *Raintree County,* a novel of nineteenth-century Indiana.

Of all the New Deal agencies, the WPA was the most criticized and the cultural projects of the WPA were among the most controversial. Stories about make-work efforts abounded; jokes about WPA bees whose stings ended every ambition for work were common; and indignation about waste continued long after the agency had vanished.

One of the most trenchant critics of the New Deal was a Hoosier, Benjamin Wallace Douglass, who had worked as a field agent for the Indiana Board of Forestry and then as state entomologist prior to opening a small business. Douglass had an orchard in Brown County in conjunction with which he operated a small canning factory.

Collecting sugar water from maple trees to make syrup.

Threshing wheat with steam engine outfit.

John Dillinger at his family home, Mooresville, April 1934, holding the wooden gun that he used to break out of jail.

Cole Porter, born in Peru in 1893.

The Porter family home, Peru.

Hoagy Carmichael, born in Bloomington in 1899, with Indiana University friends.

Writing in the *Saturday Evening Post* articles later collected and published as *The New Deal Comes to Brown County* (1936), Douglass inveighed against the NRA, under whose provisions unionization of his canning workers took place. He attacked the Resettlement Administration, which was trying to identify submarginal land in Brown County, as well as the AAA, which limited farmers in the county to a maximum of 3,800 acres of wheat when, according to Douglass, no more than 500 acres had been planted in wheat in the last ten-year period. Douglass, in common with many conservative Hoosiers, believed that the major objection was that the New Deal was leading America to communism:

> The New Dealers, being dissatisfied with the old order in America, propose to replace it with a planned economy copied from Russia. The country with the highest standard of living on this earth proposes to scrap its very existence in order to copy a ghostly dream that arose in a country having the lowest standard of any civilized people. Our race has fought for individual liberty for a thousand years; why should we copy from a race that never knew, or apparently desired, liberty either under the czars or under the red dictators?

But the New Deal did not occupy all the space in Hoosier minds; other issues and other names crowded the newspapers and radio. By the 1930s commercial radio stations filled the airways with music, comedy, and news. Among those composers whose tunes were the most common were two Indiana-born ones, Hoagy Carmichael and Cole Porter.

Hoagy Carmichael was an alumnus of Indiana University who graduated with a Bachelor of Laws degree in 1926. Even in his six years at I.U., Carmichael's main interest was jazz. In his autobiography, *Sometimes I Wonder* (1965), the name taken

John Wooden, Martinsville,
All-American basketball player at
Purdue, 1930–32.

Amelia Earhart with Purdue's President E.C. Elliott at the
Purdue airport.

from the first line of his most famous composition, *Star Dust,* Carmichael says, "We saw jazz, already into lives and moving into speakeasies, set the tone and color of the country. We all dreamed of super jazz bands." In the Book Nook, a student hangout of the 1920s, Carmichael reputedly began to work out his songs. While his initial effort to interest Paul Whiteman in his music in 1929 failed, Carmichael soon became a nationally known songwriter whose melodies were sung by the leading crooners of the day. It was a rare year in the 1930s when such songs as *Star Dust, Ol' Rockin' Chair, Lazy Bones, Lazy River, Come Easy, Go Easy Love* did not appear on the Hit Parade.

But Carmichael was not the only Hoosier whose tunes were being sung nationwide. The other one was Cole Porter, who made his reputation in that most indigenous American art form, the Broadway musical. Porter was born in Peru in 1893 and, like Carmichael, originally planned to become a lawyer. However, he changed his mind and entered the Harvard Music School instead. His musical education continued under the French composer Vincent D'Indy. This exposure to French culture, augmented by Porter's service in the French Army in World War I, has been cited as the reason for his sophistication.

Following World War I, Porter began writing musical comedies (he was unusual in that he composed both the tunes and the lyrics). Although some of these, notably *Hitchy Koo* (1921), *Greenwich Village Follies* (1923), and *Fifty Million Frenchmen* (1929), were quite successful, those of the 1930s and early 1940s—*Anything Goes* (1934), *Jubilee* (1935), *Red, Hot, and Blue* (1936), *Du Barry was a Lady* (1939), *Panama Hattie* (1940), *Let's Face It* (1941), *Something for the Boys* (1942), and *Mexican Hayride* (1943)—were more famous. Nor was that the limit of his talent; he also composed music for such movies as *Born to Dance* (1936), *Rosalie* (1937), *Broadway Melody* (1940), and *You'll Never Get Rich*

Boy Scouts saluting the flag, Fort Wayne.

Library, James Whitcomb Riley Hospital for Children, March 5, 1930.

Children at a day nursery, Fort Wayne, 1936.

Boys at the Wheatley Center, Fort Wayne, 1936.

Girls at the Wheatley Center, Fort Wayne, 1936.

(1941). While Porter continued to write in the 1940s and 1950s and did some of his best work then— *Kiss Me, Kate* (1948), *Can Can* (1953), and *Silk Stockings* (1955)—his great decade was the 1930s. No one who lived through that era can forget the familiar strains of *Begin the Beguine* or *Night and Day.*

Porter represented the sophisticated side of the Indiana character; still another Hoosier represented the rustic, naïve side. For many Hoosiers, he was more famous than Carmichael or Porter and, for a time, his name could more often be found in headlines. He was John Dillinger.

Born on a farm near Mooresville, Dillinger became the most wanted bank robber in the early 1930s. Three factors led to this notoriety: the cheap motor car and country roads on which to escape (Dillinger specialized in robbing small-town banks lacking adequate police protection), the press of the day which publicized his exploits and the FBI which made him the most wanted, and the image conveyed by the newspapers of a simple farm boy matching his wits against the wily bankers (who were convenient villains in the Depression). In the months between the day that Dillinger broke out of the penitentiary at Michigan City in 1933 and the day he died in front of a Chicago theater in 1934 after being identified by "the lady in red," he had become immortal. As John Bartlow Martin said, "To most people elsewhere, as to the cop who turned him in on a tip from a whore, Dillinger seemed just another gangster; but to Hoosiers he seemed more like Robin Hood."

Shortly after his death, Dillinger was memorialized in countless county and state fairs on tawdry midways where tents containing one of his cars or the overweight charms of "the lady in red" could be found. The fair, another Hoosier tradition, loomed large in the 1930s, as more foreign pleasures became too expensive for Depression-ridden citizens of the state.

Main Street, west side of the square, Spencer, Owen County.

The fair had already been marked as a typical Indiana institution by such writers as Theodore Dreiser, who described the Knox County Fair in Vincennes in *A Hoosier Holiday* (1916), but perhaps the Hoosier-born writer who captured the spirit of the Indiana county fair in the late 1930s best was Jean Shepherd. His "County Fair" appeared originally in *Playboy* magazine in the 1960s and can be found in a collection of his essays entitled *Wanda Hickey's Night of Golden Memories and Other Disasters* (1971).

Shepherd begins his story in his home in the East where he is watching the late-late movie *State Fair,* which even though it takes place in Iowa, Shepherd transfers to Indiana, and which contains all the clichés of the bucolic past—the trotting race, the innocent girl, and an "Indiana countryside, dotted with quaint corn shocks and tinted with lurid oranges and greens!!!" These were not what Shepherd remembered from his boyhood experiences in the Calumet Region where the sky was dimmed with the smoke and ash from the steel mills.

For Shepherd the county fair meant rides and food and automobile racing for "dirt track racing is as much a part of an Indiana county fair as applesauce, pumpkins and pig judging." The Shepherd family went to the fair, Shepherd recalled, in a hot, traffic-slowed ride, arriving in time to watch its favorite driver, Iron Man Gabruzzi, win. Then the Shepherds began a tour of the grounds, a tour that, characteristically, is a litany of food and drink. While his father was drinking Blatz beer, Shepherd and his brother were drinking Nehi orange and Hines root beer and consuming popcorn balls, Girl Scout cookies, corn on the cob, peanuts, pumpkin pie, hot dogs, pickles, crullers, baked beans, taffy apples, angel food cake, black-walnut fudge, vanilla angel's breath, and even Purina Chicken Chow. After taking in such sights as the show pigs, the prize-winning goat, and the fortune-telling chicken,

Surface coal mine, showing the steam-powered equipment in the pit.

An old preparation plant of Maumee Collieries, later acquired by Peabody Coal Company.

242

School buses at Knox, Starke County, about 1938.

Women volunteers preparing apples for charitable use, Muncie.

Kalorama Grocery on the north shore of Tippecanoe Lake, Leesburg.

Lake County fair, Crown Point.

Snowplowing an Indiana road.

W.G. Irwin, Columbus
industrialist and entrepreneur.

Some cars made in Indiana:

—Auburn Boattail Speedster, 1931.

Mired in the mud of a southern Indiana road, 1933.

—Cord L-29 Cabriolet, 1931.

—Duesenberg Convertible, 1932.

The Stutz Bearcat was also made in Indiana. Sitting on the running
board of the 1932 model are William F. Fox, *Indianapolis News,* and
Paul D. (Tony) Hinkle, Butler University.

Eddie Rickenbacker, driving the Pacemaker car, bought the Indianapolis Motor Speedway in 1927.

Clessie Cummins, Columbus, in the diesel racer that completed the 1931 500-mile race non-stop, the first time this had ever been done.

A 500-mile race in the 1930s.

Wilbur Shaw, Vernon, is congratulated by Harvey Firestone, Jr., after winning the 1939 500-mile race. He also won in 1931 and 1937.

the pumpkin which resembled Franklin Delano Roosevelt, and the world's largest cheese, the family went to the Midway where, once again, the members tried their hand at ringing the bell, throwing baseballs, and riding the Rocket Whip. The latter culminated in the inevitable; the Shepherd boys vomited all over their father's new pongee shirt. Headed home after this incident, all proclaimed the fair was better than ever.

Despite the obvious hyperbole, Jean Shepherd's recollections of the fair are not completely idiosyncratic. The fair was, like Indiana, a combination of the old and the new; it was caught between the modern and the traditional world. It mirrored the friendliness and the neighborliness of Hoosiers, even in the raw industrial region, just as Ernie Pyle recalled these same qualities in rural Dana in 1939. Home to visit his mother, who had had a second stroke, Pyle recounts how friends and relatives brought in food, flowers, and offers of help. They scrubbed the floors, cooked the food, and washed the dishes. "On Sunday there were thirty-eight people at our house," Pyle remembered.

The era of the Depression brought poverty and hardships to many; it was a time of worry and grief. Yet a sense of community persisted along with a sense of the past which helped to overcome the problems which existed as well as those which were soon to come.

The Lanier Mansion, Madison, during the Ohio River flood, January 1937.

Aerial view of the Ohio River flood, Evansville, January 30, 1937.

Bridge over the Ohio River, New Albany, 1931.

Over There and Back Home
— Again

The U.S.S. *Indiana* in 1942.

T HE SECOND WORLD WAR DID NOT ENGENDER THE DIVISIONS WHICH THE FIRST WORLD WAR HAD CREATED AMONG HOOSIERS. IN part, this was because the experience of the first war had demonstrated the loyalty of the German-Americans to their adopted country. In part, it was because of the nature of the enemy; Nazi Germany, Fascist Italy, and Imperial Japan exemplified totalitarianism far more than Imperial Germany had.

Not all Hoosiers supported the idea of participating in another foreign adventure. Indeed, there was much isolationist sentiment in the United States prior to the attack on Pearl Harbor that precipitated the conflict. At the time, the isolationists presented good reasons for noninvolvement. The memory of World War I was still quite vivid for Americans of German ancestry. Many of those who were not German were disillusioned with the results of World War I. The Allies had failed to pay their war debts, Europe and America had experienced depression, and Europe had succumbed to totalitarian movements. The revelations in the 1930s that the armament industries had profited greatly from the war and had tried to influence the United States to support the Allies strengthened the isolationism of old trust-busting Progressives.

Among them were two well-known Hoosiers, former Senator Beveridge and Charles A. Beard. In the 1920s Albert J. Beveridge had come to believe that the British and the French had tricked the United States into entering World War I. Writing in the *Saturday Evening Post,* Beveridge even charged that the French had collected rent for the use of trenches on their soil. The old Progressive still had a following; many Hoosiers accepted Beveridge's assessment. His counterpart in the intellectual arena was the Indiana-born scholar-historian, Charles A. Beard, who was then living on a dairy farm in Connecticut. In a series of books—*The Devil Theory of War* (1936), *Giddy Minds and Foreign Quarrels* (1939), and *A Foreign Policy for the United States*

Wendell L. Willkie, Republican presidential candidate, 1940.

(1940)—Beard argued that the involvement in World War I resulted from the need to protect the investment American business had made in selling weapons to the Allies. Using this economic interpretation, Beard argued vehemently against once more assuming the "atlas load."

Most of the prominent isolationists were Republicans, but the party itself split on the issue. One point all agreed upon was opposition to the New Deal. Indeed, the Republican candidate chosen in 1940 to run for president, Wendell L. Willkie, was Hoosier-born and not an isolationist, as were his opponents for the nomination, Robert A. Taft of Ohio and Thomas E. Dewey of New York. Originally from Elwood, where both his parents practiced law, Willkie received an LL.B. from Indiana University in 1916. After practicing law in Rushville and serving in World War I, Willkie moved to Akron, Ohio, to join a law firm. Among the clients of the firm was Commonwealth and Southern, a utilities holding company, which recognized Willkie's talents and made him president four years later. This meteoric career earned him the sobriquet, "the barefoot boy of Wall Street."

Willkie began as a Democrat; he voted for Franklin D. Roosevelt in 1932, but by 1936 he had become disillusioned with the New Deal, particularly with those policies antagonistic to private utility interests, and had voted for Alf Landon. Not until 1939 did he become a Republican. Despite his lack of political experience, he won the Republican nomination in 1940 primarily because of the media blitz of Henry Luce's *Time* magazine, the Cowles family newspapers in the Midwest, and the New York *Herald-Tribune*. Beginning his campaign in Elwood, Willkie later made the Durbin Hotel in Rushville his headquarters. Although he worked extremely hard, Willkie lost, probably because of his lack of political experience and his poor political organization.

After his defeat, Willkie continued his new-

Willkie began his campaign at Rushville, August 20, 1940.

Senator Sherman Minton, later a Supreme Court Justice, with Henry F. Schricker and Paul V. McNutt at an Indiana University Law School banquet.

William E. Jenner
served in the Senate
1944–68.

Evansville shipyards during the Second World War.

Toluene unit at Standard Oil of Indiana, Whiting plant.

The parking lot of the powder and powder bagging plants
under construction January 1941 at Charlestown.

found political career, testifying in favor of Lend-Lease aid to Britain and France in 1941, prior to Pearl Harbor. When the war came, he proposed to President Roosevelt that he be sent around the world to visit the Allies in Europe, the Middle East, and Asia. Roosevelt agreed and Willkie embarked upon a forty-nine-day trip, the report of which can be found in his *One World* (1943). Willkie took a liberal internationalist position in the book, criticizing the attempts of the British to retain their empire, Roosevelt's use of Admiral Darlan in North Africa, and the excesses of Stalin, while speaking for an early second front and Chinese autonomy. By 1944 Willkie had antagonized enough Republicans so that he failed to gain the nomination for president, losing to Thomas E. Dewey. He died three months after the convention.

Like Willkie, Hoosiers united behind the war effort following the sneak attack on Pearl Harbor, but with noticeably less enthusiasm than in World War I. The extravagant sales techniques used to promote the sale of war bonds and the excessively emotional appeals to enlist were muted in favor of more subdued and subtle efforts.

The war itself was a longer and more painful one for the Hoosiers, with about three times as many sons and daughters serving as in World War I, 338,000 to 118,000, and about the same proportion dying, 10,000 to 3,370. It was a longer war; the National Guard had been called to duty in August 1940, and the first draftees left for camp shortly thereafter. For most Hoosiers, however, the call came after Pearl Harbor, as America built up its armed forces.

A letter of greetings from the President of the United States signaled the first step to war. The prospective serviceman then took a physical and was classified according to his age, marital status, physical condition, occupation, and religious scruples. If the candidate were 18 to 32, single, healthy, in a nonessential industry, and not a

Ernie Pyle, of Dana, makes friends with children in the South Pacific shortly before he was killed, 1945.

Elmer Davis, of Aurora, was the head of the Office of War Information during the war.

member of the traditional peace church, he was well on his way to recruit training.

The Second World War was the last great effort of American passenger trains which hauled the recruits to physicals, to training camps, and to ports of embarkation. Crowds of servicemen dressed in olive drab or navy blue were often seen, milling through the railway stations of the major cities in Indiana, drinking the coffee and eating the doughnuts provided by the women volunteers from the USO or by the Salvation Army.

Hoosiers fought in every theater and in every branch of the service, leaving their achievements for the record in unit and regimental histories as well as in the more ephemeral newspapers of the day. Two of the best known of the Hoosier wartime correspondents were Leo M. Litz, who worked for the *Indianapolis News,* and Ernie Pyle, who served as a syndicated columnist for the Scripps-Howard newspapers.

Litz wrote of those Hoosiers whom he found serving in the Pacific, individuals such as Pfc Edward J. Hogan, a 20-year-old Marine from Indianapolis who had volunteered in 1943 after working for a year in a White Castle hamburger shop and was wounded at Iwo Jima, and Flight Orderly Samuel W. Ellison, a 33-year-old native of Middletown, who had worked as a machinist at General Motors in Anderson for ten years before being drafted in 1944, when the demands of war seemed pressing, despite the dependency of his three children.

Far more famous than Litz was Ernie Pyle, who became the best-known American War correspondent of World War II. His columns, collected into two books—*Here Is Your War* (1943) and *Brave Men* (1944)—won Pyle a Pulitzer prize in 1944. Pyle did not survive the war; he died, the victim of Japanese machine-gun fire, on Ie Shima on April 8, 1945.

Pyle's vision of the war de-emphasized the

One thousand Fort Harrison soldiers marched in the U.S. Navy Booster parade, February 22, 1942.

Women playing pool in the Lathe Workers Athletic Association rooms, South Bend, October 14, 1941.

The 44th WAAC Company, shortly after arriving at Camp Atterbury, March 6, 1943.

Soldiers in front of the Science Building, Ball State Teachers College, 1944.

WAVES, SPARS, ASTS at Indiana University, August 13, 1943.

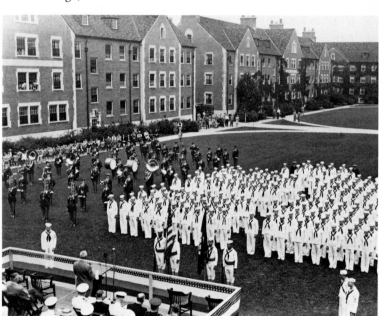

U.S. Navy enlisted trainees in Cary Quad, Purdue University, June 16, 1942.

Navy V-12 unit at Indiana State Teachers College, Terre Haute.

Dolph Crane and two of his children inspecting seed corn, Rush County, May 1942.

glory and glamor of war and emphasized the heroic qualities of the ordinary GI. Pyle was gentle and hated the war he reported. Just before he met his death in the Pacific, he wrote, "but for me war has become a flat, black depression without highlights, a revulsion of the mind and exhaustion of the spirit." Pyle did not search out Hoosiers for particular notice in his columns. Instead, he looked for universal types who represented his idea of valor and strength. One such person happened to be a Hoosier, George Thomas Clayton of Evansville, about whom Pyle wrote:

> Soldiers are made out of the strangest people. I made another friend—just a plain old Hoosier—who was so quiet and humble you would hardly know he was around. Yet in a few weeks of invasion he had learned war's wise little ways of destroying life while preserving one's own. He hadn't become the "killer" type that war makes of some soldiers; he had merely become adjusted to an obligatory new profession.

One wonders if in describing Clayton Pyle had not, perhaps unconsciously, described himself.

By an odd quirk, the official version of the war came to the American public via a Hoosier accent as well. The voice belonged to Elmer Davis, who became the spokesman of the office of War Information, which President Franklin D. Roosevelt established by executive order in 1942.

Born in Aurora, Davis was a Rhodes Scholar at Oxford prior to becoming a reporter and editorial writer for the *New York Times*. In 1924 he undertook the economically hazardous life of a free-lance writer and succeeded in that profession until 1939 when he joined CBS as a radio news analyst. By the time he was asked to coordinate the Office of War Information (OWI), he had become the Walter Cronkite of his day. Because of this image, he was an obvious choice to act as the voice of the war effort.

Cultivating a cornfield in the 1940s.

Scrap drive in front of Delaware County courthouse, Muncie.

Carole Lombard, of Fort Wayne, on a Defense Bond tour, joined Governor Henry F. Schricker (left), Will H. Hays, of Sullivan, president of a motion-picture group, and Alex Arch, South Bend, on the Statehouse lawn, June 18, 1942.

Delaware Post No. 19 Drum Corps and Color Guard, American Legion, in front of Honor Roll board, Muncie, August 3, 1943.

Bond Rally at Lebanon High School, Lebanon. Money collected at their rallies paid for 3 jeeps.

Davis's task was not an easy one. There was little unity in the armed services; there were conflicting positions among the diverse agencies of the government. In addition, there were pressures from the private sector of the economy to use its advertising talents to sell the war. Moreover, the mass media—movies and comic strips—failed, according to Davis, to present a desirable picture of either the military or home fronts. The most difficult problem was a domestic, political one. Critics of the New Deal, and these were plentiful among Hoosier Republicans, considered the OWI too active in promoting New Deal programs; their barbs were aimed at one primary target, Robert Sherwood, a close friend of Harry Hopkins and a speechwriter for President Roosevelt. As a result, the OWI became timid about stating the war aims of the United States, and congressional attacks on the agency in 1943 made it even less brave. It lasted for the rest of the war; but when Davis left to become a newscaster for ABC, he felt a sense of failure.

By 1942 the New Deal was dead, killed by the war and by the effort of its critics, among whom were Hoosier Republicans. Prominent among these was Charles A. Halleck, a second district congressman, who was elected in 1932 and served until 1968, many more years in office than any Hoosier had ever held before. Halleck led the fight in the House of Representatives to dismantle the New Deal. He was joined in the Senate by Homer Capehart in 1944 and by William E. Jenner, who was elected to serve the remaining years of the term of Senator Frederick Van Nuys, who died in 1944. Also in that year the Republicans captured the statehouse when Ralph Gates became the first Republican governor elected since before the Depression. Gates, like Halleck, Capehart, and Jenner, won on a platform which opposed "foreign-born" New Dealism.

For most Hoosiers, the demise of the CCC,

—Smiles of joy.

VJ celebration, Indianapolis, August 14, 1945:

the WPA, and the other alphabet agencies went unnoticed, for the war had accomplished what they had not, the end of the Depression. The demand for war materiel as well as for food meant prosperity for those who worked on the home front. Those automobile and truck factories left in Indiana turned out parts for tanks or built trucks or cars for military use. So many Studebaker trucks went to Russia via Lend-Lease that the story went that the Russians considered the words Studebaker and truck synonymous. The Allison Division of General Motors made 70,000 of the famous Allison engines which powered many of the U.S. aircraft. Evansville boomed, increasing in size by 45,000 persons, a 50 percent increase, as the Navy shipyards and Republic Aviation Company produced boats and fighter planes. Perhaps the greatest Indiana boom town was Charlestown, located in Clark County not far from Louisville, Kentucky. In 1940, when Du Pont and Goodyear decided to build powder plants in the town, its population was only 891. Preparing for the plants changed that; the construction workers who built the plants alone numbered 45,000. No one could live in Indiana with its war industries and its military bases, such as Camp Atterbury and Fort Benjamin Harrison, without realizing that a war was being fought.

It was ironic that although money was now far more plentiful, consumer goods were not. Two new wartime agencies, the War Production Board (WPB) and the Office of Price Administration (OPA), had taken the place of the New Deal agencies dying away. The WPB set priorities for the use of vital raw materials such as steel, rubber, and gasoline for industries, while the OPA set prices and provided a rationing system for consumer goods such as meat, clothes, coffee, sugar, and gasoline. Not that the first did not affect the second. The War Production Board set standards which influenced consumer wear. For example, the double-breasted suit, a fixture before the war, vanished because of

—"Japanese Surrender," the *Indianapolis News* headline.

—First World War veterans joined the crowds.

254

Entrance to the Indianapolis Motor Speedway, 1940s.

Tony Zale, middleweight champion, with Boy Scouts, Gary.

Mrs. Dorothy Robinson and her daughter Betty, members of Motor Maids of America, 1945.

the need to save cloth, and the WPB's edict that makers of women's swimsuits had to reduce material in each suit by 10 percent resulted in the popularity of the two-piece model.

For most of those Hoosiers who did not go to war, the memories which linger are of the shortages of gasoline, tires, meat, sugar, and shoes and the rationing these shortages necessitated. Along with the memories can be found tangible evidence such as gasoline tickets A, B, or C, or coupons for meat stored away in the attic, mute testimony to the impact the war made on almost every citizen.

The pressures which shortages were to exert after the war were already apparent near the end of the war. John Bartlow Martin, in his *Indiana: An Interpretation* (1947), wrote that he had visited Muncie and Evansville in April and November of 1944. In both places, Martin found common concerns. One was the future of unions; this was the concern of the workers who had become unionized either shortly before or during the war. The other was newfound prosperity. As one older worker put it:

> Five years ago they [the workers] could buy a hog's head and five pounds of beans and that's all. Now they can eat a dollar and a quarter steak. A man can make a hundred and fifteen dollars a week and so can his wife. What the hell do you expect them to think about? They think about spending it.

The Second World War ended in the summer of 1945 and brought a wave of spontaneous celebration on each of the special days—V-E day on May 8 and V-J day on August 14. Yet the transition from a wartime to a civilian society was not easy. Servicemen clamored to return home to their interrupted or never-begun civilian careers. A system of priorities, based upon points, went into effect. While probably necessary, it did mean low morale for those who had to wait. Leo M. Litz graphically described the feelings of one Hoosier lieutenant:

> One-Bar Bill was glum—frightfully glum. Most likely this was the first serious manifestation of unrest among our troops after V-J day. Bill had amassed 80 points toward the magic carpet trip and 85 points was the current requirement. Surveying the situation by dead reckoning, he thought it would be well past corn planting time, perhaps wheat harvest, before he would be seeing his Fountain County farm again, and had so advised his sister, Mrs. W.F. McKenna, Veedersburg.

As the serviceman proceeded through separation centers, such as Camp Atterbury, he received his back pay, his "ruptured duck" (a lapel pin in the form of an eagle symbolizing active service), and the necessary discharge papers. Back in civilian society, he looked for new clothes, a job, or a place to go to school. All were in short supply.

Clothes were scarce and the sight of an individual dressed in a khaki overcoat with the stripes and regimental badge removed was common as late as 1947. While federal law mandated that returning veterans had first claim on the jobs they had left, the law failed to cover all cases. Many had no jobs to return to, either because the war had closed their employer's doors or because they were jobless at the time they had gone into the service. For those unemployed veterans, the answer was to join the 52–20 club, a name applied to those eligible for grants of $20 per week for up to a year while seeking a job, or to go to college or vocational school under the GI Bill which paid for books, tuition, and supplies, plus a subsistence allowance of $65 a month for single veterans and $90 for married ones.

The veterans created a boom at Hoosier colleges, one which is only now ending. All institutions, private and public, shared in the growth. Ball State Teachers College is a good example of the trend. In the fall of 1945, Ball State had 1,010 students, over half of whom were women; a year later, enrollment had more than doubled and men predominated.

Nor were these the only institutions strained by the swell of postwar veterans and prosperity. The construction industry boomed because of the demand for housing, both for those who could not afford it before the war and for those persons who had married during the war or after the war was over. The new families led to demands for more

The Monon Railroad (C.I. & L.R.R.) celebrated its centennial in 1947. The station in New Albany proudly displayed the news to its patrons.

Allan C.G. Mitchell, head of the physics department, standing beside the Indiana University cyclotron, August 7, 1945.

Three well-known geneticists at Indiana University, May 21, 1946: Tracy Sonneborn, Ralph E. Cleland, and Herbert Muller.

cars, more refrigerators, toasters, and radios as well as for baby clothes, baby food, and eventually elementary schools.

All this led to inflation and general discontent as expressed by strikes, such as the one at the General Motors plant in Anderson in 1946, and by a Republican landslide that same year which returned William Jenner, an extreme conservative, to the U.S. Senate, where he became a thorn in President Truman's side. Jenner joined Capehart and Halleck in attacking the vestiges of the New Deal, particularly those elements which seemed left wing when the Cold War focused attention on the communists.

Despite the concern over inflation and the growing fear of communist aggression, the latter years of the decade were years of peace and growing prosperity. Consumer demand eased as factories poured out goods; long waiting lists for cars shrank. Studebaker brought out a new line of cars which were well-designed and which struck the consumers' fancy, and entrepreneurs in Elkhart, Terre Haute, Indianapolis, Evansville, and other cities began tract housing, the new auto suburbs. Laid out in large developments, with houses in the new ranch type or the older story-and-a-half Cape Cod, the suburbs attracted much unfavorable attention for their raw look, their lack of trees, and especially their homogeneity. To those who lacked housing, they looked very desirable.

By 1948 Indiana had returned to a more normal situation, politically as well as economically. Although the Republican candidate for president, Thomas E. Dewey, carried the state, as he had in 1944, Henry F. Schricker, the Democratic candidate for governor, won that office, thus becoming the first person to serve two nonconsecutive terms as governor. His second term saw the end of another long tradition, the legal segregation of schools. Under Indiana statutes, schools designed for one race were legal; Crispus Attucks, the black high school in Indianapolis, was built in the 1920s. In 1949 the General Assembly outlawed such practices, anticipating by five years the U.S. Supreme Court decision.

The war had tried Hoosiers but its successful conclusion, along with the transition to a more prosperous economy, ushered in a period of optimism, one in which growth seemed given and the more abundant future seemed sure. Hoosiers were better fed, better housed, better educated, and they wanted more.

Woodlawn Trailer Courts for veterans and their families, Indiana University, 1946.

A trailer courts family, 1948.

NCAA basketball champions in Kansas City: Indiana University team, after defeating University of Kansas 60–42, March 30, 1940.

Chevy night at Memorial Stadium, Terre Haute, August 31, 1947.

Coach John Wooden with the Indiana State basketball team; they were NAIB runners-up in 1948.

Big Ten football champions at Bloomington: Indiana University team and Coach Alvin (Bo) McMillin, after defeating Purdue 26–0, November 24, 1945.

Coach Bo McMillin and the Indiana University football team were dreaming of the first Big 10 championship in November 1945. Cartoon by William Mullin.

Marjorie Main, a native of Indiana, and Governor Ralph E. Gates crown the Indiana Egg Queen, Phyllis Latta, Warsaw, April 7, 1947.

Raymond Loewy designed the 1949 Studebaker Commander five-passenger Starlight coupe.

Traffic in downtown Indianapolis, March 25, 1946.

Mead Johnson Terminal: river-rail-truck terminal on the Ohio River, Evansville, 1945.

Dogtown Ferry on the Wabash River between White County, Illinois, and Posey County, Indiana, 1944.

259

Happy Days

The *Delta Queen* at Dress Plaza, Evansville.

THE 1950s ARE OFTEN REGARDED AS YEARS OF DOMESTIC PEACE AND TRANQUILITY, OF MINDLESS PREOCCUPATION WITH MATERIAL possessions, and of no social protest. Those who hold that view have forgotten that the decade began with the war in Korea and that it ended with a crisis over the U-2 pilot, Francis Gary Powers, shot down in Russia. Fears of atomic war and of communist expansion permeated American society and Indiana was not immune.

The concerns of the era appeared in the political arena. Senator William E. Jenner continued to make headlines with his demands for the impeachment of Harry S Truman when the President relieved General Douglas MacArthur of his command of UN troops in the Far East in 1951 and with his support of Senator Joseph R. McCarthy in his campaign to ferret out left-wingers in government. Jenner and the other Hoosier senator, Homer Capehart, supported the more conservative Robert A. Taft for the presidential nomination rather than the more liberal Dwight Eisenhower, whom Charles Halleck championed. Eisenhower won Indiana's votes despite Jenner's attack on General George Marshall, a close friend and superior of Eisenhower in World War II, as "a living lie." Jenner's career in the Senate, however, was soon to end, for even though he won re-election in 1952, he chose to retire to Bedford in 1958. R. Vance Hartke, an Evansville lawyer and ex-mayor, ran against Harold Handley that year and won, giving Indiana its first Democratic senator in 20 years.

Indiana's reputation as a citadel of conservatism continued because of its two senators and because of its Republican Governor Harold W. Handley, who was elected in 1956. It also was the birthplace of the John Birch Society, founded by Robert Welch, a Massachusetts candy manufacturer, in Indianapolis in 1958. Welch, more conservative than Jenner, not only attacked Eisenhower but also condemned both political parties as too liberal and called for a return

261

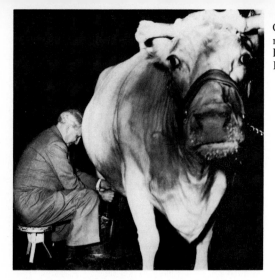

Governor Henry F. Schricker, milking a cow at the International Dairy Exposition, October 9, 1950.

Master Sergeant William Wynkoop, Indianapolis, leaving the Army at Camp Atterbury, 1951.

to a republican rather than a democratic government.

The intense conservatism symbolized by the John Birch Society was a reaction to the events of the 1950s, just as the Klan was a reaction to the events of the 1920s. The old Hoosier society seemed to be in the process of being replaced by a new society less dedicated to the small, personal institutions and more representative of large, impersonal ones. The conservative rhetoric reflected a concern over a society that seemed to become more homogeneous and national rather than heterogeneous and local. Despite the attempts to hold back the clock, those who resisted change were subtly undermined by technological changes which made Indiana less independent and more similar to the other states.

One such technological change was the advent of commercial television, the principle of which had been known since the 1920s, but the practice of which was new. In 1949 two television stations began to broadcast in Indiana; they were WTTV Bloomington, channel 4, and WFBM (now WRTV) Indianapolis, channel 6. They were joined later by channels 8 and 13. Because of the huge amount of capital required to build and operate a station and the limited number of licenses available from the FCC, television broadcasting concentrated in the large urban centers. The most watched stations were the network affiliates; these could be found in Indianapolis or Chicago or Louisville or Cincinnati and not in New Castle or Peru or Plymouth. Since the large urban areas controlled the medium, attention centered on events occurring in them and centralized viewers' information sources. National news competed with Indianapolis news, and programs filmed in New York or Hollywood far outnumbered those produced locally.

Not that familiar faces and accents failed to appear on the tube. Among those Hoosier TV personalities of the pioneering days were Red Skelton

Housing for families of soldiers at Camp Atterbury during the Korean War.

Playing checkers at the Nashville House, Nashville.

Main Street, Madison, 1959.

Indiana University School of Medicine, Indianapolis, was 50 years old in 1953.

NCAA basketball champions at Kansas City: Indiana University team, with Coach Branch McCracken, after defeating the University of Kansas 69–68, March 18, 1953.

and Herb Shriner. Born in Vincennes, Red went on the vaudeville and burlesque circuit at an early age, and then had a successful radio and movie career. His humor, based on pantomime and hyperbole, never seemed to betray his Hoosier origin. He could as easily have come from Missouri or Ohio. Not so with the Ohio-born Herb Shriner, whose forte was telling tales of rural Indiana life. In the 50s these stories seemed quaint, nostalgic, and characteristic of a society which had vanished. Other Hoosiers, then and now, have succeeded in the movies or in radio and television, such as Phil Harris, born in Linton, who appeared for many years on the Jack Benny Show; James Dean, born in Fairmount, who remains a cult figure many years after his death; and Jane Pauley, born in Indianapolis, who is co-host of the Today show. They, like Red, however, were not identifiably Hoosier.

Another homogenizing instrument was the continuing boom of the automobile after World War II. The Hoosier love affair with the car was nowhere more evident than in the new phenomenon, the two-car family. Instead of automobile sales being directly tied to new family formation, half came from families adding another vehicle to the one they already had. The two-car family resulted from the growth of the suburbs and the perceived need for one car for commuting to work and another one for the running of errands, taking children to school, or going to work in another area. It also came about because of new, car-oriented businesses. Among these were drive-in movies, restaurants, banks, and shopping centers.

Drive-in restaurants were not a new phenomenon, but the ones of the 1930s and 1940s were locally owned. Like the drive-in movies and banks which came later, they varied from community to community. In the 1950s the character of drive-in restaurants began to change. Instead of just eating at Knobby's in Indianapolis or at Custer's Last Stand in Marion, Hoosiers could go to the new fast-food place, McDonald's, which had originated in California and had spread nationwide through the merchandising genius of Ray Kroc which blended local ownership and national advertising. The familiar golden arches began to challenge smaller, less profitable operations. As a result, small local restaurants often faded away. The same kind of standardization occurred in the motel industry. Holiday Inns, begun in the 1950s, extended operations from its place of birth, Memphis, Tennessee, to all the states. Downtown hotels and small motels now felt the same pressures their restaurant neighbors had. Increasingly, all but the smallest Hoosier towns resembled each other; each had a McDonald's and a Holiday Inn.

Another development was the shopping center, usually located at a distance from the center of town, on the periphery. The first in the United States was built in Kansas City in the 1920s, but the great era of shopping plazas or malls was not to come until the decade of the 1950s. In 1953, for example, developers began building Glendale in Indianapolis. Other Hoosier cities had begun either to build plazas or to have plans for them.

The growth of the suburban shopping center helped accelerate the demise of downtown business and the growth of standardization. The enterprises found in the shopping malls were usually the large chains, either national or state, such as Penney's, Sears', Block's, or Ayres'. This meant that the new stores were not being built downtown; indeed, in many medium-sized towns the downtown stores closed and reopened in the shopping mall.

The automobile hastened the demise of the small towns as well. Now persons living in these areas could much more easily reach large stores without having to go to the center of the city. Gas was cheap, driving was fun, and highways were getting better. In 1956 the Indiana Toll Road opened, the first superhighway built in the state.

The *Majestic,* Indiana University's showboat, on the Ohio River.

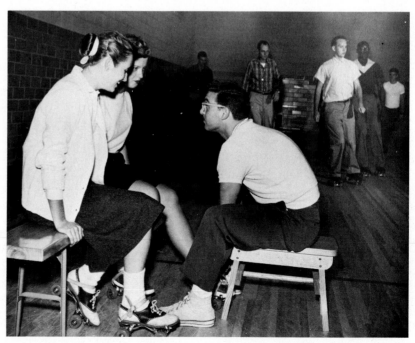

Purdue University coeds have their roller skates adjusted at the Co-Roe Gymnasium, October 31, 1957.

Woman power on an Indiana farm.

Carol Fehd, Warrick County, makes a cake while her sister Linda looks on, June 9, 1958.

But it was not to remain the sole road of this type, for in the same year Congress passed a Highway Aid Act for the construction of a system of interstate highways to be finished by 1972. The act provided that the federal government would pay 90 percent of construction costs but, for the first time, would also specify the locations of the roads. As a consequence, the interstates were designed to go near or through cities such as Terre Haute, Richmond, Indianapolis, Fort Wayne, and Lafayette, but not to many others perhaps equally important.

Revealing the optimism over the future of the automobile, the interstate highway system did spell trouble for towns not connected with it or for businesses located on such older highways as U.S. 30 or 40. It did make possible the growth of bedroom communities as workers moved farther and farther into the country, secure in the knowledge that they could drive to work and that they could escape higher city taxes.

Increasingly, the future of the older Hoosier cities seemed problematical. Indiana's industrial plant had aged, its heavy reliance on such products as iron, steel, and automobiles made it subject to obsolescence and foreign competition. The newer industries such as electronics and aerospace went to Houston or Orlando, attracted either by the warmer climate or by economic considerations. Within the state, the trend toward consolidation continued. Increasingly, national corporations absorbed local units into their systems. This could provide more capital for expansion and modernization; on the other hand, it could mean a decision to close might be made by individuals far removed from the life of the communities affected.

A glum picture of Hoosier cities in the 1950s appears in Irving Leibowitz's *My Indiana* (1964). Leibowitz cataloged the problems as he saw them: Terre Haute had not grown substantially since the 1920s, partly because of the trouble in the coal mines, but also because of the lack of leadership; Gary was corrupt, dominated by bad politicians and politically inept managers of steel companies; Muncie was a shabby town run by the Ball family; Anderson was "not as bad as its downtown looks. It's worse"; Evansville was dying in 1956—Servel had closed, International Harvester had moved to Paducah, Kentucky, and Chrysler had shifted its Plymouth assembly plant to St. Louis County, Missouri.

Despite Leibowitz's gloom, he found bright spots. Evansville had come back, thanks to the efforts of Mayor Vance Hartke (although most of its citizens believed he had not exerted himself at all) and to the sales of Metrecal, a diet aid, made by Mead Johnson. Fort Wayne, labeled the cosmopolitan and sophisticated city in the state by Leibowitz, was enjoying economic growth with International Harvester, General Electric, and Central Soya; and Indianapolis was prospering, increasing its influence and hold on Indiana life. On balance, however, Leibowitz's view of Hoosier cities was not a happy one.

The rural landscape was also changing, again in the direction of consolidation into larger units. Evidence of this could be found in both education and farming. By 1950 almost all of the one-room township schools, "the little red schoolhouses," had vanished to be replaced by consolidated elementary schools. Now the push was to consolidate these elementary and high schools into larger and larger units. Advocates of consolidation argued that larger schools could offer expanded curricula and special opportunities not available in smaller ones. Few rural schools could afford full-time music or art teachers, let alone the wide range of science and mathematics courses now in vogue. The consolidation had two consequences. Because schools now had student populations more and more distant from them, schoolbuses became more common; and because small-town life often centered in the school and its times of ritual togetherness—holiday

Crispus Attucks basketball team, Indianapolis, won the state high school championship, at Butler Fieldhouse, March 19, 1955. Ray Crowe was the coach.

Corn detasseling was a part-time summer job for high school boys in the 1950s, but by the 1970s high school girls were also doing it.

266

Alfred Kinsey, zoologist and director of the Institute for Sex Research, Indiana University.

City Hall and the *Post-Tribune* building, Gary. Steel mills are in the background.

Strikers on the picket line, Gary, 1952.

programs, basketball games, and festivals—the demise of the township school decreased community unity.

One reason for school consolidation was the continued depopulation of farms in the 1950s due to the growth of larger units. The number of full-time farmers decreased, they grew older, and their children went into other occupations. The trend toward specialization continued as equipment grew increasingly expensive. Larger tractors meant the need for more land to make their use economical, but investments in tractors and land meant no capital to invest in hogs, or dairy cattle, or poultry. The self-sufficient farm now was the exception rather than the rule.

As a result, homesteads which had once been occupied now were vacant, farmhouses were boarded up and barnlots overgrown with weeds. Because of the switch to grain farming or to confinement of livestock, many farmers no longer considered fences either necessary or desirable, allowing the once taut-woven and barbed wire fences to sag and the fence posts to rot or rust away. The growing use of insecticides, herbicides, and fertilizer made possible the continued planting of fields to soybeans or corn, with the result that fewer fields of wheat, oats, alfalfa, or clover intervened between the fields of corn and soybeans. The outbuildings once considered essential for farming—the barn to house horses and cattle along with the hay to feed them, the hog pen, and the chicken house—slowly crumbled to be replaced by the pole barn constructed of wood poles and metal panels which housed the necessary machinery or which sheltered the livestock. The whole process of replacement and change was ironic, for the very concentration of capital which made large-scale farming possible and which required such effort to attain produced a landscape which had fewer signs of human presence—fences, barns, houses—than that of earlier, smaller-scale enterprise.

267

Emily Kimbrough, of Muncie.

Ross Lockridge, Jr., of Bloomington.

Just as the trend toward larger economic units and a national rather than a state or regional audience characterized Hoosier farms, businesses, and television stations, so too did the nationalizing and centralizing of America's intellectual life change the careers of Indiana-born writers and creative artists. Hoosiers did not cease to assume cultural leadership, but they often no longer lived in Indiana, and their books came from presses in Boston or New York rather than from those in Indianapolis. Hoosiers were not writing less, nor were there fewer interested in the literary arts, but they were less identifiably Hoosiers.

Among the earliest of such persons to come into prominence were two women, Emily Kimbrough and Jessamyn West. Both were late bloomers as book writers and both utilized memories of an earlier Indiana to inform their works. Emily Kimbrough was born into a prominent Muncie family and worked as an editor for the *Ladies' Home Journal* as well as a Hollywood screenwriter before collaborating with Cornelia Otis Skinner on a light hearted account of the adventures of two young women, *Our Hearts Were Young and Gay*. Two of her other books, *How Dear to My Heart* (1944) and *The Innocents from Indiana* (1950) recall her youth at the turn-of-the-century in Indiana and her subsequent removal to Chicago. Even more famous than Kimbrough was Jessamyn West, a native of Jennings County and a cousin of Richard Nixon. West, like Kimbrough, was taken from the state as a child and later worked as a Hollywood scriptwriter. The most famous of her many books so far has been *The Friendly Persuasion* (1956), a tale based on Quaker life in Indiana during the era of the Civil War. West won an Indiana Author's Day Award in 1956 for her *Love, Death and the Ladies Drill Team* (1955), but her most recognized works have been her historical novels, such as *The Massacre at Fall Creek* (1974), which detailed the incident which happened at Pendleton in pioneer Indiana.

Robert Borkenstein, in uniform, demonstrates the use of his Breathalyzer.

Anton (Tony) Hulman of Terre Haute, owner of the Indianapolis Motor Speedway.

Kurt Vonnegut, Jr., of Indianapolis, with Governor Otis Bowen and Dean Wilfred C. Bain of the School of Music, Indiana University.

"Welcome Home" parade in Fort Wayne for Herb Shriner, who promoted Indiana in his radio and television appearances.

Carl Erskine, of Anderson, Brooklyn Dodgers pitcher. His 1953 record: 20 games won, 6 lost.

Another Hoosier who utilized Indiana's past in a creative way was Ross Lockridge, Jr. Born in Bloomington, the son of a Hoosier educator, writer, and historian, Lockridge graduated from and taught at Indiana University before going to Boston to teach at Simmons College. While in the East, he wrote the novel which attempted to capture the essence of Hoosier experience. It was *Raintree County* (1948), later made into a movie. Disappointed over its reception, Lockridge committed suicide the year of its publication.

Younger artists were just beginning their work in the 1950s, while their older peers were either at the top of their careers or fading. Among the newcomers were Kurt Vonnegut, Dan Wakefield, and Ned Rorem.

Vonnegut was born in Indianapolis of a family of German descent who operated a hardware store. After service in World War II and study and work in Chicago, Vonnegut turned to free-lance writing. Originally dubbed science fiction, his first book, *Player Piano,* appeared in 1952 and was followed by other works such as *God Bless You, Mr. Rosewater* (1965) and *Slaughterhouse-Five* (1969). By the sixties, Vonnegut was no longer just a cult figure for science fiction fans but had gained national recognition as a serious writer.

Wakefield, also Indianapolis-born, began as a journalist after graduating from Columbia University. His first books were nonfiction descriptions of the plight of Puerto Ricans and of the residents of Spanish Harlem in the late 1950s. By the late 1960s he was writing fiction. His *Going All the Way* (1970) is perhaps the best description of the decade of the 50s. In it, Wakefield recounts the story of two Korean veterans who return to Indianapolis after their tours of duty. He followed this success with such novels as *Starting Over* (1973), *All Her Children* (1976), and *Home Free* (1977).

Ned Rorem is a composer first and a writer second, but he shines in both roles. Born in

Richmond, Rorem lived in France and Morocco after obtaining his conservatory training. Returning to the United States, he became a noted composer of serious music and a writer of titillating books. His *The Paris Diary of Ned Rorem* (1966) portrayed the scandalous underlife of the famous and near-famous in that metropolis, and his *New York Diary* (1967) did the same for New York City.

The moral to this seems simple. Indiana continued to produce individuals of rare talent, but these persons found opportunities greater elsewhere. The strength of a regional cultural center was drained to bolster that of a national culture.

In another aspect of popular culture, sports, opportunities have also been found elsewhere. In basketball, the years after the Second World War were golden ones, producing legendary teams and legendary coaches. Two of the most famous coaches were Branch McCracken and John Wooden. Branch McCracken was born in Monrovia and attended Indiana University, where he was an All-American. Following professional play, he became the basketball coach at Ball State Teachers College. Returning to Indiana University in 1938, he coached there—with time out for naval service during the war—until 1965, winning the National Collegiate Athletic Association (NCAA) championship twice, in 1940 and 1953.

Another Hoosier basketball player became even more famous. John Wooden, who was born in Martinsville, lettered at guard at Purdue, where he was named to three consecutive All-American teams. Wooden coached high school basketball before becoming coach at Indiana State Teachers College. His main claim to fame, however, was the record he compiled at UCLA after he left Indiana. He made UCLA a national champion twelve times and always a threat. Like McCracken, Wooden typified the Hoosier dedication to roundball.

Only after the stress of the 1960s does the decade of the 50s seem peaceful. The process of centralization caused dislocation and pain. Although the period was prosperous, there were pockets of poverty. Although new automobiles were a necessity now, the cost of new roads and new facilities was high. In general, most Hoosiers believed it was a decade of progress, but if pressed, they recall some of the problems and tensions which also characterized a decade of change.

Sherwood Egbert of Studebaker and Raymond Loewy with the 1963 Avanti.

Harold S. Vance, president of Studebaker, and workers admire the first car of Studebaker's second century, February 1952. In the background are a Studebaker wagon and the 1902 Studebaker electric.

A Troubled Decade

College students, protesting tuition increases, demonstrate at the Statehouse, Indianapolis, May 7, 1969.

Tᴴᴱ ᴅᴇᴄᴀᴅᴇ ᴏꜰ ᴛʜᴇ sɪxᴛɪᴇs, ʟɪᴋᴇ ᴛʜᴇ ᴅᴇᴄ-ᴀᴅᴇ ᴏꜰ ᴛʜᴇ ꜰɪꜰᴛɪᴇs, ʜᴀs ᴇᴀʀɴᴇᴅ ᴀ sᴏ-ʙʀɪQᴜᴇᴛ ᴡʜɪᴄʜ ɪs ɴᴏᴛ ᴇɴᴛɪʀᴇʟʏ ꜰᴀɪʀ. Social unrest, protest marches, and effigy burning were dramatically portrayed by the media. Yet a judicious look, taken from a vantage point of ten years, reveals that under the surface there was much continuity despite the high decibels of the protest marches and rock music.

Indiana voted for Nixon in 1960, which was no surprise or change. Hannah Milhous Nixon had come from Indiana; her Hoosier roots provided the Quakerism her son frequently mentioned. But his victory did not mean that the Republicans won complete control in the state. Matthew Welsh won the governorship by the second closest margin in Indiana history, but he had to work with a Republican General Assembly. By 1962, however, the Democrats had begun to assert themselves again. In that year Birch Bayh succeeded in upsetting Homer Capehart in his bid for his fourth term as senator. In four short years Indiana had gone from a state which had not had a Democratic senator for 20 years to one which had two.

Johnson's landslide victory over Goldwater in 1964 was duplicated in Indiana as the Democrats won the General Assembly and the governor's chair for their candidate, Roger D. Branigin. Vance Hartke also returned to the Senate. The domination of state government came at an opportune time for the Democrats, as federal judges had mandated that the General Assembly redistrict the state in 1963. Although the revision of the Indiana Constitution in 1921 required reapportionment every six years, no General Assembly had ever fulfilled the requirement until the Democratic one of 1965.

Because of the reapportionment and political developments after 1965, Indiana returned to what seemed to be a more nearly two-party situation. Neither party was able to obtain the clear-cut advantage the Republicans had earlier enjoyed. In

George Wallace for president poster, 1968.

1968, when Nixon swept the state, the Republican candidate for governor, Edgar Whitcomb, won and the General Assembly was Republican again.

If state politics were the only key to the 1960s, the decade would have to be labeled a return to what many would consider normal activity. However, larger issues such as civil rights and the war in Vietnam came to the fore. The problem of civil rights had not concerned many Hoosiers until it was thrust upon them by the events of the 1960s. A brief summary of past practice will illustrate the problem.

Although there were no laws which permitted segregated facilities in the state, with the exception of those involving schools, prejudice and tradition combined to make selected private and public institutions off-limits to blacks. Nor did court action help very much. As a consequence, segregation and discrimination were common. Movie houses could refuse admission to blacks, as in Gary until 1913, or require seating in separate sections, as in Muncie until 1934 and Evansville until 1948. The city of Gary allowed blacks the use of Riverside Park, but only on a segregated basis; and the state of Indiana did not permit blacks to swim in pools at state parks or to integrate the beaches at Dunes State Park prior to World War II. Sports were also segregated; all-black schools such as Crispus Attucks were excluded from participation in contests sponsored by the Indiana High School Athletic Association until 1942.

The war years were ones of racial tension in Indiana. An example of the kinds of problems can be found in a Muncie incident of 1943. A black man was accused of attacking a white woman and robbing her; a white mob determined to search out the individual and marched into a black section of town. The local authorities did not disperse the crowd, and only when blacks threatened armed resistance did the mob members go home. The governor sent state police to restore order and even considered placing Muncie under martial law.

Mayor Richard G. Hatcher of Gary with Senator Robert F. Kennedy, 1968.

Hoosier Democrats: Senator Vance Hartke, Senator Birch Bayh, Governor Matthew Welsh; standing, Robert Rock, Marshall F. Kiser.

272

Virgil I. (Gus) Grissom, of Mitchell, the second American in space, July 21, 1961; and commander of the first Gemini flight, March 23, 1965. He was chosen to command Apollo I, but on January 27, 1967, he, along with Edward White and Roger Chaffee, died in a fire in their capsule.

The space capsule in which Grissom and John Young made the Gemini flight, in the Virgil I. Grissom State Memorial, Spring Mill State Park, Mitchell.

KC–135 Stratotankers at Bunker Hill Air Force Base, Armed Forces Day, May 21, 1966.

The immediate postwar years showed progress. Increased pressure on the part of civil rights activists, black and white, led to the gradual ending of the de facto segregation. Purdue first admitted black women in 1946 when pressured by the governor; Indiana University, although it had enrolled black students since the Civil War, opened its dormitories to black men in 1948 and to black women in 1950. Ball State Teachers College and Indiana State Teachers College also dropped their restrictions about the same time. In 1949 Indianapolis General Hospital ended its practice of segregating its wards. In 1956 Evansville and Muncie opened their municipal pools to black swimmers who had pushed for admission.

The increased pressure of blacks to achieve full equality came from their own consciousness and from the recognition by whites that blacks were becoming more and more numerous in the state. Moreover, this increased population concentrated in six of the largest Hoosier cities—Indianapolis, Fort Wayne, Gary, East Chicago, South Bend, and Evansville—which contained 80 percent of all blacks in the state.

As a result, these cities had a greater proportion of black citizens. By 1960, 20 percent of the Indianapolis population was black, while 38 percent of the Gary population was black. Moreover, the blacks remained in the older central business district because they could not move to the more affluent suburbs. Since the suburbs grew faster than the central city after World War II (in Indianapolis, for example, the central city grew 11.5 percent in the decade ending in 1960), the downtown areas became more and more black. The exodus to the suburbs had already begun.

This had several consequences. Because of lower income and latent prejudice, blacks tended to live in more crowded, older homes which required greater upkeep and which were in deteriorated neighborhoods. Because the black population was more fertile and had more children, those children

273

Open hearth furnace, U.S. Steel, Gary Works.

began to constitute an even larger proportion of the school population and schools which were once all white now were becoming more and more black. Because of the social services necessary for a population which lacked money, housing, and education, the need for tax dollars increased. But the people and businesses most able to pay those taxes had moved to the suburbs. Those businesses and industries remaining in the center of the city tended to be older ones with less need for new workers, and hence unable to furnish the jobs necessary for high employment. Moreover, the new jobs created in the 1960s were in the service sector rather than in the industrial one and required education and skills not easily obtained by deprived persons. The result was a potentially explosive situation as Hoosiers faced the possibility that increasingly their major cities might have more and more blacks. The black displacement of whites in both residential areas and in schools led to friction as competition for places to live and go to school ensued.

The 1960s were a decade of urban riots in the United States when cities such as Los Angeles, Chicago, Detroit, New York, and Washington witnessed major disturbances with looting, burning, and deaths characterizing all of them. Indiana had no such outbreaks, though the rising tensions stimulated by media reports of happenings nationally did cause Hoosiers to wonder if their cities or neighborhoods were about to explode. In most cases, however, the rumors of riots, assaults, and snipings which periodically swept Hoosier cities proved to be false.

The years of 1967 and 1968 were the most tense ones on the racial scene. In October 1967, at Southside High School in Muncie, fighting broke out between black and white students over whether to call the athletic teams "The Rebels" and to fly the Confederate flag. Several students were hospitalized and a policeman suffered a broken arm. In April 1968, when Martin Luther King was assassinated in

U.S. Steel ore carrier, *D.G. Kerr,* unloading, Gary, 1962.

Bethlehem Steel Corporation, Burns Harbor plant.

Twenty-ton capacity rope trolley unloaders, Bethlehem Steel, Burns Harbor.

Main Street, Madison, about 1965.

Downtown Indianapolis, early 1960s.

Main Street, Evansville. It was later converted to an outdoor walking mall.

Memphis, the nation was swept by a series of reactive riots. By coincidence, Robert Kennedy was in Indiana campaigning for the Democratic nomination for president and is credited with preventing disturbances in Indianapolis. Two incidents in the summer of 1968 showed how quick people were to assume that a dreaded confrontation had begun. In Gary a rumor started that blacks had sniped at police after two members of a gang had been arrested for allegedly raping a girl. The rumor had it that six persons had been hit and that Chief of Police James Hilton had been a target. Upon investigation, the riot turned out to have been the conjunction of two separate incidents. A fireman had been shot earlier by a drunk, and shots may have been fired in the air after the arrest of the two gang members. There were no snipers. That same summer in Evansville another rumor had it that snipers had fired eight shots at the police. Again, when the facts came out, only one shot could be substantiated.

The racial tensions made Hoosiers edgy and the Vietnam War added to the problem. As the war grew more intense, the protests against it mounted. These protests centered on university and college campuses in the state. Higher education boomed in the 1960s, aided by the fact that male college students could be exempt from active duty as long as they were in school. This led to resentment by those not enrolled and to charges that resistance to the war was for selfish purposes.

The protests against racial inequality and against the war converted some older persons and radicalized some younger ones. For the latter, protests were not enough and the belief grew that the whole society was at fault and should be overthrown. While these few persons never posed a serious threat to the state or nation, they added to the general unease.

Typical of those who chose this road were William and Emily Harris, who helped found the

SLA (Symbionese Liberation Army). Harris's hegira is instructive. Born at Fort Sill, Oklahoma, during World War II when his father was serving in the Army, Harris appeared to be a solidly middle-class person. He enrolled at Indiana University in 1963, joined the Sigma Alpha Epsilon fraternity, and completed two years of college before volunteering for duty with the Marines in Vietnam. Radicalized by his overseas experience, Harris returned to become vocal in his opposition to the war. He married and, after receiving his bachelor's and master's degrees, moved to California, where the SLA became notorious when it kidnapped Patty Hearst in 1974.

The general uneasiness of the times obscured the forces at work in Indiana to institute far-reaching changes. These changes involved increased political activity by blacks and attempts to restructure municipal government in order to come to grips with the problems of Hoosier cities.

In the autumn of 1967, which followed a summer when over 100 American cities had experienced violence in one form or another, voters in Gary elected the first black mayor of a "medium-sized" city in Indiana and in the United States. The man who accomplished this feat was Richard D. Hatcher, a lawyer who, by his victory, was to become a symbol of black political achievements.

The election Hatcher won was a close one for, though Gary was a traditionally Democratic area, the Democratic county chairman, John D. Krupa, did not support him. Neither did he garner much support from the Gary newspapers. Convinced his opponent was about to steal the election, Hatcher appealed to the U.S. Department of Justice, which investigated and found that the names of 5,000 black voters had been struck and the names of nonexistent white ones added to the voter rolls. So great was the reaction to the disclosure and to the possibility of violence in the election that the governor called in 4,000 National Guardsmen to Gary to

Twin tornadoes at Dunlap, Elkhart County, on Palm Sunday, April 11, 1965, at 6:30 P.M.

Tornado aftermath, Martinsburg, Washington County, April 6, 1974.

Paul D. (Tony) Hinkle, football, basketball, and baseball coach and athletic director, Butler University.

Indiana University swimming team, with Coaches Hobie Billingsley and James A. (Doc) Counsilman, 1960.

Purdue University football team, with Head Coach Jack Mollenkopf (second row, right), that won the Rose Bowl game, January 1, 1967, by defeating the University of Southern California 14–13.

forestall any disturbance on election night. Hatcher won: his victory came from black voters, and some 4,000 whites. His opponent, Joseph B. Radigan, on the other hand, received the votes of 1,000 blacks.

Hatcher's platform for renewal was that the first key to success in Gary, which was now more black than white, was money. The second was black unity. The first key started to come to Gary from the federal government, which was controlled by a Republican president, Richard Nixon. The second was to come, Hatcher argued, when blacks abandoned the false goal of integration and concentrated instead upon the control of the areas in which they lived. This meant living in the central city and not moving to the suburbs. Hatcher, however, had no grandiose illusions about the extent to which this would alter the life of blacks in Gary. As he said:

> There is much talk about black control of the ghetto. What does that mean? I am now mayor of a city of roughly 90,000 black people but we do not control the possibilities of jobs for them, or money for their schools, or state-funded social services. These things are in the hands of the United States Steel Corporation and the County Department of Welfare of the State of Indiana. Will the poor in Gary's worst slums be helped because the pawnshop owner is black, not white?

Hatcher's victory and years in office have shown that white fears of black control were unfounded. It also showed that city government is essentially conservative and difficult to change and that economic problems persist regardless of who is in charge.

Another first in municipal government occurred in Indianapolis under its Republican mayor, Richard G. Lugar. This was Unigov, the annexation of suburban communities into an enlarged metropolitan government. The move was an attempt to address the problems of a shrinking tax base caused by the movement of citizens to the suburbs. If the suburbs were included in the city,

Frederick L. Hovde, president,
Purdue University, 1946–71.

The Rev. Theodore M. Hesburgh, CSC,
president, University of Notre Dame,
1952–   , walking on campus with students.

the tax base would be increased. However, Unigov also had the effect of diluting black votes concentrated in the center city, and of increasing Republican ones. The Unigov solution was just the opposite of the Gary one.

Richard Lugar became mayor of Indianapolis in 1968, the same year Hatcher took office in Gary. Lugar's mayoral campaign was a vigorous one which featured intensive campaigning in black districts as well as white. Lugar won 10 to 15 percent more black votes than the Republicans had garnered in the preceding election year and this, with white votes, enabled him to defeat incumbent mayor Barton.

Although Lugar had mentioned Unigov in his campaign, he had not emphasized it. After taking office, he did encourage an Inter-Governmental Policy Committee to draft a bill for the General Assembly. Submitted to the 1969 General Assembly, which was Republican-dominated, the bill passed despite the opposition of both the *Indianapolis News* and the *Indianapolis Star,* which disliked the increased power the measure gave to the mayor. Democrats and some suburban whites spoke against the bills during committee hearings but there was no unified black opposition, although black representatives did attack the bill on the grounds it would dilute the vote of Indianapolis blacks. After passage of the Unigov bill, Indianapolis officially began metropolitan government on January 1, 1970. It was the only one of the twelve cities in the United States which consolidated city and county government in the past one hundred years without submitting the proposal to a public referendum.

The consolidation did have consequences. It enlarged the tax base for urban services; it diminished the overlapping governmental agencies of city and county; and it provided more services to sub-

Herman B Wells, acting president, Indiana University, 1937–38,
president, 1938–62, university chancellor, 1962–   , with his
successor, Elvis J. Stahr, Jr., in 1962.

Indiana University football team, with Coach John Pont, after
winning at Michigan State, November 11, 1967. The Big Ten
co-champions lost to Southern California 14–3, in the Rose Bowl.

278

Hoosier basketball fans fill Hinkle Fieldhouse, Butler University, to watch state high school tournament games.

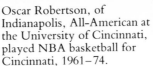

Oscar Robertson, of Indianapolis, All-American at the University of Cincinnati, played NBA basketball for Cincinnati, 1961–74.

Beginning of the 500-mile race, 1965.

Parking and traffic cause logistical problems at 500-mile race, May 30, 1964.

urban areas. It also made Indianapolis more Republican, and it laid the foundation for a continuing problem with the schools in the 1970s. The Unigov bill did not include the public schools of the surrounding area in the consolidation because sponsors feared that this would arouse too much opposition. As a result, continued litigation over the relations between Indianapolis and suburban schools plagued the next decade.

The 1960s ended with demonstrations and protests still common. Indiana had survived the crucial decade with her institutions intact and with little structural change in society. The political changes which occurred were not accomplished by revolution, but by the ballot box. The black clamor for greater equality had eased and, beyond the rhetoric, real changes had occurred. Hoosiers were more tolerant, more willing to accord full participation in their institutions to all citizens, and were trying to solve some of the problems of black and white relations. The task of constructing a more prosperous and fair society which would provide more jobs and economic opportunities remained, as it does for each generation.

Ann Sidlauskas, Indiana University student and National Intercollegiate Coed Billiards champion, 1962.

Representative William G. Bray and Patricia Abrassart, queen of Vincennes Watermelon Festival, give a watermelon to Speaker Sam Rayburn, August 25, 1960.

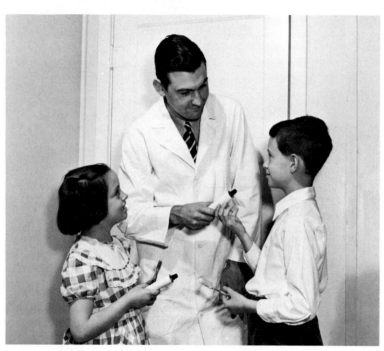

Joseph C. Muhler, D.D.S., with two children in the dental study program, Indiana University.

Rosemary Murphy, Mrs. America, comes home to Kentland, June 15, 1960. With her are her sons Mike and Steve.

Groups protesting the war in Vietnam and protesting the protest, Fort Wayne, November 14, 1969.

Students protesting tuition increases outside the Statehouse, Indianapolis, May 7, 1969.

United Grain Farmers of America made an overnight stop at Brazil on their Tractor Drive to Washington, D.C., 1969.

LOVE, the famous sculpture by Robert Indiana, on the grounds of the Indianapolis Museum of Art.

Zoe Libera at the demonstration protesting production of three millionth bomb for Vietnam War, outside Naval Ammunition Depot, Crane, February 27, 1969.

Woman at parking meter, surrounded by about 350 students in front of the Monroe County Courthouse, Bloomington.

Children in demonstration at NAD, Crane, February 27, 1969.

Today

Agriculture is an important part of the Indiana economy.

THE DECADE OF THE 1970s IS OVER, BUT THE ASSESSMENT OF ITS MEANING HAS JUST BEGUN. AS ALWAYS, THE DECADE IN MANY ways resembled the earlier ones from which it sprang.

Politically, the situation in Indiana resembled that of the 60s in that neither party was able to dominate the state completely. In the off-year election of 1970, Vance Hartke kept his seat in the U.S. Senate by barely beating off the challenge of Republican Richard Roudebush; and in 1974 Birch Bayh defeated the attempt by Richard Lugar to move from the position of mayor to that of U.S. senator. On the other hand, Nixon swept Indiana in the presidential election of 1972 and Otis Bowen, a Bremen physician and state legislator, frustrated the hopes of former Democratic Governor Matthew Welsh of duplicating Governor Schricker's feat of two nonconsecutive terms in office. In 1976 Bowen won again, to become the first governor of Indiana in modern times to succeed himself. Richard Lugar, in the same year, became a senator, defeating Vance Hartke, whose fabled luck finally ran out. Gerald Ford also carried the state. But Indiana was still not a completely Republican state as Democrats and Republicans swapped control of the houses of the General Assembly, neither side being quite able to overwhelm the other.

It is difficult to determine what has happened in Hoosier politics. Was it safe to say that the Republican control which seemed so much a part of the early twentieth century was gone forever? Was Indiana to return to being a swing state as it was one hundred years ago? Or was the situation indicative of a movement away from party politics toward single-issue politics? No issue since the Depression and the New Deal had polarized Hoosier politics. On civil rights, for example, Senators Bayh and Hartke were supportive, but so also were Governor Bowen and Senator Lugar.

On the local level, politics was much the same.

Governor Otis R. Bowen,
M.D., with Lieutenant
Governor Robert D. Orr,
served as Indiana's governor
from 1973–81.

In Gary, Hatcher seemed the perennial mayor, winning elections with ease and continuing to search for means to accomplish the rejuvenation of the city. In 1978, after ten years in office, he revealed his Genesis Plan. The keystone of the plan was a Civic Center to contain historical museums and exhibition halls, meeting rooms, a sports arena, and such support facilities as restaurants and snack bars. Other features included opening the defunct Holiday Inn as the Gary Sheraton, building a 300-car parking facility and a transportation terminal, and, in general, sprucing up the city. Hatcher's goal was to restore the cultural excitement of Gary and to further its economic development by making it a convention center for blacks. The plan was ambitious, but except for the proposed concentration on black business was not unconventional.

Indeed, the development in Indianapolis could have served as a kind of pattern for Gary. Under the administrations of Richard Lugar and his successor, William Hudnut, also a Republican, the construction of Market Square Arena provided a place calculated to attract sports fans to the city to see high school, college, or professional sports. Similarly, the construction of the Convention Center, as well as the Indianapolis Hyatt-Regency and the Hilton, brought more conventions into the city.

The question of the shape and destiny of Hoosier cities remained unanswered in the 1970s, but trends begun in the 1950s continued. The downtown centers increasingly displayed vacant spaces where once flourishing businesses existed. Sometimes these spaces were parking lots or mini-parks, but often they were not used at all. The density of the central city had diminished along with the hustle and bustle of shoppers who had meant prosperity to the area. The result was a downtown retail area which was less and less prosperous. A few retail specialties—jewelry stores, drugstores, flower shops, gift shops, and shoe shops—remained but increasingly the downtown depart-

Mayor Richard Hatcher marches with the Rev. Jesse Jackson in Gary.

Richard (Red) Skelton, of Vincennes, and Mayor Richard G. Lugar of Indianapolis received honorary degrees, May 11, 1975, from President Alan C. Rankin (left) of Indiana State University.

United States Gypsum
Company, Shoals.

World's largest smokeless fluid bed
incinerator, Standard Oil Company of
Indiana, Whiting, 1972.

Aerial view of the Indianapolis Power and Light Company plant.

National Gypsum Company, Gold Bond Building Products
Division, Shoals.

Worker in gypsum mine, Gold Bond Building Products Division.

285

Stone carver works on a Salem limestone block at a limestone mill near Bloomington.

Surface coal mining in Indiana.

Coal miners in AMAX Coal's deep mine under the Wabash River.

Limestone Quarry, near Oolitic.

Hydroplane, Madison Regatta.

Friendly Cafe, Bloomingdale.

Zaharako's Confectionery opened its doors, October 20, 1900, in Columbus. It is still operated by members of the family, Lewie and Manuel Zaharako.

ment stores, once the anchor of retail business, either closed their doors or retracted their operations as they were eclipsed by branches in suburban shopping centers.

Another trend of the 1950s that continued into the 1970s, which had profound effects upon the shape of Hoosier cities, was the continued presence of automobiles and their concomitant support facilities, particularly highways. The Interstate Highway system was to have been completed in 1972; it was not, but almost all of the projected mileage had been finished by the end of the decade. As originally conceived, the highways were not tied in with the existing city streets or transit systems. Not until the 1960s was any thought given to the possible impact of the superhighways on cities. As a result, as these highways came through cities such as Indianapolis, the primary criterion for location was economic, not social. The engineers planned the highways to go through the area where land was cheapest, often splitting existing communities.

The omnipresent automobile, however, came to be regarded as an asset as planners tried out stratagems to revive downtown areas. As better highways made longer commuting trips possible, these planners came to believe that middle-class persons might be attracted back to downtown areas if facilities for their cars were plentiful and if streets were widened and traffic patterns rationalized. In every Hoosier town of any size, parking lots and garages, private and municipal, proliferated.

Another way in which planners hoped to improve the appearance of Hoosier cities was through urban renewal. Although the first act which proposed to provide federal funds for the clearance of slum areas under municipal direction passed in 1949, the full impact of urban renewal came along in the 1960s. Urban renewal had at least two facets. The first was the razing of dilapidated buildings, and the second was building new ones to replace those destroyed. No one could deny that, in prin-

Traffic, looking north on Walnut Street from First Street, Bloomington.

ciple, the idea was a good one. Blighted areas in Indianapolis or Terre Haute or Fort Wayne needed clearing. Practice was another matter. Unfortunately, many of the buildings destroyed were in marginal areas and occupied by blacks. Urban renewal soon earned the name of black removal.

The persons displaced were not usually able to move into the newly constructed buildings which replaced the older ones. The new construction was either devoted to such public buildings as government offices or university campuses or such private ones as apartment buildings. The new apartment buildings, like the highways and parking garages, had in part the purpose of attracting the middle class back into the city. Few poor persons, black or white, could afford the rent.

Because of these reasons and others, the optimism which had first been felt when interstate highways and urban renewal had begun waned. By the 1970s neither was very popular and any attempt to implement either one met with significant citizen resistance. Neither had accomplished what the proponents had hoped. They had, in fact, added to the problems.

Not that urban construction ceased in the 1970s. It continued but for different clients. Private buildings downtown took the form of office towers utilized by banks, insurance companies, and corporations rather than department stores or factories. These towers joined the sports arena or the convention center as typical of the new central city. Oddly enough, the design of these structures tended to be forbidding. Either a glass skyscraper with everything on view or a stone- or brick-faced building with few windows, and those slits, these new edifices did not appear to welcome the casual visitor.

The changed physical character of Indiana's larger cities meant changes in their uses. Since the downtown buildings were governmental, commercial, or recreational rather than retail, pedestrian traffic was intermittent. Persons working in banks

Monroe County Courthouse, Bloomington.

Market Square Arena, in the background, and the City-County Building, under construction, Indianapolis.

288

Some Elkhart people and places:

—Houses.

—Half the nation's band instruments come from this city.

—General Telephone Company operators.

—Public housing.

—The state's first phosphate sewage treatment plant.

George McGinnis, of Indianapolis, was the Big Ten basketball scoring champion at Indiana University (1970–71). He then played professional basketball for the Indiana Pacers (1971–75), Philadelphia 76ers (1975–78), Denver Nuggets (1978–79), and has now returned to the Pacers.

NCAA basketball champions at Philadelphia: Quinn Buckner, Coach Bob Knight, and Scott May, after the Indiana University team defeated Michigan 86–68, March 29, 1976.

Larry Bird, of French Lick, goes up for a basket. The Indiana State University team went to the 1979 NCAA finals.

Neil Armstrong, a Purdue graduate, with a group of students, Purdue University, February 19, 1970.

Butler University campus, Indianapolis.

Tommy John, of Terre Haute, attended Indiana State University before he became a pitcher for the Cleveland Indians in 1963. Since then he has pitched for the Chicago White Sox (1965–71), the Los Angeles Dodgers (1972–74, 1977–78), and the New York Yankees (1979–   ). Pioneering surgery was performed on his arm in 1974.

Dennis Christopher, hero of the movie *Breaking Away*, filmed in Bloomington, 1978.

Kurt Thomas, a great gymnast, on the rings, Indiana State University.

or the post office were off the streets except when going to or from work and when going out to eat. People going to a sports arena could park in adjacent high-rise parking towers.

In order to encourage the remaining retail shops and to increase pedestrian traffic downtown, Indiana cities began to imitate the shopping centers which had proven to be such strong competition by creating pedestrian malls off-limits to vehicular traffic. The principle of the downtown mall was that shoppers would return if they could walk amid pleasant surroundings, attractively designed, with plenty of green spaces, with benches for the weary, and with restaurants and entertainment for all. By the end of the 1970s it was rare to find a medium-sized city without a mall. In some form or another, they could be found in such cities as Anderson, Huntington, Richmond, Fort Wayne, Evansville, and Indianapolis.

Nor was this the only way in which Hoosier cities were changing their physical form. One city was unique enough to earn a national reputation as a showplace of modern architectural design. That was Columbus, which, under the leadership of Cummins Engine Company and its head, J. Irwin Miller, attempted to make each of its new public buildings—schools, fire stations, churches—as imaginative and outstanding as possible. These, combined with those built by corporate citizens, have given Columbus an urban vista matched by few other cities.

Curiously enough, the attempts to attract people downtown and to increase urban density relied upon returning to forms which were pre-automobile—the walking city, the small shop, the downtown hotel. Nor was this the only return to the urban past, as increased interest in historic preservation, in neighborhoods and in whole towns, typified the decade.

In areas of Indianapolis, Fort Wayne, Anderson, and Muncie, private citizens created historic preservation districts to save old residential or commercial sections. Aided by municipal ordinances, these citizens tried to attract businesses or residents that would restore old buildings to their original state which, in turn, would provide the focus of a better community. Places such as the Landing in Fort Wayne or Lockerbie Square in Indianapolis have become more and more numerous and fashionable.

In some smaller communities, the entire town participated in the rejuvenation. Such a restoration has occurred in New Harmony, where the community founded by Rapp and bought by Owen is more nearly what it was one hundred and sixty years ago than at any time since its demise. Centerville, whose major prosperity seems to have ended when Richmond eclipsed it for the county seat and when Interstate 70 ended the businesses inspired by the traffic on U.S. 40, has come back as antique shops inhabit the fine old buildings left over from the era of the 1830s. Metamora, an old canal town on the Whitewater River, has undergone a similar metamorphosis. Occupied in the summertime by antique dealers and craftsmen, the terminus of a narrow-gauge railroad ride from Connersville, Metamora has become a town based upon the past.

"Old Canal Days" in Metamora typifies another facet of the renewed interest in the past. Festivals abound in Indiana; their growth in the 1970s centered on the material remains of not-so-recent history. "The Feast of the Hunter's Moon" commemorates the French control of Fort Ouiatenon, just as the "Three Rivers Festival" in Fort Wayne celebrates the era of the fur trade and the wars between the French and the English. The "Covered Bridges Festival" in Parke County features those hundred-year-old bridges so vital to the transportation system of that time as well as the reconstructed Billie Creek Village. At Conner Prairie, open in the summer and at select times in the winter, Indiana life remains as it was in 1836 for the many visitors to this excellent pioneer restoration. Nor are all the

High school girls basketball team.

High school girls rugby team.

Brookville High School girls performing routine at football game, 1975.

Amateurs perform circus acts at the
Circus City Festival, Peru.

Little League baseball, Elkhart.

Bill Monroe and his mandolin.

Sharon Smiley, Greencastle,
"Little Miss Bluegrass."

Bill Monroe's Bluegrass Festival, Bean Blossom, June 8–16, 1974.

Young fisherman at Bonneyville Mill, near Elkhart.

Fisherman with large catfish.

Boy with baby pig.

Tractor pull contestant, Indiana State Fair, August 24, 1971.

Hampshire hogs on the Ben Johnson farm, near Connersville.

Walking an Angus down the road.

festivals devoted entirely to old artifacts; some, including the Bluegrass Festival at Bean Blossom, feature music of an earlier, simpler, more rural society.

The interest in the Hoosier past has a significant consequence. At the same time that national trends have made Indiana cities seem more like those in other parts of the United States, the process of historic restoration and commemoration has emphasized the uniqueness of communities in the state. Hoosiers became more like other Americans and yet retained an older, regional identity.

The same mixture of old and new characterized Hoosier agriculture. The trend toward larger and larger units, begun in the 1950s, continued as land and implement prices shot up in the 1970s, making it difficult for those lacking capital to enter. Economies of scale were necessary. Little land came up for sale; when it did, the demand to add land to that already owned squeezed out those not already financially strong. The result was to depopulate rural areas of farmers, as evidenced by slackening fences or no fences at all and vacant, unused farm buildings.

Suburban sprawl, however, continued to push into rural areas, forcing land prices up and competing for available space. Single units or whole developments sprang up, adjoining fields of soybeans and corn. Along highways connecting cities, strip development became common, characterized by single dwellings, often no more than one lot deep, lining the pavement for miles. Increasingly, it was difficult to separate rural from urban, for where did the city stop and the farm begin? Yet in the more isolated areas of rural Indiana the depopulation and the absence of fences, like the historic preservation district, led to a landscape more similar to that of earlier times.

The basic question which remains, however, concerns the persistence of a Hoosier identity. Was it still possible to recognize Americans on the basis of differences between state and region?

Heritage Days parade, Huntington.

Superficially, the answer would have to be no. The old distinctions between rural and urban Indiana have vanished with the advent of consolidated schools and sophisticated communications media. Little of the dialect of the early Hoosier remains, though a few Hoosierisms are heard, mainly in the speech of older residents of more isolated areas. Nor is the dress a clue. Hoosiers dress as well or as simply as other Americans. After all, some of the most famous American contemporary fashion designers have Hoosier backgrounds—Bill Blass was born in Fort Wayne, Halston (Roy Halston Frowick) grew up in Evansville, and the late Norell (Norman Levenson) was born in Noblesville.

If the answer were based upon other criteria, it might be less negative. If the question were phrased in terms of whether the experiences of Hoosiers have altered their fundamental value system—their belief in individual effort, self-determination, work, religious institutions, and patriotism—the answer would be different.

Here, behavior and values clash. Two examples will suffice. Hoosiers still speak of the need for self-help and local determination, yet, according to a study of Muncie's city financing, by 1975, 53 percent of the general revenue came from government sources—county, state, and federal—outside the city. So much for local autonomy.

Nor are city dwellers alone in being inconsistent. Farmers use the terms "family farm" and "an unregulated market" to describe their goals for agriculture. When Earl Butz, a native-born Hoosier and dean of the School of Agriculture at Purdue prior to becoming President Nixon's controversial Secretary of Agriculture, did succeed in getting some governmental controls removed from crop production, Hoosier farmers applauded. Yet in the second half of the decade, when farm prices declined, Hoosier farmers protested, solicited government aid, and urged a strike to withhold commodities from the market.

Connersville, 1975.

Fayette County Farm Bureau Co-op, Connersville.

Migrant workers on the Norman Eickhoff farm, near Carthage, August 4, 1973.

Roadside stand, near Goshen, 1975.

Old woman and her garden, Bloomington.

Spencer fur market, 1975.

Amish couple in buggy, near Etna Green.

Pennsylvania Railroad station, Gosport, June 1976.

Cornfields and farm buildings.

Case Tractor and Chisel-Planter.

I–275 bridge over the Ohio River, Lawrenceburg.

Perhaps these examples demonstrate the conviction with which Hoosiers cling to older values, despite their temporal experience. If so, they would confirm the findings of two scholars—Theodore Caplow and Howard M. Bahr—who gave the same test to high school students in Muncie in 1977 that the Lynds had given in 1925. They were astonished to find that the values had changed little:

> What we do report is that in this one midwestern community, selected originally for its lack of unusual features, we have not been able to find any trace of disintegration of traditional social values that is commonly described by observers who rely on their own intuitions. It is hard to believe that the young people of even one midwestern community are as strongly imbued with religion, patriotism, and the Protestant ethic as their grandparents were at the same age but that is what the data seem to be telling us.

Since their findings probably do hold true for the rest of Indiana, we can agree with George Ade, who wrote by intuition in 1922: "Just as the Hoosier emerges from the cradle he is handed a set of convictions and learns that he must defend them, verbally and otherwise. . . . Here's to Indiana, a state as yet unspoiled! Here's to the Hoosier home folks, a good deal more sophisticated than they let on to be!"

Northeast Interchange in center of Indianapolis: I–65 and I–70.

Barge traffic is heavy on the Ohio River.

Burns Waterway Harbor, Portage, provides access to the Great Lakes and the St. Lawrence Seaway.

Southwind Maritime Centre, Indiana's first riverport, Mount Vernon.

The Indianapolis Symphony Orchestra, with John Nelson, music director, celebrated its 50th anniversary, 1979–80.

Aerial view of the Indianapolis Museum of Art.

Bartholomew County Courthouse, built in 1875, has been renovated.

First Christian Church, Columbus, Eliel Saarinen, architect, built in 1942, with "Large Arch," 1971, by Henry Moore, in the foreground.

North Christian Church, Columbus, Eero Saarinen, architect, built in 1964.

"Chaos I," 1974, created by Jean Tinguely, in The
Commons, Columbus, shopping mall, Cesar Pelli, architect
of Gruen Associates, Inc., which was built the year before.

Lillian C. Schmitt Elementary School, Columbus, Harry Weese,
architect, built in 1957. It was the first building in the Cummins
Engine Foundation architectural program.

W.D. Richards Elementary School, Columbus,
Edward Larrabee Barnes, architect, built in 1965.
On the playground 12 sculptured miniature
horses, created by Constantino Nivola, encircle
an ash tree.

ACKNOWLEDGMENTS AND CREDITS

Front Matter. 1: University Press of Kentucky, Roger W. Barbour, photographer. 2–3: Indianapolis Museum of Art, Theodore Groll, artist. 4: Map, Indiana Geological Survey and Indiana Academy of Sciences. 5: Map, Indiana Geological Survey, Henry Gray.

The Land. 6: a/b, c, © Bill Thomas. 7: a/b, © Bill Thomas; c–1, c–2, *Outdoor Indiana,* William A. Barnes. 8: a/b, *Outdoor Indiana;* c, © Bill Thomas. 9: a/b, © Bill Thomas; c, *Outdoor Indiana,* John Bacone. 10: b, Indiana Geological Survey, R.D. Rarick; c, *Outdoor Indiana.* 11: *Outdoor Indiana,* Dennis Bogden. 12–13: a, *Outdoor Indiana,* Dennis Bogden. 12: b/c, *Outdoor Indiana,* Dennis Bogden. 13: b/c, © Bill Thomas. 14: b, © Bill Thomas; c, © Dave Repp. 15: b, © Bill Thomas; c, *Outdoor Indiana,* Dennis Bogden. 16: b, Indiana Historical Society Library, George Winter; c, Russell E. Mumford.

The First Inhabitants. 17: Glenn A. Black Laboratory of Archaeology, Indiana University, Bloomington. 18: b–1, b–2, Ball State University; b–3, Black Laboratory, © Dave Repp; c–1, c–2, Black Laboratory. 19: b–1, b–2, c–1, c–2, Black Laboratory. 20: a, Black Laboratory; b–1, b–2, Black Laboratory, © Dave Repp; c, Black Laboratory. 21: a, b, c, Black Laboratory. 22: a, Black Laboratory, Dave Repp; b, Black Laboratory. 23: Michigan State University, Vergil E. Noble, Jr., and Tippecanoe County Historical Association, Lafayette.

Explorers, Fur Traders, and Empire Builders. 24–25: Tippecanoe County Historical Association. 26: a–2, *Outdoor Indiana,* Dennis Bogden; b, c, Northern Indiana Historical Society, South Bend, Dave Repp. 27: a, Byron R. Lewis Historical Library, Vincennes University, Dave Repp; b–1, b–2, Lewis Historical Library; c, Indiana Historical Society Library. 28: a–1, Black Laboratory; a–2, b, c, Michigan State University, Richard A. Knecht. 29: a, b–1, b–2, c–1, c–2, Michigan State University, Richard A. Knecht. 30: Michigan State University, Richard A. Knecht.

The Americans. 31: Indiana State Library, George Rogers Clark Memorial, Vincennes, Hermon A. MacNeil, sculptor. 32: a–1, Virginia State Library; a–2, a–3, Indiana Historical Society Library; b/c, Lewis Historical Library. 33: b/c, Indiana Historical Bureau, George Rogers Clark Memorial, Ezra Winter, artist. 34: a–1, Indiana Historical Society Library; a–2, Robert D. Parker Collection, Fort Wayne, Dave Repp; b, Indiana Historical Bureau, Frederic C. Yohn, artist; c, Indiana Historical Society Library. 35: a, Allen County Public Library, Fort Wayne, Dave Repp; b, Lewis Historical Library, Dave Repp; c, Chicago Historical Society Library. 36: a–1, Francis Vigo Chapter, Daughters of the American Revolution, Vincennes, attributed to Rembrandt Peale; a–2, b, D.A.R., Vincennes; c, © Dave Repp. 37: a–1, Indiana State Library, James Peale; a–2, *Indianapolis Star* Magazine, George McCormack; b, *Outdoor Indiana,* Dennis Bogden; c, Lewis Historical Library, Dave Repp. 38: b, Indiana Historical Society Library. 39: b, Tippecanoe County Historical Association; c, Indiana State Library. 40: a, Allen County Public Library, Dave Repp; b, Map, Clark Ray; c, Allen County Public Library, Dave Repp. 41: a–1, Parker Collection, Dave Repp; a–2, Indiana Historical Society Library; b, Indiana State Library; c, Indiana Historical Society Library. 42: a/b, Indiana State Library; c, Indiana Historical Society Library, Dave Repp. 43: a–1, © Dave Repp; a–2, Tippecanoe County Historical Association; c, Indiana State Library. 44: a–1, a–2, Allen County Public Library, Dave Repp; a–3, Northern Indiana Historical Society; b, Map, Clark Ray; c, Tippecanoe County Historical Association, Dave Repp. 45: a–1, a–2, b, c, C.G. Ball and Tippecanoe County Historical Association, George Winter.

The Pioneers. 47: Indiana Historical Society Library. 48: b, c–1, c–2, Indiana State Library; 49: b, Basil Hall Manuscripts, Lilly Library, Indiana University, Bloomington; c, Herbert L. Heller, Greencastle, Bruno Lundgreen. 50: a, Ball State University; b, *Outdoor Indiana,* Ken Williams; c, © Bill Thomas. 51: a, b, c, Ball State University. 52: a, *Outdoor Indiana,* Dennis Bogden; b, J.C. Allen and Son, West Lafayette; c, *Outdoor Indiana,* Dennis Bogden. 53: a, *Outdoor Indiana,* Dennis Bogden; b, Northern Indiana Historical Society, Dave Repp; c, J.C. Allen and Son. 54: a, Indiana State Library, George Winter; b, Allen County Public Library, Dave Repp; c, Indiana State Library, Christian Schrader. 55: a, Allen County Public Library, Dave Repp; b, Indiana Historical Society Library, Karl Bodmer; c, Indiana Historical Society Library, George Winter. 56: a, Allen County Public Library, Dave Repp; b, Indiana State Library, Christian Schrader; c, Archives, Indiana University, Bloomington, Theophilus Adam Wylie. 57: a, Madison-Jefferson County Public Library, Dave Repp; b, *Outdoor Indiana,* Dennis Bogden; c, Indiana University Archives, Theophilus Adam Wylie. 58: a–1, Don Blair, New Harmony; a–2, The Long Island Historical Society; a–3, b, c, Indiana Historical Society Library. 59: a–1, a–2, Indiana State Library; a–3, b, Indiana Historical Society Library; c, Workingmen's Institute, New Harmony, Josephine M. Elliott. 60: b, American Philosophical Society, Charles-Alexandre Lesueur; c, Muséum d'Histoire Naturelle du Havre, Charles-Alexandre Lesueur. 61: a, Indiana State Library; b–1, American Antiquarian Society, Karl Bodmer; c, Maximilian-Bodmer Collection, © Northern Natural Gas Company, Joslyn Art Museum. 62: a, Lewis Historical Library, Dave Repp; b, Frances Trollope, *Domestic Manners of the Americans* (1832); c, Indiana Historical Society Library. 63: a, b, Hope Moravian Church, Hope, Dave Repp; c, Indiana State Library. 64: a–1, a–2, Indiana State Library; b, Wabash College Archives, Gladys Otto; c, Archives, Lilly Library, Earlham College. 65: a, Indiana State Library; b–2, Wabash College Archives; c–1, Indiana University Archives; c–2, Allen County Public Library, Dave Repp.

Unity and Division. 66–67: Indiana State Library, Christian Schrader. 68: a–1, a–2, Muséum d'Histoire Naturelle du Havre, Charles-Alexandre Lesueur; b–2, Indiana Historical Society Library, George Winter; c, Indiana State Library. 69: a, Indiana State Library; b/c, Map, Clark Ray. 70: a, Basil Hall Manuscripts, Lilly Library; b, Lefevre Cranstone Manuscripts, Lilly Library; c, Indiana State Library. 71: b, Tippecanoe County Historical Association, Wils Burry; c, Tippecanoe County Historical Association, Dave Repp. 72–73: a, Indiana State Library, Christian Schrader. 72: b/c, Madison-Jefferson County Public Library, Dave Repp. 73: b/c, Map, Clark Ray. 74: a, Madison-Jefferson County Public Library, Dave Repp; b, Indiana Historical Society Library; c, Indiana State Library, Christian Schrader. 75: a, New Albany-Floyd County Public Library, Dave Repp; b, Madison-Jefferson County Public Library, Dave Repp; c, Indiana Historical Society Library. 76: b, New Albany-Floyd County Public Library, Dave Repp; c, New Albany-Floyd County Public Library. 77: a, Indiana State Library; b, Indiana Historical Society Library; c, Indiana State Library. 78: a–1, Lewis Historical Library; a–2, b, Vigo County Public Library, Dave Repp; c, Lewis Historical Library. 79: b, c, Indiana State Library, Christian Schrader. 80: Indiana Historical Society Library. 81: a–1, a–2, Allen County Public Library, Dave Repp; b/c, Parker Collection, Dave Repp. 82: a–2, b, c, Indiana State Library. 83: a–1, a–2, Madison-Jefferson County Public Library, Dave Repp; b, © Dave Repp; c, *Outdoor Indiana.* 84: a–1, a–2, Indiana State Library; b, c, Lefevre Cranstone Manuscripts, Lilly Library. 85: a, b, c, Lefevre Cranstone Manuscripts, Lilly Library. 86: a, Indiana State Library; b, Wilbur D. Peat; c, Lewis Historical Library, Dave Repp. 87: a–1, a–2, Indiana Historical Society Library; a–3, Indiana State Library; b, Allen County Public Library, Dave Repp; c, Tippecanoe County Historical Association, Dave Repp. 88: a–2, a–3, b, Indiana Historical Society Library; c, *Frank Leslie's Illustrated Newspaper,* August 8, 1863. 89: a, Indiana Historical Society Library; b–1, *Harper's Weekly,* November 8, 1862; b–2, Lewis Historical Library, Dave Repp; c, Indiana State Library. 90. a, Indiana Historical Society Library; b, Northern Indiana Historical Society, Dave Repp; c, Indiana Historical Society Library. 91: b–1, b–2, c, Indiana Historical Society Library. 92: a–1, a–2, a–3, a–4, b–1, Indiana Historical Society Library; b–2, c, Indiana State Library.

Politics and Social Change. 93: Indiana State Library. 94: b, *Harper's Weekly,* October 14, 1876; c, Indiana Historical Society Library. 95: b, c, Indiana State Library. 96: b, Indiana State Library; c, Indiana Historical Society Library. 97: b, Ball State University; c, Wayne County Museum. 98: a–1, Indiana State Library; a–2, Indiana Historical Society Library; a–3, Indiana State Library; b, Lewis Historical Library, Dave Repp; c, Hohenberger Collection, Lilly Library. 99: a–1, a–2, Indiana State Library; b, C. Warren Vander Hill; c, Miami County Historical Museum and Puterbaugh Museum, Peru. 100: a, b, Indiana State Library. 101: b, Miami County Historical Museum; c, Indiana State Library. 102: Special Collections, Purdue University Libraries, West Lafayette. 103: b, Eugene R. Bock, Brookville, Ben F. Winans; c, Indiana State Library. 104: b, New Albany-Floyd County Public Library, Dave Repp; c, Eugene R. Bock, Ben F. Winans. 105: b, Indiana State Library; c, Don Blair. 106: Indiana State Library.

Down on the Farm. 107: J.C. Allen and Son. 108: b, Lewis Historical Library, Dave Repp; c, Indiana Historical Society Library. 109: b–1, Christopher Oppy; b–2, Maurice L. Williamson, Purdue Agricultural Alumni Association; c–1, Eugene R. Bock, Ben F. Winans; c–2, J.C. Allen and Son. 110: b–1, b–2, c–1, c–2, J.C. Allen and Son. 111: b, Herbert L. Heller, Bruno Lundgreen; c, Indiana State Library. 112: b, Eugene R. Bock, Ben F. Winans; c, Maurice L. Williamson. 113: a, b–1, b–2, J.C. Allen and Son; c–1, Indiana Historical Society Library; c–2, Studebaker Historic Vehicle Collection, Discovery Hall Museum, South Bend. 114: b, c–1, Maurice L. Williamson; c–2, J.C. Allen and Son. 115: b, c, J.C. Allen and Son. 116: b, c, J.C. Allen and Son. 117: b–1, J.C. Allen and Son; b–2, Indiana State Library; c–1, Herbert L. Heller, Bruno Lundgreen; c–2, J.C. Allen and Son. 118: a, Maurice L. Williamson; b, Indiana State Library; c–1, c–2, Maurice L. Williamson. 119: a, J.C. Allen and Son; b, Maurice L. Williamson; c, J.C. Allen and Son. 120: a, Indiana Historical Society Library; b–1, Crawfordsville District Public Library, Dave Repp; c–1, Rumely Manuscripts, Lilly Library; c–2, Crawfordsville District Public Library, Dave Repp. 121: a–1, Maurice L. Williamson; a–2, *Indianapolis Star;* b–1, Indiana State Library; b–2, *Postmaster General's Report,* 1899. 122: a, Allen County Public Library, Dave Repp; b–1, Studebaker Collection, Discovery Hall; b–2, Maurice L. Williamson; c–1, Center for Middletown Studies, Ball State University, Roger Pelham, Swift Photographic Studio; c–2, Indiana State Library.

Transformation of the Town. 123: College of Architecture and Planning Libraries, Ball State University, David Hermansen. 124: b, c, Architecture Libraries, David Hermansen. 125: a, Indiana State Library; b–1, Architecture Libraries, David Hermansen; b–2, Indiana State Library; c–1, Architecture Libraries, David Hermansen; c–2, Indiana State Library. 126: a–1, Vigo County Public Library, Terre Haute, Dave Repp; a–2, Indiana Historical Society Library; b–1, Vigo County Public Library, Dave Repp; b–2, c, Herbert L. Heller, Bruno Lundgreen. 127: a–1, a–2, Indiana State Library; b, Herbert L. Heller, Bruno Lundgreen; c, Indiana State Library. 128: a, b, *Indianapolis Star* Magazine; c, Indiana State Library. 129: a–1, Allen County Public Library, Dave Repp; a–2/b–2, Fred Garver, Fairland, Dave Repp; b–1, Purdue University Libraries; c–1, Allen County Public Library, Dave Repp; c–2, James M. Guthrie, Bedford. 130: a, Allen County Public Library, Dave Repp; b–1, Vigo County Historical Society, Terre Haute, A.R. Markle; b–2, Paul Frisz Collection, Terre Haute, Dave Repp; c, Indiana State Library. 131: b, Indiana State Library; c, Herbert L. Heller, Bruno Lundgreen. 132: a, Indiana State Library; b, Miami County Historical Museum; c, Indiana Historical Society Library. 133: a–1, Lewis Historical Library; a–2/b–2, Indiana State Library, Jack Householder; b–1, James M. Guthrie; c–1, Parke County Historical Society Inc., Museum, Rockville, Dave Repp; c–2, Indiana State Library. 134: a, b–1, Indiana State Library; b–2, Indiana Historical Society Library, Dave Repp; c, Indiana State Library. 135: a, Studebaker Collection, Discovery Hall; b, Parker Collection, Dave Repp; c, *Indianapolis Star* Magazine. 136: a–1, Wabash *Plain Dealer;* a–2, Don Blair; b, Allen County Public Library; c, New Albany-Floyd County Public Library, Dave Repp. 137: a, Indiana State Library; b, c, Miami County Historical Museum. 138: a–1, a–2, Herbert L. Heller, Bruno Lundgreen; b–1, Madison-Jefferson County Public Library, Dave Repp; b–2, Indiana Historical Society Library, Dave Repp; c–1, Herbert L. Heller, Bruno Lundgreen; c–2, © Dave Repp.

Business and Industry. 139: Standard Oil Company (Indiana). 140: a, *Indianapolis Star* Magazine; b, Indiana Historical Society Library; c, Allen County Public Library, Dave Repp. 141: b–1, Madison-Jefferson County Public Library, Dave Repp; b–2, c, Indiana State Library. 142: b–1/c–1, Indiana State Library; b–2, Ball State University; c–2, Ball Corporation, Muncie. 143: a, Ball Corporation; b, c, Indiana Coal Association, William Beeman. 144: a, James M. Guthrie; b/c, Indiana Geological Survey, R.D. Rarick. 145: a–1, a–2, Studebaker Collection, Discovery Hall; b–1, b–2, Allen County Public Library, Dave Repp; c–1, Discovery Hall; c–2, Studebaker Collection, Discovery Hall. 146: a–1, a–2, Herbert L. Heller, Bruno Lundgreen; b–1, Madison-Jefferson County Public Library, Dave Repp; b–2, Indiana State Library; c–1, *Spencer Evening World;* c–2, Madison-Jefferson County Public Library, Dave Repp. 147: a, Stokely-Van Camp, Inc.; b, Indiana State Library; c, Ball State University. 148: a, b–1, Archives, Eli Lilly and Company; b–2, Indiana Historical Society Library; c–1, c–2, Archives, Eli Lilly and Company.

Iron and Automobiles. 149: James B. Lane, Calumet Regional Archives, Indiana University Northwest, Gary. 150: a–1, Gary *Post-Tribune;* a–2, b, c, James B. Lane. 151: b, c, James B. Lane. 152: b, c, James B. Lane. 153: b, Indiana Historical Society Library, Thelma Confer, artist; c, *Haynes Pioneer,* July 1918, Wallace Spencer Huffman, Kokomo. 154–155: *Horseless Age,* Wallace Spencer Huffman. 156: a, b–1, b–2, c, Indiana Historical Society Library. 157: a, J.C. Allen and Son; b, c, Studebaker Collection, Discovery Hall. 158: b, Indiana State Library; c, Indiana State Highway Commission. 159: a–1, Herbert L. Heller, Bruno Lundgreen; a–2, Indiana Historical Society Library; b, Herbert L. Heller, Bruno Lundgreen; c–1, Indiana Historical Society Library; c–2, Indiana State Highway Commission. 160: a, b–1, b–2, Indianapolis Motor Speedway, Inc.; c–1, Bureau of Public Roads, National Archives; c–2, Indiana State Library. 161: a, Indianapolis Motor Speedway; b, Indiana Historical Society Library, Bass Photo, Dave Repp; c, Indianapolis Motor Speedway. 162: a–1, a–2, b, Herbert L. Heller, Bruno Lundgreen; c–1, Allen County Public Library, Dave Repp; c–2, Indiana Historical Society Library, Dave Repp; c–3, Purdue University Libraries.

The World of Work. 163: National Archives, Lewis Hine. 164: a, James M. Guthrie; b, c, Indiana State Library. 165: b, c, Discovery Hall. 166: b, Studebaker Collection, Discovery Hall; c, Indiana Historical Society Library. 167: a, Indiana State Library; b, Indiana Historical Society Library; c, Indiana State Library. 168: b, c, National Archives, Lewis Hine. 169: a, Indiana State Library; b, National Archives, Lewis Hine; c–1, c–2, James B. Lane. 170: a–1, a–2, b, c–1, c–2, Eugene V. Debs Foundation, Terre Haute.

Toward A Better Life. 171: Indiana Historical Society Library, Dave Repp. 172: a–1, Indiana State Library; a–2, Hohenberger Collection, Lilly Library; b, Indiana State Library; c, New Albany-Floyd County Public Library, Dave Repp. 173: a–1, a–2, b, Indiana State Library; c, J.C. Allen and Son. 174: a–1, b, Herbert L. Heller, Bruno Lundgreen. 175: a–1, Indiana State Library; a–2, New Albany-Floyd County Public Library, Dave Repp; b, Allen County Public Library, Dave Repp; c, DePauw University. 176: a–1, a–2, b, Hanover College; c, Wabash College Archives. 177: a–1, a–2, University of Notre Dame Archives; b, Allen County Public Library, Dave Repp; c, Hanover College. 178: a–1, Herron School of Art, Indiana University-Purdue University at Indianapolis; a–2, Hohenberger Collection, Lilly Library; b, News Information Services, St. Meinrad Archabbey; c, *Outdoor Indiana*, Dennis Bogden. 179: a, Indiana State Library; b, Lewis Historical Library; c, Earlham College Archives. 180: a–1, Lewis Historical Library; a–2, *Evansville Courier;* b, Indiana State Library; c, University of Notre Dame Archives. 181: a–1, Ball State University; a–2, b, Purdue University Libraries; c, Indiana State University Audio Visual Center. 182: a, b, Purdue University Libraries; c, Maurice L. Williamson. 183: a, Purdue University Libraries; b, c, Indiana University Archives. 184: a–1, a–2, b, c, Indiana University Archives. 185: a, J.C. Allen and Son; b–1, Lewis Historical Library; b–2, Indianapolis Hebrew Congregation, Mrs. Robert Romer, Lester E. Ayres; c, Joseph Levine, The Indiana Jewish Historical Society, Fort Wayne. 186: a–1, Wilbur D. Peat; a–2, Madison-Jefferson County Public Library, Dave Repp; b–1, b–2, Indiana State Library; c–1, Wabash College Archives; John T. McCutcheon, *The Mysterious Stranger and Other Cartoons* (1905). 187: a–1, a–2, b–1, b–2, b–3, Indiana State Library; c–1, Indiana Historical Society Library; c–2, Indiana State Library. 188: a–2/b–2, McCutcheon, *Mysterious Stranger;* c–1, Vigo County Historical Society; c–2, Dreiser Collection, Lilly Library; c–3, Indiana State Library.

Recreation and Leisure. 189: Madison-Jefferson County Public Library, Dave Repp. 190: a, Tippecanoe County Historical Association, Dave Repp; b, Madison-Jefferson County Public Library, Dave Repp; c, Vigo County Public Library, Dave Repp. 191: a, Allen County-Fort Wayne Historical Society; b–1, Indiana State Library; b–2, Indiana University Archives; c–1, c–2, Frisz Collection, Dave Repp. 192: a, Indiana University Archives; b–1, Parke County Historical Society, Dave Repp; b–2, Madison-Jefferson County Public Library, Dave Repp; c, University of Notre Dame Archives. 193: b, Purdue University Libraries, F.E. Quick; c, Purdue University Libraries, Sutton's Photo. 194: b, c, Indiana University Archives. 195: a, Madison-Jefferson County Public Library, Dave Repp; b–1, Indiana State Library; b–2, Crawfordsville District Public Library, Dave Repp; c, Herbert F. Schwomeyer, Indianapolis. 196: b–1, Indiana University Archives; b–2, Madison-Jefferson County Public Library, Dave Repp; c–1, Herbert L. Heller, Bruno Lundgreen; c–2, Indiana Historical Society Library. 197: b, Indiana Historical Society Library, Dave Repp; c, Indiana State Library. 198: a, Madison-Jefferson County Public Library, Dave Repp; b, Studebaker Collection, Discovery Hall; c, Indiana Historical Society Library, Dave Repp. 199: a, Indiana State Library; b–1, Indiana Historical Society Library; b–2, Indiana State Library; c–1, Indiana Historical Society Library, Dave Repp; c–2, Ball State University. 200: a–1, a–2, Indiana Historical Society Library; b–1, Lewis Historical Library, Dave Repp; b–2, Indiana Historical Society Library, Dave Repp; c–1, Hanover College; c–2, Parke County Historical Society, Dave Repp. 201: a, Discovery Hall; b, Indiana State Library; c, Allen County Public Library, Dave Repp. 202: a, b, Herbert L. Heller, Bruno Lundgreen; c–1, c–2, Miami County Historical Museum. 203: a, Miami County Historical Museum; b–1, b–2, Herbert L. Heller, Bruno Lundgreen; c–1, Indiana Historical Society Library, Dave Repp; c–2, Miami County Historical Museum. 204: a–1, a–2, b–1, Indiana Historical Society Library; b–2, Indiana State Library; c–1, New Albany-Floyd County Public Library, Dave Repp; c–2, Indiana Historical Society Library, Dave Repp.

Over There and Back Home. 205: Northern Indiana Historical Society, Dave Repp. 206–207: a, Indiana State Library. 206: b, c, Indiana State Library. 207: b, Indiana University Archives; c, Indiana State Library. 208: a, Indiana University Archives; b, *Indianapolis Star* Magazine. 209: a, Standard Oil Company (Indiana); b, Indiana State Library. 210: a, Indiana State Library; b, *Indianapolis Star* Magazine; c, Indiana University Archives. 211: a, b, c, Indiana State Library.

The Twenties. 212–213: Herbert L. Heller, Bruno Lundgreen. 214: b, Herbert L. Heller, Bruno Lundgreen; c, Indiana Historical Society Library, Dave Repp. 215: a, Hohenberger Collection, Lilly Library; b–1, Eli Lilly and Company Archives; b–2, Indiana State Library; c–1, Ball State University, Swift Photographic Studio; c–2, Ball State University. 216: a, Allen County-Fort Wayne Historical Society, Dave Repp; b, c–1, Indiana State Library; c–2, Swift Photographic Studio. 217: a, b, c, Swift Photographic Studio. 218: a, Swift Photographic Studio; b, Allen County-Fort Wayne Historical Society, Dave Repp; c, J.C. Allen and Son. 219: a, Indiana State Highway Commission; b–1, Purdue University Libraries; b–2, c–1, c–2, Indiana State Highway Commission. 220: b–1, Hohenberger Collection, Lilly Library; b–2, Indiana State Library, Frank M. Hohenberger; c–1, *Indianapolis News,* November 25, 1921, Gaar Williams; c–2, *Indianapolis News,* April 18, 1925, Charles Kuhn. 221: a, Allen County Public Library, Dave Repp; b, James B. Lane; c, J.C. Allen and Son. 222: b, c, Purdue University Libraries. 223: b–1, University of Notre Dame Archives; b–, Indiana Historical Society Library; c–1, Purdue University Libraries; c–2, Bloomington *Herald-Telephone,* Sinclair Photo. 224: Indiana State Library. 225: a, J.C. Allen and Son; b, Swift Photographic Studio; c, J.C. Allen and Son. 226: b, c, J.C. Allen and Son. 227: b, c, J.C. Allen and Son. 228: a, b, c, J.C. Allen and Son. 229: a, Indiana State Library; b–1, Indiana Historical Society Library, Dave Repp; b–2, © Dave Repp; c–1, c–2, J.C. Allen and Son.

The Lean Years. 230–231: James B. Lane. 232: a, b, Indiana State Library; c, Allen County Public Library, Dave Repp. 233: b–1, Indiana State Library; b–2, Roy Stryker Collection, University of Louisville Photographic Archives; c–1, Indiana State Library; c–2, Northern Indiana Historical Society. 234: a, b–1, b–2, Stryker Collection, University of Louisville; c–1, Hohenberger Collection, Lilly Library; c–2, Stryker Collection, University of Louisville. 235; a, b, c, Rural Electrification Administration (REA). 236; a, J.C. Allen and Son; b, REA; c, J.C. Allen and Son. 237: b–1, b–2, c, J.C. Allen and Son. 238: a, b, c, J.C. Allen and Son. 239: a–1, a–2, b, Indiana State Library; c, Photographic Service, Audio-Visual Center, Indiana University, Bloomington. 240: a–1, Purdue University Sports Information Office; a–2, Purdue University Libraries; b, Allen County Public Library; c, Indiana State Library. 241: a, Allen County Public Library; b, c, Allen County Public Library, Dave Repp. 242: a, Allen County Public Library, Dave Repp; b, c, Indiana Coal Association, William Beeman. 243: a, Indiana State Library; b–1, Ball Corporation; b–2, Allen County Public Library, Dave Repp; c, Maurice L. Williamson. 244: a–1, Indiana State Highway Commission; a–2, Cummins Engine Company, Inc.; b–1, J.C. Allen and Son; b–2, b–3, b–4, Auburn-Cord-Duesenberg Museum, Auburn; c, Herbert F. Schwomeyer. 245: a–1, Cummins Engine Company, Inc.; a–2, b, c, Indianapolis Motor Speedway. 246: a, Madison-Jefferson County Public Library, Dave Repp; b, *Evansville Courier;* c, Indiana State Highway Commission.

Over There and Back Home.—Again. 247: Allen County Public Library, Dave Repp. 248: a–1, Indiana University Archives; a–2/b, Indiana State Library; c, Indiana University Audio-Visual Center. 249: a–1, Indiana State Library; a–2, Dr. Charles F. Leich, Evansville; b, Standard Oil Company (Indiana); c, *Indianapolis Star* Magazine. 250: a–1, Department of Journalism Library, Indiana University, Bloomington; a–2, Indiana State Library; b, *Indianapolis Star* Magazine; c, Discovery Hall. 251: a–1, *Indianapolis Star* Magazine; a–2, Ball State University; b–1, Indiana University Aduio-Visual Center; b–2, Purdue University Libraries; c, Indiana State University Communications Services. 252: a, b, Maurice L. Williamson; c, Ball State University. 253: a, Indiana State Library; b, Ball State University; c, Indiana State Library. 254: a, b, c, Indiana Historical Society Library. 255: a, Indiana State Highway Commission; b, James B. Lane; c, Hohenberger Collection, Lilly Library. 256: a, Indiana State Library; b, *Indianapolis Star* Magazine; c, Indiana University Audio-Visual Center. 257: b, c, Indiana University Audio-Visual Center. 258: a, Indiana University Audio-Visual Center; b–1, Frisz Collection, Dave Repp; b–2, Indiana State University Communications Services; c–1, Indiana University Audio-Visual Center; c–2, Indiana University Sports News Service, Bloomington. 259: a–1, a–2, b–1, *Indianapolis Star* Magazine; b–2, Metropolitan Evansville Chamber of Commerce; c, Standard Oil of New Jersey Collection, University of Louisville Photographic Archives.

Happy Days. 260–261: Metropolitan Evansville Chamber of Commerce. 262: a–1, a–2, *Indianapolis Star* Magazine; b, *Indianapolis News,* Steve Smith; c, Hohenberger Collection, Lilly Library. 263: a, Madison Area Chamber of Commerce; b, c, Indiana University Audio-Visual Center. 264: b, Indiana University News Bureau; c, Purdue University Libraries. 265: b, c, REA. 266: b, Herbert F. Schwomeyer; c, *Indianapolis Star,* William A. Oates. 267: a, Indiana State Library; b, c, James B. Lane. 268: a–1, Ball State University; a–2, Vernice Noyes; b, *Indianapolis Star* Magazine; c, Indianapolis Motor Speedway. 269: a, *Indianapolis Star;* b, Allen County Public Library, Dave Repp; c, Frisz Collection, Dave Repp. 270: a, b, Studebaker Collection, Discovery Hall.

A Troubled Decade. 271: © Dave Repp. 272: a, © Dave Repp; b, Gary *Post-Tribune;* c, Indiana State Library. 273: a, Indiana State Library; b, *Outdoor Indiana,* Ken Williams; c, *Indianapolis Star.* 274: a, b, Indiana State Library; c–1, Bethlehem Steel Corporation; c–2, Allen County Public Library, Dave Repp. 275: a, Madison Area Chamber of Commerce; b, *Indianapolis Star* Magazine; c, Metropolitan Evansville Chamber of Commerce. 276: b, Lawrence A. Schaal, Purdue University, Paul Huffman; c, © Dave Repp. 277: a, Butler University; b, Indiana University Audio-Visual Center; c, Purdue University Sports Information Office. 278: a–1, Purdue University Photographic Service; a–2, University of Notre Dame Archives; b, Indiana University Audio-Visual Center; c, Indiana University Sports News Service. 279: a–1, Herbert F. Schwomeyer; a–2, Vigo County Public Library, Dave Repp; b, Indianapolis Motor Speedway; c, *Indianapolis News,* Robert Lavelle. 280: a–1, a–2, *Indianapolis Star* Magazine; b–1, Indiana University Audio-Visual Center; b–2, *Indianapolis Star* Magazine; c–1, c–2, Allen County Public Library, Dave Repp. 281: a, Indiana State Library; b, © Dave Repp; c, Allen County Public Library, Dave Repp. 282: b–1, b–2, b–3, c, © Dave Repp.

Today. 283: Maurice L. Williamson. 284: a, Indiana State Republican Committee; b, James B. Lane; c, Indiana State Library. 285: a, United States Gypsum Company; b–1, *Indianapolis Star* Magazine; b–2, © Dave Repp; c–1, c–2, Gold Bond Building Products Division, National Gypsum Company. 286: a, b–1, Indiana Geological Survey, R.D. Rarick; b–2, AMAX Coal Company; c, Indiana Geological Survey. 287: a, Madison Area Chamber of Commerce; b, © Dave Repp; c, Columbus *Republic.* 288: a, b, © Dave Repp; c, *Indianapolis Star* Magazine, James C. Ramsey. 289: a, b–1, b–2, b–3, c, Greater Elkhart Chamber of Commerce. 290: a, Indiana Pacers; b–1, Indiana University Sports News Service; b–2, Indiana State University Communications Services; c–1, Purdue University Libraries; c–2, Butler University. 291: a, New York Yankees; b, *Indianapolis Star* Magazine, Fred Cavinder; c, Indiana State University Communications Services. 292: b, c, *Indianapolis Star* Magazine. 293: b, © Dave Repp; c–1, Circus City Festival, Inc., Peru; c–2, Greater Elkhart Chamber of Commerce. 294: a–1, a–2, b, c–1, © Dave Repp; c–2, Greater Elkhart Chamber of Commerce. 295: a–1, a–2, b, c, © Dave Repp. 296: a, b, c, © Dave Repp. 297: a, b–1, b–2, © Dave Repp; b–3, *Spencer Evening World;* c, © Dave Repp. 298: a, *Spencer Evening World;* b, c, Maurice L. Williamson. 299: a, b/c, Indiana State Highway Commission. 300: *Evansville Courier;* b, c, Indiana Port Commission. 301: a, Indianapolis Symphony Orchestra, Don Cushman; b–1, Indianapolis Museum of Art; b–2, c–1, c–2, © Balthazar Korab. 302: a/b, c–1, c–2, © Balthazar Korab.